The Agent

The Agent

PERSONALITIES, PUBLISHING,
AND POLITICS

Arthur M. Klebanoff

TEXERE

Copyright © 2001 Arthur Klebanoff

Published in 2002 by

TEXERE LLC
55 East 52nd Street
New York, NY 10055

Tel: +1 (212) 317 5511
Fax: +1 (212) 317 5178
www.etexere.com

In the UK

TEXERE Publishing Limited
71–77 Leadenhall Street
London EC3A 3DE

Tel: +44 (0)20 7204 3644
Fax: +44 (0)20 7208 6701
www.etexere.co.uk

This publication is designed to provide accurate and authoritative information in regard to the subject matter covered. It is sold with the understanding that the publisher is not engaged in rendering legal, accounting, or other professional services. If legal advice of other expert assistance is required, the services of a competent professional person should be sought.

Designed by Elliott Beard

Library of Congress Cataloging in Publication Data is available.

ISBN 1-58799-104-7

Printed in the United States of America

This book is printed on acid-free paper.

10   9   8   7   6   5   4   3   2   1

To my father, who was very much a principal; my wife, a life partner; and my sons, in the hope that they find their own way

PREFACE

....

This is a book I would like to have read when I was twenty, thirty, forty, or even recently when fifty. In a world of ever larger institutions, I have chosen to be on my own. I work interactively every day, often with very accomplished (and sometimes celebrated) people. My "intellectual diet" is constantly changing, so my career path has been unplanned with unpredictable twists and turns. My fundamental goal is personal challenge and with it the opportunity to effect change. Sometimes I win and sometimes not, but each new challenge benefits from the past and brings forth a new energy and satisfaction level.

This is not "how to be a literary agent," nor is it a publishing memoir. It is a story of transitions and challenges. Every entrepreneur meets transitions and challenges their own way. These are mine and I hope they will resonate for you. If you are thinking of pursuing your own path, may you find in these pages the confidence to take the plunge—or the assurance that following your current course is wiser.

It is difficult in today's volatile business world to define the meaning of "career security." For me, it is some combination of education, life experience, relationships with talented people, mentors and mentoring, and willingness to take risks. Each person will measure these elements on his or her own terms.

The Agent

ONE

··

Cease and Desist

Agents try very hard to sell as many rights as they can, in as many creative (and remunerative) ways as they can. They also try not to sell the same right twice to different people at the same time. Just such a mistake in 1998 put me unexpectedly in the position of becoming an electronic publisher. I had acquired the fifty-year-old Scott Meredith Literary Agency in 1993. The agency continued to represent dozens of estates with hundreds of titles, arranging translation editions, permissions for excerpting, and new editions for titles that were out of print.

One of these titles was the novel *Red Alert* by Peter George, rarely read today but a very good book nonetheless. The title's claim to fame was that it was the basis for Stanley Kubrick's classic film *Dr. Strangelove*. We sold the publishing arm of Barnes & Noble a license to publish a trade paperback edition of the book, with worldwide

English rights and permission to sublicense. Barnes & Noble sublicensed Souvenir Press to publish a British edition. In an inadvertent error made by my foreign rights staffer, months later we gave a direct license for the British edition to Prion Books, for placement in a line of books which had become classic films. To make matters worse, Souvenir and Prion scheduled their editions for the same season in 1999 and learned of each other's plans from their respective catalogs.

Of course, neither Souvenir nor Prion were happy and we were caught in the middle. Barnes & Noble did a lot of licensing business with Souvenir and was less concerned with this title than the relationship. Prion had already printed 5,000 jackets and was not interested in throwing out its investment and announcement. John Kelly, the Barnes & Noble publisher, threw the problem into my lap. After many transatlantic exchanges, I worked out the Solomonic solution that Souvenir would publish first, Prion's publication would become a sublicense from Souvenir, and I would personally pay a modest amount to compensate Prion for its legal fees. John Kelly was very grateful.

For some time I had been considering a business idea that would make me a publisher. It was in many ways a natural progression. I had no idea at the time that it would lead me into the middle of one of the most contested rights-conflict cases in my nearly thirty years in publishing. Ironically, the challenge to my business idea became that authors were selling rights twice: once to their original publisher, and later to the business I would form.

My idea was to form an electronic publishing company focused on acquiring exclusive electronic rights to the premier backlist titles. From my experience in the business and from close study of the Scott Meredith contract files, I was convinced that the authors owned the electronic rights to any title when the prime publishing contract was silent on electronic rights. I helped Richard Hurwitz, a young entrepreneur, explore the electronic rights marketplace with agents, and was satisfied that the the general view of agents was the same as mine—their authors controlled the rights. Some publishers, like Simon & Schuster, had adopted electronic rights clauses in the mid–1980s. Others, like Time Warner (owner of Little, Brown and Warner Books), had not adopted clauses until the mid–1990s. While some authors had granted electronic rights to their older titles when they were relicensed or renewed, the vast majority of books in copyright—works published since 1923—were silent on electronic rights, since neither publisher nor author had foreseen the electronic world in which we now live.

There was some gossip in the community that publishers would begin to seek to acquire these rights. Bn.com ultimately announced a full-fledged effort to acquire rights for both backlist and frontlist titles. Time Warner formed an electronic publishing unit, iPublish, which originally was a competitive answer to iUniverse.com but rapidly positioned itself to publish electronic editions of Time Warner books and other titles it could acquire. Simon & Schuster formed an electronic unit and was the first to make front-page news with the publication of an original electronic novella, *Riding the Bullet* by Stephen King. They also moved to tie up electronic rights for some of its most important backlist properties, such as the works of Ernest Hemingway.

I thought an independent electronic publisher would have certain advantages no major trade publisher could offer. The trade publishers were interested in controlling titles for the life of copyright, just as their prime contracts did for print. The authors and agents were understandably nervous about long-term commitments to the unknown. Trade publishers placed their promotional interest on their frontlist titles. Preeminent backlist titles often have not been promoted for years. Authors and agents know this and resent it. A company dedicated to the backlist could give these titles and their authors the promotion they deserve. On the other hand, trade publishers had to be concerned first and foremost with their retail relationships. For many, the Internet is at heart a direct-selling vehicle. A company that took every advantage of the Internet as a medium for direct-selling opportunities could build an on-line following that no retail-oriented company could afford to pursue. Trade publishers are very concerned with maintaining the higher price points of the paper editions, particularly the hardcover books of the frontlist. Since electronic reading is in its infancy, my view was that attractive pricing and pricing models (rental, subscription, free trial, and so forth) would be key. By focusing on books whose paper editions were already paperbacks at lower price points, we had more flexibility. As far as I could determine, trade publishers were also not prepared to pay an advance for the electronic rights. Even a modest advance payment would make an impression on the agent and author community.

I wanted a chance to pitch my idea to Barnes & Noble and thought that John Kelly could arrange it. Kelly worked closely with both Len and Steve Riggio, the brothers who were the principals of Barnes & Noble. Len Riggio ran the parent company, while Steve ran the electronic affiliate, barnesandnoble.com. Steve Riggio got the idea that Easton editions, which were available only through direct response from Easton Press, could be successfully marketed on barnesandnoble.com. Kelly was asked to see how that might be achieved.

In light of my handling of *Red Alert,* Kelly was willing to let me deal directly with Steve Riggio on Easton. It was unusual in my experience for a literary agent to deal directly with a senior executive of a bookseller or book wholesaler. Publishers jealously guarded those relationships for themselves. The chance to deal directly with Steve Riggio presented an opportunity on which I planned to maximize. Kelly introduced me as an expert in handling rights. I cleared with Easton that they would at least meet to explore a relationship. When I got my chance to talk to Steve Riggio by telephone, we agreed to set two meetings—one with Easton Press, and another at his suggestion with Richard Tam, the chief executive officer of iUniverse, then a company focused on publishing unpublished authors. Barnes & Noble then owned 49 percent of iUniverse. Tam potentially needed some rights assistance.

The meetings with Easton ultimately went nowhere. Easton Press and its parent, MBI (whose other divisions included the Danbury Mint and Postal Commemorative Society), had grown very successfully over the years by controlling their own marketing. MBI and Easton also were proceeding very slowly with Web-based marketing. The meetings with Steve Riggio and Richard Tam, however, spun into a number of interesting directions.

Tam had developed two infrastructures. The first dealt with using electronic systems to bring the publishing process into the twenty-first century. Part of such a system would come to be called *digital rights management* (DRM). The digital world required DRM for a number of reasons—encryption (that is, master files which could be transformed into otherwise incompatible digital delivery systems), download tracking, which would enable financial monitoring, and the like. Another part would track and produce a manuscript from acquisition through editorial and copy editing through the printing process. The second infrastructure took this electronic content and used servers and specialized printing and binding machines to produce as few as one book at a time (so-called print-on-demand). The hardware had originally been built by IBM to accommodate government document needs. Now there was a cost-affordable way to produce trade books with a similar technology.

The largest independent distributor in trade publishing was Ingram, which formed a unit called Lightning Source to produce and distribute print-on-demand editions. The appeal for publishers was that thousands of titles which sold relatively few copies each year could now be kept in print indefinitely, without having to maintain inventory. Barnes & Noble had tried to buy Ingram, but the effort was blocked by the U. S. Justice Department. Tam had forged an alliance with Lightning Source, which gave him access to booksellers, production, and order fulfillment.

Tam had already labeled his offer to publish anyone in a print-on-demand edition for $100 "the new face of publishing." The Scott Meredith Literary Agency had read the manuscripts of unpublished authors for a fee for nearly fifty years. At its peak in the 1980s, that agency alone read more than 4,000 manuscripts annually. Unlike iUniverse, which offered to publish all comers, Scott Meredith offered a critique that concluded with whether or not a manuscript was commercially saleable to a trade publisher—in the agency's judgment it was rarely was, and, indeed, manuscripts rejected by the program were very rarely published at all.

Tam planned to capture the publishing business down to people who wanted to publish their children's efforts for a birthday party. To make his effort more credible, he needed as many professional titles as possible. Some of those would come from the rare titles that iUniverse would publish electronically and Barnes & Noble would sell at retail. Tam thought that he could extend the model by publishing hundreds of print-on-demand editions from the backlist of trade publishers.

Tam retained me to help iUniverse develop these licensing relationships, much as I had done for nearly 2,000 titles for Easton Press. We would seek print-on-demand rights from publishers who controlled these rights for their backlist titles. Print-on-demand rights, which created paper books, were typically controlled by publishers for their entire backlists and could be licensed unless the publisher was inclined to develop the rights itself. At this stage of my career, I was far more interested in equity than fees, and as an agent I had worked for contingent commissions for more than twenty-five years. I delivered what Tam wanted—licenses which would have given iUniverse depth in quality science fiction, mystery, and romance. Typical for Web companies, Tam was evaluating his next steps with his investors as my negotiations firmed up. In the end, he declined to go forward with the licenses, but honored his deal with me by delivering stock options in the company. Over the months, iUniverse backed away from its original strategy of treating authors as their customers, in favor of a corporate strategy which delivered print-on-demand and electronic book services for publishers and large corporations.

When I first met Steve Riggio, I was on the Board of a then privately held company called Webcasts.com. Webcasts.com was one of a few companies specializing in the emerging technology of broadcasting video signals over the Web and particularly Webcasts with an interactive character. Barnes & Noble had produced dozens of short videos promoting categories of reading, often with a focus on a particular author or set of titles. Riggio was considering Webcasting these videos on his site, and I was able to arrange meetings for my team. Webcasts.com also explored outfitting the flagship store of Barnes & Noble in New York as a studio, where visiting authors would participate in live and taped Webcasts. Ultimately, nothing came out of these discussions.

The Easton Press, iUniverse, and Webcasts.com discussions gave me an opportunity to interact with Steve Riggio somewhat frequently in 1999. Steve Riggio was and is messianic on the subject of electronic books and how they will change trade publishing. Since Amazon.com had gotten a substantial head start on Barnes & Noble selling paper books over the Web, Riggio was determined to position Barnes & Noble as a leader in electronic books. Early efforts of barnesandnoble.com had cost more than $100 million. Before I met Steve Riggio, Barnes & Noble had invited Bertelsmann, to join as a partner. The resulting company, referred to as bn.com, is 40 percent owned by Barnes & Noble, 40 percent by Bertelsmann and 20 percent by the public. When he and I began talking, Steve Riggio was acting chief executive officer, a position in which he was renewed in May 2001.

I shared the view that electronic publishing would be a watershed change for trade publishing. I had represented the Vatican Library and seen their extraordinary collection of handwritten bibles. With his invention of movable type, Johannes Gutenberg had brought the bible to the masses nearly 500 years ago (roughly when the Vatican Library was formed). Whatever one thought of the new paper printing technology or even print-on-demand, the experience for the consumer was the same—a physical book in your hand. And the publisher had to find a way to produce and deliver that physical book.

Electronic publishing changed all of that: delivery to the consumer by almost instantaneous download; a reading experience limited only by the pace of new technology, with the appliances and software packages which make it work; easily adjusted font size for those who prefer larger type; search engines that find words in context, anywhere throughout a book, instantly; dictionaries that define and even pronounce a highlighted word; on-screen note taking and highlighting, used to collect and summarize information for writing papers; and a storage capability equal to forty books in a single hand-held device, with compression technologies coming to market which will multiply that amount by ten.

I quickly realized that my interaction with Steve Riggio could be my chance to create the electronic publishing company I had been thinking about. Riggio was excited when I first described the idea. He told me that as part of bn.com's discussions to align with Microsoft, they had discussed with Bill Gates the effectiveness of an independent company to gather rights. Both Microsoft and bn.com as huge companies could have image and practical problems as rights buyers in the agent and author community. I decided that I should approach Riggio with a fully realized, credible business plan rather than with a pitch that he could turn back into a job offer. I had already spent a few years with Mark McCormack's International Publishing Group after a head hunter recruited me, and, as much as I admired IMG, I had promised myself when I bought Scott Meredith that I was done working for other people. For a business plan to be convincing, I would need partners, partly for capital and partly for expertise.

I turned to Marshall Sonenshine, a forty-year-old investment banker who had begun as a partner at James Wolfensohn and stayed with the firm through its sales to Bankers Trust and later to Deutsche Bank. His specialty was media. I knew Marshall since we had served for several years on the Board of a wonderful New York City arts-in-education organization, ArtsConnection. I had been involved with ArtsConnection for nearly twenty years, ever since I had been recruited by Linda Janklow, its founding and continuing chairman.

By coincidence, Marshall was setting up his own investment banking boutique just as I was meeting with Steve Riggio. Marshall's partner was Rafael Pastor, who had run a major part of Rupert Murdoch's international operations and who had extensive experience in media-related companies. Both were lawyers and close friends. The firm opened its doors as Sonenshine & Pastor (later Sonenshine, Pastor & Appel) and SP Capital. Its business model was to invest its own capital in appropriate early stage companies, while paying its overhead with consulting and transactional banking assignments. By May 2001, Sonenshine & Pastor had raised significant equity for PC on Call, a company which brought computer services to the door of businesses and represented Structural Dynamic Research Corp. in a $1 billion sale to EDS, the huge data processing company founded by Ross Perot.

We had our first planning breakfast in the fall of 1999, before Marshall and Rafael had committed to their Rockefeller Center offices and hired their first Yale BA/Harvard MBA staffers. After days of discussion, we decided to form a company and begin by trying to recruit bn.com and Bell & Howell (a corporate client of Marshall's) as strategic investors. Bell & Howell had a $100 million division that electronic products distributed on-line to 50,000 schools. I had never prepared a serious business plan before. It took us until January 2000 to finish a presentation that everyone liked.

Marshall, Rafael, and I presented to Steve Riggio and his financial officer, Marie Toulantis. On the substance of our slide show, we certainly got no argument, since bn.com was making significant investments on the same assumptions. We showed that substantial electronic companies such as Microsoft, Adobe, and Palm were investing a great deal of money in e-reading and that over the next several years electronic reading would have a substantial market. We pointed out that about 40 percent of the revenues of the nearly $25 billion–annual trade publishing business were from the backlist, and that most of those sales were sourced in perennially selling titles. We shared with Riggio a list of nearly 1,000 titles we thought would be appropriate to acquire. Of course, Barnes & Noble's database was one of the industry's best for sales patterns of titles from all publishers. We estimated that of 1.5 million titles published since 1923, at most 25,000 met our definition of quality e-reading. And we projected high-margin sales with annual revenues well over $100 million over the next five years. Our company would only acquire electronic rights for reading on screens, in part to give us a clear focus and in part out of necessity—for any in-print title, the paper publisher would obviously control the print rights (and for many out-of-print titles as well, if the rights had not been formally reverted to the author).

Steve Riggio was focused in these and later meetings. He told stories of how other Barnes & Noble investments came about: iUniverse was a last minute substitute for near deal with Xlibris, a company Random House ultimately funded. He shared his experiences with the early days of Rocket Books, when its founder Martin Eberhardt, showed him a mock-up of the device and Riggio committed on the spot. We discussed the pros and cons of limited exclusivity for bn.com if it became an investor. Riggio openly shared his competitive feelings about Amazon. He gave us financial follow-up assignments for spreadsheets and detailed projections. We clearly had his attention.

We went through what turned out to be a multimonth process with bn.com and Bell & Howell that almost resulted in having both companies as strategic investors. Three problems ultimately doomed the strategic investments. The first was valuation: We were discussing this investment as the markets began to collapse around us. The second was exclusivity: Both parties wanted significant exclusivity for their channel of distribution in exchange for the investment. We felt strongly that we should be licensing rights exclusively from authors and selling nonexclusively through distributors and retailers in order to maximize the opportunity for the company. The third problem was the most vexing. Bn.com and Bell & Howell believed that we would be successfully licensing rights, but we didn't control any rights at the time. In other words, we were asking them to trust us with their money to succeed in rights acquisitions. Both companies had extensive rights buying capabilities of their own. Eventually, both companies said to call them back when we had the rights, even if an investment at that time would be much more expensive.

In the summer of 2000, Marshall, Rafael, and I decided that if we believed in our plan, we would have to execute it ourselves. We decided that betting our own money would let us acquire titles and build a demonstration of the business. It was early enough in the adoption curve for electronic rights that top quality titles could be acquired for an advance of $5,000 or less. Our concept was to raise a round of financing based on the demonstration after the end of the year, and then solicit a much larger round of funding twelve to eighteen months thereafter.

I knew that one of the most important challenges would be building a brand and that the first step would be a strong name and logo. Initially, my branding and design adviser Christopher Johnson and I came up with the name "Yourclassics.com." As Marshall and Rafael got more involved in the company, we looked for another name. Rafael's telling comment was, "I don't like 'your,' I don't like 'classics,' and I don't like '.com.'" Christopher and I went back to plan and, in one long conversation, settled on "RosettaBooks" and, later, "Rosetta Stone," a character who would act as an electronic "librarian" and sharp-tongued spokesperson for our Web site. Christopher followed the naming with one of his typically wonderful logos and now everyone was excited.

RosettaBooks worked for us on a number of levels. While the actual Rosetta stone was not universally known, it was certainly well known among educators, and it drew, with the Elgin marbles from the Parthenon, crowds in the millions each year at the British Museum. The stone itself was a "portal" in its own way to ancient Egypt. To the extent we would connect quality writing of the past with the technology of the present, the analogy seemed apt. Also, while others were selecting gibberish names which were soon to communicate here today but perhaps gone tomorrow (Questia, Xlibris), RosettaBooks seemed to suggest that we had been in business for some time, or, in any event, planned to be.

We made another fundamental decision at the outset—RosettaBooks would be an author-centric business. I knew that the main complaint of authors and agents for their backlist books was lack of attention and promotion by publishers. RosettaBooks would offer broad promotion which would help both the electronic and the paper edition sales, since the paper editions were so underpromoted. We would also focus on the quality backlist and celebrate fiction. I thought that the large publishers would need to focus on their frontlists, which are very diverse. Also, they would try to issue public domain programs, an initiative which in my judgment would be overwhelmed by offers of free titles (this is already the case on Amazon and through the University of Virginia, among others). Rosetta could show the agents and authors a clear mission.

We meant several things by "author-centric." The first was the look and feel of the Web site and the product itself. We learned how to present a uniform Rosetta typeface across all commercial Internet delivery platforms. Christopher Johnson and his team created the first "electronic jackets" intended to be clearly visible in thumbnail and resized to fit full-screen depending on the format of delivery. The jackets typically seen on Amazon or bn.com are identical to the hardcover or softcover jackets. Those jackets are rarely designed with the Web in mind—in fact, you often can't clearly read the author's name or the title in electronic thumbnail view. Our e-jackets "popped" in the size intended and emphasized the author, title, or corresponding Hollywood movie as appropriate.

We commissioned original copy about the author, the title, and, if the book had been made into a film, the movie. And we took advantage of the Web by researching and presenting the RosettaBooks Connections, a set of hyperlinks to sites related to the author, content, or context of the title. We also gave the author the opportunity to place his or her own hyperlink on our site and to offer "news" which we would promote. We presented the authors as "legends" and their work as an "electronic festival."

More important than presentation would be our approach to distribution. A passive listing on a bookseller site with hundreds of thousands of titles did not seem to be worth much. Our guiding principle became the exposure for our e-jackets. We sought exposures in the millions. As we looked out over the embryonic state of the e-book business our plan would consist of two things: a promotional presence on the bookseller sites and aggressive alliances with hardware and software makers and with high-traffic Web sites that did not normally sell e-books. Of course, to make this happen, we would need high-profile titles.

Our first major title signing success was with the estate of Aldous Huxley for *Brave New World* and *Brave New World Revisited*. Scott Meredith was co-agent for the books with Dorris Halsey, who represented the estate. Aldous Huxley's grandson Trev Huxley was a co-founder of Muze.com, a leading electronic database company for the music, film, and publishing businesses. We satisfied Trev Huxley, who was extremely sophisticated about electronic issues, that we were the right company to bring his grandfather's work to the electronic marketplace. My key conversation, however, was with Aldous Huxley's third wife, now eighty-eight-year-old Laura. Laura Huxley was a concert violinist with Arturo Toscanini, a renowned psychoanalyst and author of a book about Aldous Huxley. She grilled me for an hour about many issues, including details of the contract. I knew the conversation was a success only when the contracts were finally signed.

Pat Conroy is the lead fiction writer being represented by International Management Group. I was able to negotiate a four-book license, including *The Prince of Tides, The Great Santini,* and *The Lords of Discipline.* Kurt Vonnegut had been a leading Easton Press author for fifteen years. I negotiated a five-book license with his lawyer, Donald Farber, that included *Slaughterhouse Five, Cat's Cradle,* and *Breakfast of Champions.* In science fiction, we acquired *The Puppet Masters* by Robert Heinlein and, from Russell Galen, Scott Meredith's former lead agent, short stories by Ray Bradbury and Arthur C. Clarke. In mystery, we acquired Agatha Christie's *And Then There Were None* and Ed McBain's *Fuzz.* We added *An American Tragedy* by Theodore Dreiser and three award-winning books on the American Experience by the former Librarian of Congress Daniel Boorstin. Our first success among London agents was the six-volume Winston Churchill's World War II set. George Orwell's *1984* followed. In all, we lined up from several dozen representatives nearly one hundred titles in science fiction, mystery, movie tie-ins, and fiction and nonfiction classics.

Our progress was the result of a great deal of effort and the strong advice from my partners to hire good people before we needed them. Our first hire, Leo Dwyer, was a Harvard MBA with extensive entrepreneurial experience but no background in publishing. Since almost all electronic publishing issues were by definition new, Leo could use his general business experience. As a very effective chief operating officer, Leo made us look like a much bigger company to those with whom we dealt. Our second hire, Dorothy Kauffman, came to us after years of senior profit-and-loss responsibility at Bertelsmann's BMG music clubs. Dorothy helped us create a Web site whose content, functionality, and appearance compared favorably with companies who had spent many times our investment. As our chief marketing and editorial officer, she became a talented rights recruiter as well.

Why did authors license to us when we were so clearly a start-up? My credibility and access to the author representatives helped. More important was our preliminary Web site, which confirmed what we planned to do and our specific exposure opportunities. Our very visible advisory board was a plus, as was the momentum of persuading one agent/author based on the commitment of another. Fundamentally we succeeded when agents and authors were ready to experiment with electronic editions and where our model—including favorable license terms and an advance—was appealing. As Bill Hamilton, the agent for George Orwell's estate said when Dorothy and I visited him in London, "I thought someone would come to talk to me about this sooner or later."

One of Leo's early tasks was to figure out how we would digitize, securitize, and serve our titles to the consumer and through various alliances. On Leo's recommendation, we hired Reciprocal as our Digital Rights Management (DRM) company. Their clients included Random House, Time Warner, Pearson, and many others. The rapidly changing technology permitted us to serve a wide range of commercial platforms and consider an ever more intricate set of options for marketing (free samples, jackets placed on other Web sites for automatic orders, time-limited offers, etc.) Also, their volume capability— millions of downloads in a day—gave us the chance to consider high volume and secure promotions. Reciprocal later signed AMS, the major wholesaler to the warehouse selling clubs, Baker & Taylor, a leading independent wholesaler, and hardware companies as clients. These developments made coordinating promotions easier.

As part of our commitment to brand building, we decided that one of our most important team members would be our public relations adviser. We decided to retain Burson-Marsteller, the world's largest public relations company. Our team, led by Robert Grieves was very effective getting us early attention and invaluable when Random House decided to sue us. They helped large companies feel comfortable with us.

I decided that our credibility would be enhanced with many constituencies, particularly the schools, if we could recruit a diverse advisory board. I had rarely asked any important people in my life for help, certainly operating on the principle "Never ask big people for small favors." However, this seemed like a good time to start asking and, fortunately, people responded positively: Bill Bradley, whom I had helped in politics for thirty years (starting when he decided not to run for statewide office in Missouri); the world-renowned sociologist Nathan Glazer, who had used my college work in revised editions of *Beyond the Melting Pot* (and who happened to be my uncle); the celebrated political scientist James Q. Wilson, who had been a client for a successful textbook project; the Nobel Laureate in Medicine Dr. Joseph Murray, whose moving memoir I had been an adviser for; two Pulitzer Prize winners, Paul Goldberger in architecture (a friend since college) and David Kennedy in history (thanks to another Board member, William Lilley, my college mentor); Sheila Lukins, my client who had sold 10 million cookbooks; Checker (Dr. Chester E.) Finn, Jr., one of the leading opinion makers in education and a fellow Moynihan staffer in Nixon's White House; Bryna Sanger, a leading student of government administration (a friend since college); Bernice Kanner, a marketing jack-of-all-trades for Bloomberg and others; and Stephen Hess, a Brookings Presidential Scholar and Moynihan's White House deputy.

Distribution and marketing would be the key to our success. If we could gain enough exposure for our book jackets, we would be a leader in e-book sales as the adoption curve grew. The exposure itself would build our brand and make title licensing easier. And each high-profile promotion would make the next promotion easier to execute. Our strategy was simple. We wanted high-profile exposure on bookseller Web sites and as many high traffic promotions as we could muster.

Steve Riggio and his team, led by Michael Fragnito, worked out an arrangement for RosettaBooks to have a "boutique" on bn.com, meaning that Rosetta would be listed among relatively few publishers on bn.com's e-book home page. When the consumer clicked on our listing, they would go straight to a page which highlighted a group of Rosetta titles. This was, of course, meaningfully more visible than a simple listing on bn.com. Bn.com provided a boutique in both Microsoft Reader and Adobe Glassbook formats.

Amazon initially offered us standard listings (we refused). Later we worked out very visible promotions. We strengthened our access to Amazon through our relationships with Microsoft and Adobe, each of whom established substantial alliances with Amazon. Smaller e-book sites such as Powells and Contentville were happy to give prominent placement to showcase our titles.

We were very interested in establishing distribution to the educational marketplace. Folletts, a multigenerational family-held company, is the leading book distributor to the 100,000 school libraries in the United States. Like most book companies, Follett saw the need to enter the e-book marketplace to stay competitive. They established e-folletts in cooperation with Overdrive, an e-book marketing company whose principal investor was Microsoft. For the launch of e-folletts, we provided *The Prince of Tides* and *Brave New World* in exchange for promises of prominent promotion on five hundred college campuses.

Baker & Taylor, second only to Ingram as an independent wholesaler of books, is a $700 million annual sales unit of the enormous venture capital firm The Carlyle Group. In business for nearly 150 years, they serve nearly 25,000 publishers (although close to 90 percent of their business is with the top 400). Although the leader in book distribution to the 9,000 public libraries in the United States, Baker & Taylor was playing catch-up to Net Library, a well capitalized Web start-up, in e-book sales to libraries. Rosetta was the first electronic publisher invited to meet the senior Baker & Taylor team to discuss how our titles could help their electronic library initiative. As a result of these meetings, we permitted them to use *Brave New World* to demonstrate their e-book lending system at the 2001 American Library Association Convention.

Despite Baker & Taylor's importance as a wholesaler to major publishers, no other publisher had permitted them to demonstrate titles in the new electronic system. The system was different than standard DRM systems (which permitted only a single user) because it enabled both lending (one copy at a time) to users and time-limited use (an e-book for a month, for example). Rosetta was inclined to participate in all legitimate new electronic business models. The Baker & Taylor model, which effectively created an "electronic library edition" of a title, justified a higher retail price.

We scrambled to take advantage of visible alliances. DataPlay, a privately held company backed by Toshiba and Universal Music, had developed a compression technology which delivered five hundred megabytes on a disk the size of a quarter. For e-books, this was the equivalent of five hundred titles on one disk; for audiobooks, thirty-four hours of recorded voice; for MP3 quality music eleven hours, and for studio-recorded music six hours. The technology was striking enough that DataPlay won most of the major awards at the 2001 Consumer Electronics Show. Several major recording labels (including EMI and BMG) agreed to publish with DataPlay technology. Microsoft agreed to release games. But at the Consumer Electronics Show (and six months later), RosettaBooks was the only e-book partner. Our edition of *Brave New World* appeared in all of DataPlay's advertising opposite Disney photography, Garth Brooks, Sting, and the Toshiba logo on blank disks.

We also demonstrated the first ever e-book and unabridged audiobook on the same platform—a presentation with implications for learning to read, particularly those for whom English is a second language. This demonstration led DataPlay to invite Rosetta to assemble audiobook recordings for issue on DataPlay technology. Since a typical unabridged audiobook runs between fifteen and twenty-five hours on multiple disks, the distribution and pricing implications of reducing the delivery to one quarter-sized disk are substantial. The DataPlay alliance brought us early favorable exposure. Leo Dwyer and I manned our section of the space-age DataPlay booth at the Consumer Electronics Show in front of mock-ups of our most attractive titles and met dozens of people who could help our business development. Leo chaired a Microsoft-sponsored presentation for the audiobook industry at the 2001 BEA convention in Chicago which took this e-book/audiobook technology to another level.

We had targeted Microsoft, Adobe, and Palm for promotional marketing projects from the moment we closed our early title licenses. All had the same basic problem. For the consumer to order e-books, they first had to download (at no cost) the enabling software. Even by the summer of 2001, relatively few consumers had, in fact, elected to download the software—several hundred thousand for Palm (out of more than 10 million machines), perhaps one million for Adobe Glassbook (versus 170 million Acrobat users), and at most double that for Microsoft Reader (but still less than one percent of the Windows-installed base). To push the adoption of e-reading (trade books or textbooks, newspapers, magazines, and other professional materials) would require aggressive consumer marketing and education. Over time, new appliances would come preloaded with reading programs, but until they did and dominated the market, consumers would have to be encouraged to add software to their current machines.

We wanted Palm, Adobe, and Microsoft to use our titles promotionally for millions of exposures. Adobe was the first to respond. In January 2001, Leo was able to arrange twenty-four-hour delivery of a Ray Bradbury short story *The Playground,* which, supported by the circulation of 3 million e-mails, became a bestseller on bn.com. Our quickness in meeting Adobe's needs and the quality of our title list led them to offer us a slot in each of their next five promotions including a "time-limited" offer—ten hours for one dollar of Agatha Christie's *And Then There Were None.* We gave Microsoft a short exclusive on *Brave New World* and in exchange they promoted the title on their newly redesigned home page for MS Reader. Our high-profile promotions with Palm after their purchase of Peanut Press included our Pat Conroy offers.

We tried to group our efforts around an official launch of the RosettaBooks Web site on February 26, 2001. Adobe's promotions, Microsoft's break of *Brave New World*, bn.com's boutique, and Overdrive's e-follett announcement were all coordinated roughly to fall in the same window of time. About forty of our titles were available for downloading from our site in three formats and negotiations were underway to extend distribution to Gemstar's REB 1100 (formerly known as RocketBook). That day started particularly well, with the final confirmation from London that we could proceed with Agatha Christie's *And Then There Were None* (often known as *Ten Little Indians*) and two other Christie titles. Since this was one of Agatha Christie's leading titles, acquiring the electronic rights was a great coup for us and suggested that the London title pitch trip which Dorothy and I had recently completed would indeed bear fruit.

By mid-morning, our day took a very unexpected turn. Random House's lawyers, Weil, Gotshal, hand-delivered a letter claiming electronic exclusive electronic rights to Rosetta's William Styron, Kurt Vonnegut, and Robert Parker titles and demanding that we cease and desist publishing those titles in twenty-four hours. They also demanded that we not seek to acquire rights from any of the more than 20,000 Random House backlist titles. It was clear that they would sue in the morning if we didn't comply. If we had so attracted the attention of the largest English-language publisher in the world, we had certainly succeeded in making our demonstration project look important.

Marshall, Rafael, and I decided during the day that to back down to Random House—which had nearly a one-third market share in the United States and whose sister company Random House Group had a similar market share in the United Kingdom—would inevitably mean that other large publishers would take the same position and block our electronic rights licensing. I was confident that our fundamental position—that authors owned electronic rights unless contracts specifically conveyed them to publishers—was sound. Now we would have to fight to prove it and put our fledgling company at risk to do so.

Our immediate problem on Tuesday was that Random House sued RosettaBooks corporately and me personally and went to the media to characterize us as Napster-like pirates even before we received the papers. From a public relations point of view, Burson-Marsteller stepped in and pointed out that we had signed contracts with the authors, so our case bore no resemblance to Napster (Napster never had or claimed any rights). They made me available to journalists throughout the day and early evening, and as a result the first-day coverage, particularly in the *New York Times* (which ran a strong supportive quote from Paul Aitken, executive director of the Authors Guild) and the *Wall Street Journal,* was balanced or positive.

We needed to be represented in Federal Court on Wednesday morning and as of Tuesday morning we didn't have litigating attorneys. Marshall had prior experience with David Boies's law firm, perhaps the most sought after law firm in the United States. As a courtesy to a client, the firm stepped in Tuesday afternoon, worked late Tuesday night, and by Wednesday morning one of their talented partners, William Isaacson, was well prepared to argue in front of Judge Sidney Stein. Weil, Gotshal sought an immediate hearing date. Isaacson successfully argued that the importance of the case, the size of Random House's filing in terms of affidavits and briefs, and the rather nominal and easily measured flow of actual e-book sales all argued for a reasonable response date, which the judge set for April 20.

As we reviewed our options, Kay Murray, general counsel of the Authors Guild, called to offer the organization's full support. The Authors Guild had a proud history dating back to 1912, and in 2001 boasted nearly 7,000 members and a professional staff of a dozen, mostly attorneys. As we talked, Kay Murray suggested that I check with the Philadelphia law firm of Kohn, Swift & Graf and its partner Michael Boni. She was very pleased with the work the firm was doing on another electronic rights matter. The firm specialized in David and Goliath cases and had quite a track record representing David. They also had current experience opposite Weil, Gotshal and Bertelsmann, Random House's parent company. Random House may have been hoping that our young corporation couldn't or wouldn't stand up to them. They may also have calculated that naming me as a personal defendant would complicate my life as a literary agent. If so, both the hope and the calculation turned out to be wrong.

The decision to name me as an individual defendant made it easier for Burson-Marsteller to interest the media in interviewing me. Inside.com (immediately before its sale to *Brill's Content*) profiled me in an article titled, "The Accidental Crusader." Many widely read Web columns described the case at length—one even using the David and Goliath analogy to say that we were about to place a rock into Random House's ample forehead. Ultimately, the *Wall Street Journal* filed a front-page marketing section piece about the litigation the day before the court hearing on the preliminary injunction and validated the interest of the major media in covering the case—and Rosetta.

Of course, the main arena had to be the courtroom, not the media. We began in a large planning session at the Authors Guild. Paul Aiken, the executive director, and Kay Murray led the Guild team. Their outside counsel, led by David Woolf, would prepare the amicus brief. The Association of Authors Representatives (AAR) was represented by its president, agent Donald Maass, and its able outside counsel for the past several decades, Ken Norwick. Robert La Rocca, Mike Boni's partner, led our legal team. The meeting opened with Kay Murray's comment that she couldn't recall a time when a publisher sat in its offices with issues at stake of such importance to the authors' community. I chimed in that we were an author-centric publisher, so it seemed appropriate.

The Guild and AAR team worked very hard to help our four-person legal team. Leo, Dorothy, and I did whatever we could to back up our lawyers (and contributed our own affidavits). Rafael offered the benefit of his experience as deputy counsel at CBS and other relevant experiences in major litigation. We got a major break when Cathy Fowler, who had run Random House's reference and electronic unit in the 1990s, called and offered her testimony. She was, in effect, the Insider. Her testimony in essence was that she went to work at Random House after helping Simon & Schuster establish an electronic program in the late 1980s. Her first assignment was to study the rights picture. She concluded that Random House's standard publishing agreements, which were silent with respect to electronic rights, could not be construed to convey electronic rights. A number of electronic rights licenses to older titles were negotiated so that Random House could acquire the rights. Ultimately, in 1994, Random House adopted a new contract form with explicit electronic rights clauses. This contract was implemented contentiously in the community.

Major agents contributed powerful affidavits, which essentially laid out the history of trade custom and contract interpretation in the publishing business. The agents for William Styron, Kurt Vonnegut, and Robert Parker submitted strong affidavits supporting Rosetta. Of course, if Random House was right, their authors had licensed the same rights twice. I guess Random House thought it had enough of a public relations issue on its hands with the test cast against us without suing its authors. Or perhaps they thought Rosetta would bring the authors into the case. We never seriously considered that option, since our business is pro-author.

The Authors Guild and the AAR put in an eloquently argued joint amicus brief, the first joint brief in their histories. In addition to the legal argument, the brief pointed out that publishers including Random House were "warehousing" the electronic rights since their electronic publication plans impacted only a small percentage of the titles they did control. Among the 3,000 new titles published annually and all contracts since 1994 with an electronic rights grant clause, Random House seemed to have a pretty deep supply of titles. Not to mention its ability to seek to license the electronic rights to any backlist titles they wished.

Random House sought and gained a two-week delay when they saw our papers, an unusual step for a plaintiff seeking a preliminary injunction (the plaintiff is supposed to be worried about the urgency). As Random House filed their reply brief, Simon & Schuster, Time Warner, Penguin, and Perseus joined to file an amicus brief for Random House. Now we had by my count about $5 billion of sales lined up against us. I commented to some reporters that we should be flattered that a start-up like Rosetta was already perceived as such a threat.

Random House and their supporters argued that the basic rights grant to "print, publish, and sell in book form" included e-books, even though the grant had been made at a time when neither buyer nor seller could visualize a desktop computer, let alone an e-book. Random House relied heavily on several movie cases, including a claim by the owners of Igor Stravinsky's *The Rite of Spring* symphony that when they licensed in 1940 to Disney for *Fantasia* they did not contemplate videocassette distribution as it developed in the 1980s. Movie rights grants are broad and tend to be a flat fee; book rights grants are narrow and royalty specific. Also movies are collaborative and expensive efforts, with creative components merged. Books are the creative act of an author and relatively inexpensive to produce and market. No one was challenging Random House's rights to the printed physical editions (even though under the new copyright act they would run almost one hundred years from initial publication). Random House would earn profits from them for generations.

Random House also claimed that e-book editions would compete with the sales of printed books. This had been the movie industry's concern when videocassettes and television licensing became commonplace (would people still go to theaters)—the answer was that more people went to theaters. In the book industry, the growth of the audiobook—to nearly ten percent of the sales of trade books—had come over a fifteen-year period when the growth of hardcover book sales had never been healthier. Also, the book clubs paid publishers a fraction per title of what they could earn by making the sale themselves. Yet publishers routinely licensed their best titles to the clubs, viewing the visibility and the channel of distribution as incremental sales opportunity. And that was all for the frontlist title. Our view was that the promotion of backlist e-books, which would reach millions, could only accelerate the buying patterns for printed editions which essentially were not otherwise promoted.

While we had tacit informal support from the major electronic companies and some visible authors, most people were understandably loath to get involved in the litigation and upset the publishers whose cooperation they needed for title licensing. Ironically, bn.com (whose 40 percent owner was Bertelsmann, Random House's parent company) stood to benefit since they were trying to license precisely the same community of rights on the same theory that the authors owned the rights. We were able to secure a very powerful affidavit from the author James Gleick, which dramatically illustrated these conflicting interests. He attached his contract with Random House for *Genius* (the bestseller about the physicist Richard Feynman) which had no electronic rights clause, his contract with Penguin (an amicus publisher) for his bestseller *Chaos* which had no electronic rights clause, and his electronic rights contract with iPublish (the Time Warner amicus publisher) to publish those titles electronically!

Of course, Random House was not about to sue bn.com or AOL Time Warner on the same theory they sued RosettaBooks. Bn.com was corporately related to their parent Bertelsmann by ownership. AOL Time Warner was part of a joint marketing agreement with Bertelsmann for the Book of the Month Club, the Literary Guild, and Doubleday Book Clubs. And they later joined together to acquire an electronic company to help them expand the printed book clubs to e-book editions. Since the nearly $1 billion in book club sales dominated the book club markets and created only one buyer for book club rights, the publishing community in general had conflicts as well. Challenging Bertelsmann was potentially angering the book clubs, one of their significant sources of subsidiary rights revenue and title visibility.

By suing RosettaBooks, Random House had the test case they wanted. Since our company and business model was at risk, we chose to make this the test case we wanted. Civil court filings are public documents, but it takes some burrowing at the courthouse to get a look at them and make copies. We published the papers—both sides—electronically on our Web site and announced to the media and publishing community that the information was available. Hundreds visited this area of our site daily. For the media, this projected confidence in our position—and made their homework much easier. For the publishing community, this led to an ever broadening circle of agents, lawyers, intellectual property lawyers, technology experts, and others curious about the litigation—and one well enough informed to express a view which was far more often favorable to us. I felt strongly that the more the dispute was framed in its historic importance, the more likely the author/agent (and therefore Rosetta) position would prevail. Let Random House and the other publishers argue that they couldn't compete to acquire these electronic rights today.

The preliminary injunction hearing was May 8, 2001. The courtroom was a bit like a wedding where neither side approves of the match. One side of the aisle had a team of Random House executives and lawyers and enough Weil, Gotshal lawyers to send a bill equal to a significant electronic rights acquisition budget. The other side had the Authors Guild, AAR, and Rosetta team. There were perhaps a dozen journalists, including reporters for the *Wall Street Journal,* the *Washington Post,* and Bloomberg News. Before we reached our matter, the judge addressed two criminal motions. One defendant, arrested for dealing cocaine, faced a twenty-year sentence and was trying to change his guilty plea. Another, a teacher, was in jail for fraud and was apparently suicidal. The question was if her husband's bond alone would be sufficient for bail. Watching these first motions certainly placed our issues in context. I could lose a company and some money; life had more challenging issues to offer.

Judge Stein was thoughtful and frequently questioned both teams of lawyers during three hours of oral argument. His opening questions established that both sides agreed that neither party had contemplated e-books when these contracts were signed and that the contracts were silent about electronic rights. Perhaps his most interesting questions were those that pressed Bruce Rich of Weil, Gotshal on just how far Random House's definition of a book (and therefore its rights) would go. The judge asked, "What if Kurt Vonnegut's *Slaughterhouse Five* were written on the walls of the courtroom, is that a book? What if it were written in chalk on an East Side sidewalk, is that a book?" Both times, Rich said, "Yes." Rich argued that the Rosetta electronic editions were "flat" rather than multimedia (with hyperlinks, video, audio, and so forth). But he then went on to argue for books from 1923 forward that Random House controlled the multimedia rights in any event and Rosetta would be infringing even if the presentation of the titles was "multimedia."

From a legal perspective we could only wait for the decision on the injunction. From a business point of view there was much to do. The lawsuit was filed days before we planned to begin the process of raising additional capital. With our updated offering memorandum, we began the process of raising more money with the expectation that the typical investor would want to wait for the outcome of the preliminary injunction. Bill Bradley was a founding member of our Advisory Board, a thirty-year colleague, and after his presidential race loss, a managing director at Allen & Co., a leading investment firm in the entertainment industry. Bradley led an Allen & Co. investment in Rosetta before the preliminary injunction was decided, a tremendous credibility boost for us.

We pushed hard for our business concept of "the publisher's electronic publisher." None but the largest publishers chose now to invest in the infrastructure of electronic publishing and the myriad of distribution relationships that were necessary. We could offer significant visibility, links to sites that sold the printed versions, and a maximized electronic sales result without the investment of money or staff time from the publisher. The network we were building for our own titles could easily be extended to others. Our first targets were Reader's Digest and Kensington Publishing (the primary competitor to Harlequin in romance publishing)—I knew both decision-makers well. Also, Baker & Taylor had promised to make appropriate introductions for us.

We also worked to develop forms of electronic publishing that would be outside the boundaries of the litigation, since we could not predict the course of the litigation or its impact on our ability to acquire rights. I had worked several years before with David Clark, a talented young promoter who worked in "cause marketing" with not-for-profits, with the cooperation first of visual artists and later musical performers.

I proposed to David Clark that Rosetta become the "official electronic program" of his events. The electronic program would be for free. We would try to get sponsors for the program and the downloads, both for the visibility and for the necessary free download of the reading software before the program could be received. Also, a multimedia program, which included soundtracks and perhaps a video clip would demonstrate the capabilities of the sponsor's software package. Our first effort became a worldwide AIDS day broadcast with MTV in December, 2001

The demonstration site we had built, the quality of our titles, the fact that they were standing up to Random House and the other publishers effectively and the branding visibility that the fight had brought us all combined to make us look like a formidable independent force in electronic publishing in the summer of 2001. If the lawsuit didn't bury us, we would be at least two years ahead of our business plans because of it. By May 2001, the major mass market retailing sites all took us seriously. Everyone we approached at least explored a high-profile way to align.

We had to wait nine weeks from the oral argument to read Judge Stein's opinion on July 11, 2001, but it was well worth the wait. The judge not only denied Random House's request for an injunction, he also reached substantive issues in the case and, in a twenty-page opinion, concluded that the authors were the beneficial owners of the backlist electronic rights. We immediately made the full text of the opinion available for electronic download from our Web site. There was worldwide press coverage of the opinion, including a front page story in the *New York Times*. The *New York Times* followed up with a front-page business page story, with my color picture in front of a computer screen displaying the Rosetta logo and e-jackets. CNNfn, Bloomberg TV, and the BBC all followed with on-camera interviews.

Random House, of course, announced its intention to appeal the decision, but as a practical matter the world viewed us as the leading independent electronic publisher. With the injunctive request decided in our favor, we were free to build our financing, alliances, rights, and brand visibility. The large publishers continued to seek backlist electronic rights for life of copyright commitments without an advance in the context of a electronic publishing program that was frontlist oriented. We took every opportunity to emphasize that we would pay a competitive advance for a relatively short-term license and that our efforts were highly promotional and backlist oriented.

The litigation, of course, made the major publishers appear to be anti-author. Our support from The Authors Guild and the literary agents' association in the United States and their equivalents in England reinforced our business model as an "author-centric" publisher. The litigation also made rightsholders throughout the world aware of the potential value of their backlist electronic rights and that a Federal judge had concluded, at least in a preliminary opinion, that the authors, rather than the publishers, owned the rights. This would, of course, make the rights more competitive and possibly more expensive to acquire.

Since the aggregate annual revenues of Random House and the amicus publishers aligned against Rosetta were more than $5 billion, the litigation looked like a David and Goliath case. The large publishers in general had small electronic publishing programs with limited backlist title issuances and an unwillingness to license electronic rights to third parties. At every opportunity, my teammates and I emphasized our pro-author highly promotional commitment and the importance of experimentation in building the adoption of electronic reading. Key industry forums responded with invitations for us to make presentations. Any company shopping for e-rights tended to call us.

Personally, I could now look forward to several years of building my dream. There were many unknowns—the rate of adoption of electronic reading, the price the consumer would pay for titles, Rosetta's ability to execute its plan, the impact of competitors—in other words, all of the risks of an entrepreneur with a start-up business. Professionally, I had never felt more excited whatever the outcome.

RosettaBooks was the result of thinking for some time about a business which would permit me to participate in the electronic revolution. I was not afraid of the personal transition and risk this venture would represent. My professional experience had first been in politics—in John Lindsay's New York City Hall and Richard Nixon's White House. I had begun in 1973 as a corporate finance lawyer and basically shed that career as the unanticipated chance to become a literary agent came along. In 1983, I struck out on my own precisely to be on my own, even though I had left behind a partnership in one of the most successful literary agencies in the world (now Janklow & Nesbit). The purchase of the Scott Meredith Literary Agency in 1993 made me a small business owner as well as a literary agent. At the time I began talking with Steve Riggio, I had already begun my first efforts as a book packager for Bloomberg Financial and Oshkosh B'Gosh. Risk, change, and challenge were my partners, and that was fine by me.

TWO

···

"Five Hundred of Your Classmates Were First in Their Class in High School"

I left for Yale College in 1965 knowing that counting money was not my sole objective in life. For my father, money was the bottom line. As an immigrant from Harbin, China, and an Horatio Alger success story, my father was obsessed with money. He would brag about paying more than $1 million in taxes in 1953 when he sold his business. When, in fourth grade, I hadn't known what to answer to the simple question, "What does your father do?" he said, "Tell them I am investor and a financier." Before I left for college, my father offered me the opportunity to join him in real estate with an assurance of a $100,000 salary within a few years—real money in the 1960s. I think this was a test since his commitment to education was, if anything, stronger than his commitment to money. My first choice to follow my own path was Yale over real estate—I have never looked back.

In high school, I took the Kuder Preference Test, which was supposed to give guidance on career choices. I finished with strong ratings in math and persuasion and a high interest in music. Their conclusion? Consider a career as a musician's business manager. In fact, the test wasn't that far off, since you could say it predicted that I should be an agent, a conclusion that took me ten more years to reach. I left for Yale interested in intellectual challenges and exposure to new things. On the eve of my departure, I stood all night for tickets to one of Maria Callas's farewell concerts in New York, an introduction in its own way to event marketing, a concept which would fascinate me later.

I had studied the large course schedule and signed up over the summer for a rather traditional set of lecture courses with no particular focus and certainly no career plan. Incoming freshmen for the class of 1969 were assigned advisers. I waited fifteen minutes as Calvin Hill (soon to be star of the Yale football team, later a Dallas Cowboy and now best known as Grant Hill's father) completed his session. I then met with William Lilley III, an associate professor of history, who changed my life in one short meeting. At our first meeting, he was the teacher and I was the student in need of guidance and inspiration. Nearly twenty years later, when he was the senior communications executive for CBS and I was launching my own business, he was my first corporate client.

Lilley looked at my high school transcripts (the highest academic record in nearly one hundred years from my high school with at least an interest in history) and at the lecture program I had elected. His first comment was, "Why would you ever want to spend your time in lecture classes? If you are interested in lectures, I will arrange for you to read mine." When I asked what he had in mind, he said that I belonged in an intensive American history seminar. His colleague Lew Gould was teaching one. By second semester, I was at the Library of Congress in Washington, D.C., reading original newspapers of the Civil War era to research southern reaction to the Crittenden compromise, an attempt to head off the War. Writing that paper encouraged me to pursue four years of research and writing, mostly under

Bill Lilley's tutelage. While I had no particular targets in mind, I certainly planned to do well academically. In my freshman year, the freshman dean looked at my transcript from high school and observed that five hundred of my classmates had also finished first in their class. He hoped that I wouldn't be disappointed to finish somewhere below the top at Yale. This encounter increased my motivation.

My appreciation for the American urban experience was formed by studying with Alexander Garvin. Garvin, an urban planner himself, taught a small class that did fieldwork in the troubled Bushwick neighborhood in 1960s Brooklyn. Like Bill Lilley, Alex Garvin became a mentor and, later, a client. When Robert Kennedy was assassinated in 1968, it was Alex Garvin to whom I turned to talk things through. Years later, he would turn to me for help with his book, twenty-five years in the making, *The American City.* The opportunity to be his adviser was a satisfying role reversal.

In my junior year, I had joined a graduate seminar in political science. One of our invited guests was Ronald Reagan, then Governor of California, who was visiting the campus as a Chubb Fellow. Our seminar group was quite liberal. We prepared to question Reagan in a way that would prove how smart we were. Reagan disarmed us with his charm. He also showed a far more specific knowledge than we did. During this two-hour session Reagan handled us without the benefit of aides or notes and convinced me that he was not to be underestimated. Nancy Reagan sat glowingly at his side, never speaking.

Aside from academics, I became active on the business side of the *Yale Daily News,* which was and still is student-managed. The *News* was a great experience. We had a chance to run our own business. The profits went to the student workers, the higher your station, the higher your return. Our editorial chairman, Reed Hundt, told me years later in his office as chairman of the FCC that his profit share from our years had permitted him to attend Yale Law School where he befriended a student named Bill Clinton. In our years, the *News* launched Garry Trudeau and the earliest versions of the *Doonesbury* cartoon, with characters inspired by the winning Yale football team.

In my junior and senior year, the *News* participated in some experiments that were forerunners to Yale's move to coeducation. Several Vassar women who were actively involved in their student newspaper joined a program to work with the *News*. Ellen Chesler was one of those pioneers. Ellen later spent nearly ten years writing the definitive biography of Margaret Sanger, titled *Woman of Valor*. I was Chesler's literary agent. Bryna Sanger was another of these pioneers. She went on to become a leading published scholar on government management at the New School and an adviser to RosettaBooks.

Issues of campus governance also attracted me. I served on the student advisory board and became active with a small faculty-student group that seriously studied how Yale could improve itself. Yale College works on a residential college system. Various faculty members are aligned with each college. Each member of the faculty tends to have an area of specialization in which he or she researches and publishes. Our published study recommended that senior Yale faculty offer seminars in their areas of specialization. Typically, these faculty members offered undergraduates only large lecture classes. In many cases, they taught only graduate students. The faculty would have to do little or no preparation. The most interested students would be attracted and the experience for faculty and student would be fulfilling. For example, in Pierson College, where I was resident, Gaddis Smith was at work on the definitive biography of Dean Acheson. His seminar offering focused on Dean Acheson while his lecture class was a broad-based review of American foreign policy.

We also recommended that Yale invite people outside the academic world to return to campus for seminars which introduced students to the worlds of the visitors' disciplines. Robert Sweet, then Mayor John Lindsay's deputy, visited Pierson College for one of these seminars and helped to excite me about what Lindsay was trying to achieve in New York. These outreach activities demonstrated that Yale's faculty and administration in the late 1960s were more open with students than other Ivy League campuses, which often had isolated students from issues of administration.

It was hard to get a quality summer job after my sophomore year. With Bill Lilley's introduction, I landed an internship with the central planning unit of the Port of New York Authority, which ran New York City's bridges and tunnels. My supervisor, Carl Franzman, a wonderfully trained planner, taught me the life lesson that any fool can project from a straight line, but that the art of projection was determining when the direction and angle of the line was changing. So, for example, in the early days of air travel you project small numbers of passengers and find yourselves without airports when everyone wants to fly. Later, you assume continued growth and fund overcapacity and so forth.

The Port Authority job helped me land an internship the following summer in New York City Deputy Mayor Timothy Costello's office. A political appointee of the Liberal Party, Costello's office was across the street from City Hall in more ways than one. Robert Sweet, the "real" Deputy Mayor, worked at Lindsay's side in City Hall. Costello was rarely granted a City Hall meeting. I thought I could document that Black and Puerto Rican voter registration was low by comparing census data with registration data at the block level. With the data in hand, we could rationalize a drive to register "low participation" voters, which was, in reality, a drive to register Lindsay voters, since his support was very strong in their groups.

Census information was collected by tract. While voter data was kept by election district. The two units didn't match geographically and there was no code to make them compatible. There was no solution to the problem other than a manual overlay. So I spent hours on the floor of the municipal building with map overlays making a hand-match code for the lines. The results in map form were clear. Higher registration areas tended to be white. Black and Puerto Rican areas were registered at less than one half the percentage of white neighborhoods. Costello was able to use his twenty-year-old Yale intern as a ticket to City Hall.

Lindsay approved a voter registration drive targeted at "low registration" areas. The arithmetic was honest and the result was politically appealing in City Hall. Since the best story to support the drive was the data I had gathered, I became a "poster child" of the campaign. The *New York Times* ran stories under the headline, "Pow

Voteman," and reproduced the maps that showed voter registration rates by neighborhood. I was quoted frequently through the series of articles and got my first hate mail ("Why would a Jew be helping those niggers?"). One of the readers of the articles was Daniel Patrick Moynihan, who referenced them in his book on the poverty program, *Maximum Feasible Misunderstanding*. I administered the drive, down to the level of approving the placement of voter registration sites. The most productive sites turned out to be those with a political base in the poverty programs.

I wanted to spend a substantial part of my senior year in City Hall, but there was no program in place to get credit at Yale for the internship. I ended up drafting an exchange of letters between Deputy Mayor Costello and Yale President Kingman Brewster that covered my case. The letters, of course, emphasized the educational element of the experience. Later, Yale formalized an urban internship program for undergraduates.

The academic portion of my work built upon my voter registration experiences. I published a pamphlet in September 1968 with the Mayor's office titled "Mounting a Voter Registration Drive." I then produced a longer essay, "The Demographics of Politics: Legislative Constituencies and the Borough of Brooklyn, 1950–1965." The essay made the case that lack of voter participation by Blacks and Puerto Ricans had distorted the electoral process, which was instead in the hands of a "white machine" that protected its assemblymen and state senators until they became judges. It was profiled in the *New York Times* and had something to do with New York City coming under the spotlight of the Voting Rights Act, which had become law just a few years earlier. Years later, the librarian for the Supreme Court of the United States requested a copy so that the essay could be cited in a voting rights case.

I met many of the Lindsay team: Lance Liebman, my boss (who would go on teach at Harvard Law School while I attended, and later become Dean of Columbia Law School), Peter Goldmark (who would go on to head the Rockefeller Foundation), Jay Kriegel (now a successful public relations executive), Sid Davidoff and his sidekick, a short kid nicknamed Squirt, as hard working and driving as anyone in the group and later known as Jeff Katzenberg of Dreamworks. They were all drawn as I was to this incredible personality. John Lindsay in 1969 had the charisma of a movie star. At an open lecture overflowing the Yale Law School auditorium, he held a student audience rapt for an hour. His press briefings in the Blue Room at City Hall were an event. His street presence, particularly in the friendlier neighborhoods, echoed a Kennedy. I was certainly under his spell.

Once I met Lindsay one on one. Dave Garth, his media guru, had engineered a weekly television show for Lindsay to focus on an issue or two. On one program, Lindsay planned to present charts and pitch for voter registration. The other subject for that show was a new subway car that, in theory, would reduce crowding at rush hour. To illustrate the difference between old and new cars, charts used black dots to indicate the spacing of people. The two charts looked remarkably alike. Lindsay told the team that had created the subway charts that they could present and defend them, but he wouldn't. It was a rare chance for me to see behind the public person, a glimpse I would fortunately repeat with a number of fascinating people.

With my background in voter registration work and a real interest in political numbers, I began to write Lindsay's team a series of memos before the Republican primary in which Lindsay faced opposition from a little known conservative state senator named John Marchi. My memos were highly critical of his political strategy and basically predicted that he would lose. One of our strategies for the primary was to consolidate Black voters, since he was so popular in their communities. I wrote a memo pointing out that there were no registered Blacks who could vote in the Republican primary. That and other memos I wrote were not popular with the Lindsay team. I was a twenty-year-old writing unsolicited advice and didn't really expect anybody to take it.

Lindsay, of course, lost the Republican primary and was forced to run on the Liberal Party line against Republican John Marchi and Democrat Mario Proccacino. Richard Aurelio, a thoughtful and very competent person, was appointed campaign manager with centralized authority. Dave Garth was the media man. Tully Plesser was the pollster. Peter Goldmark called me shortly after the primary results and said, "Okay, smartass, what do we do now?" At least then I knew that someone had been reading my memos. I said, "Give me ten thousand dollars and I will build a computer model that will define strategy for the campaign." This was a rather brash statement since I had never worked with a computer, didn't quite know what I would do with the money, and hadn't specifically outlined what I would build. But I knew enough from the work I had already done that something valuable could be achieved.

Political campaigns then and now believed far more in polling than in studies of actual voting patterns. Today, when you watch the televised election results, the focus is on the projected winner and the exit poll, not on the turnout or the analysis of the raw vote. This, of course, was painfully apparent in election night coverage of Florida and other states during the 2000 presidential election. From studying registration numbers and reviewing some voting models that had been done for Kennedy's 1960 campaign, I felt that much more could be achieved with the use of a voter study rather than a poll.

Peter Goldmark decided that he was not going to let a maverick kid run around with campaign strategy money without a savvy supervisor. William Josephson, a partner at the law firm Fried, Frank, Harris, Shriver & Jacobson, had long been involved in Democratic politics. Josephson was the first counsel to the Peace Corps, close to Sargent Shriver and the Kennedy family and active for unions and educational institutions where Democratic constituencies were based. He volunteered to work for Lindsay after the primary defeat, but only if a serious assignment could be carved out. Peter Goldmark offered him me.

Josephson, a very careful person, would certainly have checked me out. I doubt he believed that a twenty-year-old would know enough to make a strategic difference in a high stakes political race. He debriefed me over a period of several days. I learned how someone must feel after an interrogation. My answers and statements were checked with friends he trusted. At first we worked as colleagues, but quickly became friends. We began by selecting a series of races we thought would indicate Lindsay's potential strengths and weaknesses. We had the advantage of a recent highly polarized vote on a civilian review board for the police. Those who hated Lindsay had voted against it overwhelmingly. We could use the mapping codes I had developed for the voter registration project. We found a wonderful team of computer consultants. Those were the days when you needed a room full of machines to achieve what a laptop can do now.

When the data finally was completed, the strategy virtually leapt off the page. We divided the city into three political camps, Lindsay friends, Lindsay enemies, and everyone else. Unfortunately, there weren't enough Lindsay friends to get him elected. The Lindsay enemies were a lost cause. This was easily confirmed by the Lindsay personal appearances, which required good police protection. Everyone else was up for grabs, although they clearly started out with an anti-Lindsay bias. Richard Aurelio, Tully Plesser, and Dave Garth paid careful attention to our presentation and recommendations and basically acted upon them. The key was to appeal to the "swing" voters who were opposed to Lindsay, but not steadfastly so. Garth developed the contrite commercial we called, "I made mistakes." It was rumored that there were many takes before Lindsay sounded sincere. What those mistakes were—how Lindsay handled education issues, or cleaning up after a big snow storm, or, indeed, just being too friendly to the aspirations of minorities—no one ever said. But the implicit apology appealed. He also developed a great campaign theme, calling the position of being New York City's mayor "the second toughest job in America."

Josephson and I built a poll-tracking model from a handful of the districts in the swing group. By regular focused polling we were able to track the pick up of voters for Lindsay. We also built a citywide model with about thirty election districts that called the race on election night within a few percentage points of the actual result.

In the midst of my intensive work for Lindsay, I graduated from Yale on June 9, 1969, Phi Beta Kapa, Magna Cum Laude, with Honors with Exceptional Distinction in American Studies. I also won the

Alpheus Henry Snow Prize, which by tradition meant leading the commencement processional. A group of Students for a Democratic Society walked out of graduation in protest, presumably because I somehow symbolized cooperation with the faculty and administration when confrontation was best. Earlier in the spring of my senior year, the *Yale Daily News* had published a column by the head of Students for a Democratic Society which referred to me by name as a "house nigger" for helping the faculty throw bones to the student body. John Hersey, the writer and Master of my college, took me aside and offered to write a response letter to the editor or to help me write a reply. I declined, saying "What am I supposed to do, explain I am not a 'house nigger'?"

When I returned to my City Hall job the Monday morning after graduation I told Lance Liebman that I had won the Snow Prize. He asked how much cash I received. I told $770. He said, "When I won, it was seven hundred dollars." I am reminded of this whenever I am tempted to feel too full of myself. That summer, I shared an apartment with Michael Kramer, who went on to be a noted political writer, Orin Kramer, a friend from Yale, now a major Democratic fundraiser, and a quiet Dewey Ballantine legal associate whose name was George Pataki. Both Kramers were not too motivated about their work at Columbia Law School, but certainly were lively. Orin was not beyond letting women confuse him with Bill Bradley. Michael, who wrote nothing at the time, later had to remind himself in a profile piece of Pataki that they had been roommates. Pataki had left no more of an impression on me.

I graduated from Yale consumed by my work for Lindsay, giving little thought to my future. My writing and research work at Yale offered me a chance to pursue a Ph.D., which Bill Lilley and others I admired on the faculty had done. I applied to law school but learned later that I had won the Mellon fellowship to study abroad and deferred my acceptance to Harvard. In the summer of 1969, I assumed that I would be going in the fall to Clare College, in Cambridge, England, as a Mellon Fellow. A call placed by the White House operator changed my plans.

THREE

····································

"You're Not Working for the Yale Daily News Anymore"

I had never felt much of a need to stay on the expected path. At Yale, that had meant research opportunities to challenge conventional wisdom and a contribution to lasting legacies in the college seminar and urban intern programs. With Lindsay, it had meant the chance to put theory into action both by dramatizing the need for higher voter registration patterns and by using a voter study in a unique way to help set campaign strategy. I preferred writing my own rules.

While working the summer of 1969 for Lindsay, I was also targeting another opportunity. The man I most admired for his work on urban causes was Daniel Patrick Moynihan, a Harvard professor who had become a senior White House counselor to Richard Nixon with the new administration that January. My voter registration work had come to Moynihan's attention and was quoted in his book on the poverty program *Maximum Feasible Misunderstanding*. He had also written for Nathan Glazer the Irish chapter in the classic sociology book *Beyond the Melting Pot*. With my uncle Nathan Glazer, bloodlines didn't mean as much as achievements. Since my work had passed muster with Moynihan, my uncle set up a meeting and I spent an afternoon in Cambridge walking and talking with Moynihan.

Afterward, I lobbied again and again for a position on his staff. He would call from time to time (the White House operator can track you practically anywhere—I once received a call when sleeping at a friend's apartment with no recollection of telling anyone where I was); meanwhile I would get polite rejection letters which he had signed but had been drafted by his staff. Finally, a call came in the late summer to see Moynihan in Washington. I had to meet another White House aide, Peter Flanigan, for some kind of vetting that I was not a Nixon enemy. Flanigan never asked me flat out if I was a loyal and active Republican. Perhaps anyone who was an enemy of the Students for a Democratic Society looked like a friend of Nixon's. In any case, I wasn't a Nixon enemy. Flanigan cleared me and asked me to become the junior man on staff.

My strategy work for Lindsay was largely done, except for the outcome. I declined my Mellon Fellowship. Moynihan had worried about this. I told him I thought I could learn a lot more from a year with him in Washington than from a tutor in Cambridge, England. Both Yale and the Lindsay team were surprised to learn of my change of plans, but were supportive. To get me paid for my months of work for Lindsay, I was sworn in as a pothole inspector and received back pay. If the pothole budget was going to the likes of me, it might explain some of the bumps in the road.

Pat Moynihan in 1969 was a forty-two-year-old man in a hurry. He kept a staff of three secretaries busy around the clock just dealing with the more mechanical details of his work. Three or four speaking invitations, up to one hundred telephone calls, and stacks of mail, mostly from the public, came daily to his office. His staff was a very talented policy-focused group. Steve Hess, his deputy (now the presidential scholar at the Brookings Institute) brought good judgment, humor, and moderate Republican credentials. John Price (now a managing director of Chase Manhattan) was immersed in welfare issues, his interest in which stemmed from his more liberal Republican Ripon Society background. Checker (Chester E.) Finn (now one of the leading educational policy voices) had been with Pat at Harvard, as had Richard Blumenthal (now attorney general from Connecticut). Chris Demuth (now head of the American Enterprise Institute) had also been with Pat at Harvard. There were two interns—Frank Raines (now head of Fannie Mae), who was completing an incredibly successful undergraduate career at Harvard, and Marty Fischbein, who made his way to Rupert Murdoch's team before tragically dying in a car crash with Jessica Savitch.

Everyone had staked out a policy area since January. As the last to arrive, I got the most junior assignment, which was to make sure that Moynihan's day worked smoothly. That meant handling the mail, the calls, the schedule, and making sure the right papers were in his hands at the right time, and so forth. From day one I spent very little time on policy and a lot of time with Moynihan, which was just fine with me. I ate on the early shift in the White House Mess, had an office in the Executive Office Building across the driveway to the West Basement, carried a White House pass and even a title—assistant to the counselor for the President, had use of the White House car and driver pool, and had the chance to get the White House operator to place calls if need be.

My rental apartment was at Dupont Circle within an easy walk of the White House. Typically I was at work by 8 A.M. and often didn't leave until close to 8 P.M. Saturday was a bit shorter and Sundays sometimes half a day off. While exhilarating, it was also tiring. One morning I overslept and got to the office an hour late. Moynihan had an early morning speech at the Pentagon and had to find his own papers. He was not happy. When I arrived, he was on the phone from the Pentagon with a one-liner I will never forget: "Klebanoff, you're not working for the *Yale Daily News* anymore." That has since been my rallying cry whenever it looks like something may go wrong.

Moynihan's immediate team worked well together. I grew to admire other senior Nixon staffers Len Garment, Ray Price, and Bill Safire, all of whom I later got to know better. Kissinger's staff wouldn't talk to the domestic staffers. Moynihan would tweak Kissinger each time I saw them pass in the West Basement (their offices were directly across from each other), usually with a line like "Well, Henry, what have you done for peace today?"

Shortly after I started, I had the chance to draft a speech for Moynihan to deliver in front of the Association of Newspaper Publishers in Hartford. I prepared a rather straightforward defense of what I understood to be Nixon's domestic agenda, much of which was being shaped by Moynihan. Moynihan threw out the draft and, within hours of our scheduled departure, turned to his own typewriter and drafted what he wanted to say. I had to handle duplication of the speech for handouts to the media. The White House car took us directly onto the tarmac at Andrews Air Force Base where we were met by two saluting pilots. We were airborne within moments. The speech as delivered was incomprehensible. I asked Moynihan on the return flight why he had rewritten the speech. His response: "If I had wanted to say anything, I would have." When we exited the plane, Moynihan left a small amount of cash for the pilots. When I later asked why, he explained that the soft drinks and sandwiches were out of pocket for the pilots. This was a good introduction for me to how the government could find the money to fly and drive us to Hartford, but not the cash for a Coke.

I kept actively in touch with the Lindsay general election race. Steve Weisman was a friend from my *Yale Daily News* days and was working for Richard Reeves at the *New York Times* city desk. I became an active source since my voter study numbers were useful for some of their stories. Election Night 1969 was spent in New York analyzing the victory at the Port Authority bus terminal as I waited for an early morning departure back to Washington. I wrote memos for Moynihan and others on how to interpret the Lindsay victory. That Sunday's *New York Times* "Week in Review" led:

The man from the White House came into New York on Tuesday with a briefcase full of computer printouts on past city elections. He worked through the night, pushing stacks of returns onto the floor as he plotted jagged lines on graph paper. By seven A.M. he was on the air shuttle and by nine A.M. a report on the election's national significance was ready for President Nixon.

"There's just not very much national significance—at least no immediate significance. New York tends to be unique," said the man from the White House. . . . The election should focus some real attention on political polling at two levels—the brilliant use of private polls by candidate Lindsay and the wild inaccuracy and effect of public polls.

So the twenty-one-year-old brand-new college graduate who had never seen a computer in action was by November "the man from the White House" with computer printouts.

While on Moynihan's staff, I continued to pursue my interest in New York City electoral issues. I tried without success to get my Yale senior thesis published. Parts of my voter registration analyses were quoted in a new introduction to Glazer and Moynihan's *Beyond the Melting Pot*. Since that book was widely read on college campuses, I felt privileged to be included. Somehow between Nathan Glazer and Pat Moynihan, Norman Podhoretz invited me to write a piece in *Commentary* on the Jewish vote in the 1969 Lindsay race. My theme was that there were several "Jewish votes" and that they were not all liberal. I also argued that Lindsay had not used a traditional ethnic vote strategy in his race, but had instead focused on centrist issue appeals. In effect, Lindsay won the votes of most of the liberal Jews, enough of the centrist Jews, and relatively few of the conservative Jews. Podhoretz then asked me to write on the subject of quotas, utilizing my numbers interests to attack the concept of quotas. I declined, since it was clear enough to me that this was a step into an ideological battle that was not mine. Podhoretz lost interest in me immediately. The piece was assigned to Elliot Abrams. Abrams later rented a room in Glazer's house when we were at Harvard Law

School together, married Podhoretz's daughter, and made plenty of news during the Iran Contra events in the Reagan administration.

Before I returned on the shuttle that November postelection morning, I learned that there had been a Moynihan staffing realignment. All of the policy staffers would no longer report to Moynihan. In his new position, Moynihan could retain one staffer of his own. I was selected, I guess because I was closest to helping his day-to-day life in the office. This staffing change meant that for the coming months I would spend many more hours a day at Moynihan's side. The pace quickened, since it was hard to both be with him and get the assigned work done at the same time. My exposure broadened, since I was often in meetings with Moynihan and others, heard at least his end of interesting telephone calls, and got to read memos intended for very few eyes.

Moynihan had made writing a memo for the President into an art form. I was allowed to read his memo book from January forward. The subject range was broad and clearly encouraged by Nixon based on notes and responses. Topics ranged from anti-Semitism to architecture in Washington, welfare, education, and even the military. Moynihan found the opportunity again and again to return to the theme of the significance of ending the War in Vietnam. The memos were a body of work of which any public figure could be proud. One memo volunteered Moynihan would never write of his White House years, a promise I hope Moynihan no longer feels obliged to keep.

One memo that became famous (or infamous depending on your point of view) urged Nixon not to stir the racial waters in the nation's cities. The memo quoted a British phrase that racial passions could best be addressed by a period of "benign neglect." What Moynihan meant was that Presidential comment on racial issues during a time of such raw emotions could only make matters worse, no matter what Nixon said. Moynihan and Nixon were both fighting for a minimum national income. Moynihan certainly didn't mean for benign neglect to reflect the policy commitments to helping the poor, Black and white alike. Moynihan had once before been in the center of a racial controversy over his 1965 report on the Black family and the problems on single parenthood and out-of-wedlock births. Nixon had his own image problems in the Black community. When Moynihan got a call that the *New York Times* had been read the benign neglect sentence out of context, there was a problem.

Moynihan leaned on editors of the *New York Times* to publish the text of the entire memo, so that the argument could be seen in context. They did and a potential maelstrom became more of a teapot tempest. The White House press office had duplicated a copy of the memo with Nixon's handwritten comments in the margins (it was Nixon's habit to respond to these memos with handwritten marginalia). What they hadn't noticed was that Nixon had written "right" next to the benign neglect phrase. Moynihan caught the discrepancy in time and substituted a "clean" version of the memo. Had the Nixon comment circulated, we can only guess at the press field day that certainly would have followed.

There were other opportunities to learn Moynihan's strategy for managing the press. Moynihan worked on a White House conference on hunger. The chairman was Jean Mayer, president of Tufts, a friend of Moynihan's but not much of a Nixon supporter. Mayer would get trapped by the press into comments that appeared critical of administration policy, which would, of course, put Moynihan in an awkward position. I spent one car ride to National Airport hearing Moynihan lecture Mayer on managing the press: Say one thing, say it again and again and say nothing else. Very good advice indeed.

Moynihan could also be very practical. In 1969, Washington still had an afternoon daily newspaper, the *Washington Star*. The paper dropped off all of its White House copies each afternoon in the hall outside Moynihan's West Basement office. One day, when the front page story was particularly distressing from Moynihan's point of view, he collected and trashed all of the White House copies. His theory, I guess, was that what you don't know won't hurt you.

We didn't often get time to reflect, but at one dinner with several members of the team, Moynihan gave us his view of how best to pursue government service. His argument was that you should always have a career or place you can return to—a safety net, in effect.

Everyone in government service should be prepared to quit on principle or be fired at any time. If you didn't have that other place, you could compromise yourself during your public service. If you were dependent on the favors of your superiors, you could bring nothing meaningful to government service and ultimately corrupt yourself. Moynihan himself went to great lengths to hang onto his tenured chair at Harvard until he won a Senate seat from New York.

During these months, I was able to observe Nixon a number of times. It was totally apparent that his public speaking without notes was very impressive, entirely different than his television image. I had only two closer, but incredibly brief, encounters with Nixon. Sooner or later staffers, whatever their religious persuasion, were invited to the White House for Sunday morning services. My turn came. It was a beautiful late fall Washington day. After the service, there was a receiving line to shake hands with the dignitaries (an astronaut) and Nixon. When I reached Nixon I said, "Mr. President, it is a beautiful day for a walk. You should get outside." He looked like he didn't know what to say in response and finally said, "Would I need a coat?" A few months later while working late in the West Basement, I went into the hall and practically collided with Nixon. I am reasonably certain he had no idea who I was. After a moment's pause, he said, "The Marine Corps band is playing tomorrow on the White House lawn. You really ought to hear them." So much for my relationship at the time with the President of the United States. My turn for a real meeting would come two decades later.

Moynihan was in many ways Nixon's opposite. Moynihan was never at a loss for an endearing anecdote or a comeback line. In public presentation Nixon was rehearsed while Moynihan often spontaneous. Nixon would always be clear and careful in public; Moynihan was often unclear and frequently very quotable. Whatever advice Moynihan had offered Jean Mayer, he completely projected his own style. Of course, the media took to Moynihan's persona more than Nixon's. But Moynihan was very careful not to upstage his boss in public.

After the staffing shift, I worked next door to Moynihan in the

West Basement. It meant the chance to observe things not seen across the way in the Executive Office Building. For instance, the day Kirk Douglas came to meet Nixon and created more of a stir than a head of state. Or the day that Bud Krogh, an Ehrlichman staffer who would later go to jail after Watergate, waved around the FBI report on Nixon's Supreme Court nominee Harold Carswell. They needed a nominee who was absolutely financially clean. A good judge, Clement Haynsworth had been rejected by the Senate on largely political grounds with some argument over personal financial dealings. Carswell was to be the replacement nominee. They neglected to check Carswell's opinions and background or they would have found him positioned awfully close to the Ku Klux Klan. Carswell's candidacy was voted down by the Senate for eminently good reasons.

Moynihan usually returned to Cambridge, Massachusetts, for the weekend since he never moved his family to Washington. Each Cambridge trip meant a bundle of papers made their way from the office to one closet or another in Moynihan's Cambridge house. Moynihan was fully capable of voicing his personal views. In preparing to publish one of Moynihan's books, Random House sent back a copyedited manuscript that marked up nearly all of Moynihan's (convoluted) sentences. Moynihan called his editor, Jason Epstein, and said that they could publish the book the way he submitted it, or not at all. They published. Had I followed the same approach for this book, I can promise you a far more convoluted account than you are reading now.

By the spring of 1970, Vietnam became a central focus. I accompanied Moynihan to the department in the Pentagon that monitored domestic demonstrations and violence in the event that the military needed to be called into action. The visit made me feel all too close to a power center I didn't care to understand. Moynihan asked how they went about getting their information, since any domestic spying should have been the responsibility of the FBI. The General in charge pointed to UPI and AP wire machines in the room and said that anything that concerned them concerned crowds and that crowds would be covered on the wires as they gathered. It was not the most convincing answer, but the only answer made available to us.

In April and May, the Vietnam War protesters came to Washington involving me personally. Black Panther leader Bobby Seale went on trial in New Haven, and Yale University and the city of New Haven found themselves surrounded by ten thousand federal troops. For New Haven, Yale had a faculty/student team in charge of trying to keep the peace. The White House had a team on Ehrlichman's staff coordinating deployment of federal troops to contain potential urban violence. I became an informal liaison for the Yale group and the White House group, would speak several times a day with faculty on the scene in New Haven, and synthesize their views for Bud Krogh, who was coordinating matters for Ehrlichman. Since the stakes were whether ten thousand troops would actually put bayonets on their rifles and march into town, my role, while not that of a policy maker, was stressful enough.

For the first March on Washington, young White House staffers were asked to coordinate with its leaders. To try to keep the march peaceful, there was a command center staffed with one White House and one march leader representative. Communication was by walkie-talkie to police or Secret Service teams. As one of the junior most staffers, I drew the graveyard shift from midnight to eight A.M. One of the more dramatic moments was the candlelight march in front of the White House with one candle per marcher for each dead soldier in Vietnam. The candlelight march was to be over by a certain time around dawn so that buses could surround the White House and serve as a protective shield against the possibility of the main march getting out of hand later in the day.

The candlelight march started in Arlington and went single file until it reached the White House in a predictable amount of time. As the time neared for the march to end, there was still a stream of marchers in front of the White House and as far as the Secret Service could see. My walkie-talkie picked up the conversation of the Secret Service and the police planning the arrest of everyone left on line, which could have become a bloody encounter. My counterpart march leader with his walkie-talkie knew when the last marcher had left Arlington and therefore approximately when that marcher would pass the White House. They needed a thirty-minute extension to finish. I shouted to everyone I could find to check for the end of the march line and allow the extension. The Secret Service and Washington police held back and let the candlelight march peacefully.

In May, Nixon scheduled a major television address to announce the Cambodia incursion. The speech included that strange line, "The United States will not be a pitiless giant." Typically, any follow-up for evening presidential addresses was handled in the communications office and others on the White House staff could watch the speech on television at home. That night, all staffers were asked to stay late. The White House Mess served a formal meal with candlelight. Everyone (not including me; I was to assist Moynihan) was asked immediately after the speech to call friends to ask for reaction, so that a controlled poll, obviously intended to be positive, could be in Nixon's hands that night. Moynihan called David Riesman, the Harvard sociologist, and another Harvard friend or two, and purposely stayed on the phone a long time with each call hearing a complete attack on Nixon's Vietnam policies. Moynihan contributed his few negative responses to the office poll, which preserved his integrity at least, if not the poll's.

The demonstrations and shootings at Kent State took place soon after Nixon's address. The Bobby Seale trial was ongoing. There were frequent smaller Washington demonstrations. In one near Dupont Circle, I ended up teargassed as I tried to get home one night. The next major march on Washington threatened to be violent. I had decided to quit in May. Moynihan said that he wished he had a good argument to talk me out of quitting, but he didn't. I promised not to make a public fuss over quitting so as not to embarrass him. Moynihan later wrote that he went to Nixon at this time to resign as well, but Nixon talked him into staying to try and save the Family Assistance Plan, which Moynihan had worked so hard to make a reality.

On my way out, I got sworn in at the Office of Economic Opportunity so that I could get paid. As in New York City, no one had managed to get me formally on a payroll for more than nine months.

I wondered if I would still get my autographed picture with Nixon from a recent cabinet meeting on youth issues (I did). William Kristol, now a leading conservative figure, took my job.

Meanwhile, just before leaving, I had confided my plans to Lance Liebman, who without my permission told Steve Weisman at the *New York Times*. The front page right hand lead read, "Youth aide quits." I had no intention of becoming part of a media circus. The *New York Times* piece left the clear impression that I had resigned in protest of Nixon's Vietnam policies, which was fine by me, but the article didn't quote me. An NBC reporter reached me at home and tried to convince me to appear on one of the morning talk show since I had an obligation to the American people to "tell my story." I declined. John Osborne, the lead White House reporter for the *New Republic,* tried to interview me since he had earlier done the legwork of taking me to an introductory lunch. I declined. Osborne filed a brief story on my resignation, spelling my name several different ways in the same few paragraphs.

All of my press relationships before joining Moynihan were tied to my substantive work on voter registration and voter studies. In many instances, I acted as a numbers source for reporters. They, in turn, often quoted me in pieces which concerned registration patterns, registration drives, or voter strategy. My resignation from the White House was a chance for one moment in the media glare. This was very different indeed than commenting on political numbers or trends. My gut instinct was to duck the cameras as an act of self-preservation.

I had stayed honest with myself by resigning. But I also maintained personal relationships which were important to me. Ultimately, Moynihan would become my first professional client, Nixon my most visible client, and Haldeman my most challenging client. I later traded Len Garment and Ray Price professional advice for professional help. I also worked hard for Bill Safire, the founding client of Janklow, Traum & Klebanoff, and his friend John Ehrlichman. I didn't, of course, see this outcome at the time.

I decided while traveling that I would attend Harvard Law School in the fall of 1970. Yale Law School was an alternative, but I felt it was too small and I had been in New Haven too long. In the summer of 1970 Charles Goodell, New York's junior senator by appointment from Governor Nelson Rockefeller, was running for Senate against the Democrat Richard Ottinger and the Conservative James Buckley (Bill's brother). Goodell had taken an anti–Vietnam War position, angering his patron Rockefeller. Good people were trying to help him and I was attracted to the campaign. The campaign manager was the same Bob Sweet who had been Lindsay's first deputy mayor. In my job interview, I wanted a salary fifty dollars a week higher than they wanted to pay. He said "What's fifty bucks a week between friends?" I said "Exactly." I got the salary.

Political campaigns are often a disaster and this one was no exception. The organized meetings all seemed to deal with trivial issues. My favorite was the presentation of the campaign stationery. The colors were all brown. Goodell questioned the color. The agency presenter said, "Brown is a very sincere color." The letterhead came out brown, although not necessarily sincere.

I was able to study the polling data. Everyone who was for the Vietnam War had lined up with Buckley, giving him a core support of about 20 percent. Ottinger was narrowly ahead of both Buckley and Goodell. Very few people other than Rockefeller knew of Goodell's Vietnam positions, and the only issue that mattered was Vietnam. If Goodell ran on the issue, he would appear to be an independent Republican, prepared to buck his party and his patron. Goodell instead trimmed his sails. Ottinger was not a very effectual candidate and Jim Buckley won the three-way race. Little did I know that six years later I would be active in Pat Moynihan's challenge to Jim Buckley's reelection.

It was hard for me to tell which was my vocation, politics or the law school. Soon after I started law school, Michael Kramer called to invite me to join a political consulting group with a young Harvard polling whiz named Pat Caddell, leading to a multimonth consultancy. I spent some time flying around to various meetings. The company had everything but paying clients. Caddell eventually volunteered his services to a long shot candidate in the 1972 presidential primaries. When George McGovern prevailed, Caddell had a business even if McGovern did not. Caddell went on to become Jimmy Carter's pollster and to build a major commercial polling business.

In 1971, Bill Josephson and I decided to launch a consulting company offering Lindsay-style voter study projects to other politicians. We worked for the Democratic State Committee and helped improve their strategic support of candidates in 1972, and for Al Blumenthal, a good but ineffectual candidate for mayor of New York City in 1973. We did a study in Maine for a candidate who didn't run, thus creating the image of a consulting service that would take a potential candidate to a retreat and return with a certainty of campaign or no campaign. Another study was for a candidate in Missouri who didn't run. His name was Bill Bradley. Collecting the data for that study included a visit to Jackson County, Missouri, the county seat for Kansas City. The courthouse was built in the 1930s with a dedication plaque in the lobby signed "Harry S. Truman, County Commissioner." Harry Truman seemed like an unlikely President of the United States in 1930, and Bill Bradley was not an apparent presidential candidate in 1971.

I stayed active sourcing Richard Reeves voter data for a series of excellent articles he wrote for *New York* magazine. That, in turn, led to a chance to advise the networks on several election nights. I got to watch the legendary Richard Scammon call election results for NBC from scraps of paper hitting his desk from partial call-in results from sample precincts. I also had a chance to work at CBS and observe Warren Mitovsky build out sophisticated polling and election night result calling systems. Mitovsky would ultimately build the system that all three networks had to explain after the flip-flopping Florida results in the 2000 presidential election. One thing that was apparent early on is that all sampling systems work better when races are not close.

I used my data-oriented approach to analyze voting patterns over the years in New York gubernatorial elections. The results were published by the New School for Social Research in October 1970 and covered in the press. I found that overall New York State voting was declining, a fact confirmed when the 1970 census shifted congressional seats from New York to California, Florida, and Texas. Also, the decline of the urban vote's impact on the overall state numbers was striking. This was what ultimately got my roommate George Pataki elected even though Mario Cuomo won New York City overwhelmingly.

In my second year at Harvard Law School, Lance Liebman, who was teaching property law, said that he wanted me to meet the only person he had ever met who knew more about Brooklyn politics than I did. The first-year student he introduced me to was Chuck Schumer. We became good friends and I had the chance over the years to help a friend build his political career.

Meanwhile, there was law school. Harvard was proud that it wasn't a "trade school." Would you see a doctor who hadn't been trained in a "trade school"? Or hire an architect? You could get law school credit for courses throughout the University curriculum. I guess that law school is a good place to catch up on the great novels you missed in college, but the structure seemed to me a tacit acknowledgment of a thin law school curriculum. The faculty studied the possibility that you could get a year's worth of credit by living abroad and doing a paper on the legal system of another country, preferably in the Third World. When Lance Liebman asked what I thought of the plan, I told him that a plan to cut law school to two years since there was no curriculum sounded excellent and that, if they were short of money, they might consider simply raising the tuition.

Law Review was the standard of achievement. About twenty-five of each class of seven hundred made *Law Review,* most by grade point average and some by spots reserved for a competition. Since I wasn't paying all that much attention to my courses, my B-plus average wasn't about to make *Law Review* on grades. The competition was an editing test (one of my strengths) and an essay. I purposely chose a conservative stance in my essay, on the assumption that most would write about the welfare question presented from a liberal point of view. It worked, probably because the liberal oriented editors thought having at least a token conservative voice made sense.

My experience on the *Law Review* was not much happier than in class. The *Review* was long, turgid, and with many pieces without a point of view. I decided to research *Review*s of the past learning that in the early 1900s, the *Harvard Law Review* was short (a fraction of its current length), pithy, and always with a point of view. Four-page pieces from Brandeis would effectively develop the law of privacy. Recent issues proved hard to find anything published that made a difference. The *Review* was student run. I made a strong argument to my colleagues that we should return to our roots—cut the size of the *Review* significantly and push the contributors for a point of view or refuse to publish their pieces. This was not a popular position. Ultimately, I resigned before my third year. I couldn't support what the publication was doing and I had other plans in mind for my third year, which became a part-time job in New York City.

I had to choose a subject for a third-year paper and decided to follow up on my research on the *Harvard Law Review* by writing on the standards at the Law School. Examination questions were published back to the turn of the century. I surveyed the exams at five-year intervals. I also interviewed the forty or so members of the faculty regarding their views of the grading system. When I researched the old examinations, I found that testing had moved from specific information (answer these 100 questions; if you were not well prepared, you were dead) to generic essays, which could have been reasonably answered whether the course had been taken or not. In my essay I argued that the standards of Harvard Law School had collapsed and made it possible to sleepwalk your way to acceptable grades.

There was one catch. Would my adviser choose to challenge my own imitation of a third-year perfunctory performance? Grade examinations were read "blind"—the name of the student was not supposed to be known to the professor. For his course, not only was I relying on notes prepared by *Law Review* editors, I had not even purchased the text. On exam day, I bought the book (and returned it a few hours later) concerned that the question might require turning to a given page (it did). A friend assures me that I removed the wrapper of the book to applause in the exam room, but I have no memory of that happening. My grade was a B-plus, thereby confirming my third-year paper as well.

When John F. Kennedy received an honorary degree from Yale, he said, "Now I have the best of both worlds, a Harvard education and a Yale degree." When I graduated from Harvard Law School, I felt that I had a Yale education and a Harvard degree. I resented that the law school took itself so seriously, when its curriculum seemed so divorced from any useful purpose. For passing the bar exam, a good review course would have worked with or without law school. Just as important, I can't remember ever using knowledge or techniques acquired at law school on any problem, law or other, I have faced since. My education from Yale is life education. I use it each day. And it grows over time.

I didn't leave Harvard empty-handed. My friendship with Chuck Schumer was forged there. And but for Harvard, I would not have begun my path in New York to Janklow, Traum & Klebanoff.

FOUR

....

Practicing Law Part Time

Students at Harvard Law School thought early and often about
their first career step out of law school. Firms actively recruited at
Harvard for summer associates. The pay was relatively good and the
summer programs could be broadening experiences. Bill Josephson
asked me to work for the summer of 1972 at Fried, Frank, and I
never considered looking anywhere else. Josephson wanted me there
to use my political number skills in a lawsuit he was pushing against
the allocation of delegates to the Democratic National Convention.
We claimed, which was substantively true, that the delegate allocation process did not reflect the Democratic primary vote. Many primaries awarded the winning candidate *all* of the delegates, rather
than a proportion related to the vote. Amazingly to me, we convinced
a federal district judge to issue an injunction against the 1972 Democratic convention delegate allocation. The Democratic National

Committee raised a ruckus and the injunction was overturned on appeal. The lawsuit helped move along a party process toward more proportional representation of delegates.

The job interviewing process began in earnest in the fall of 1972. Fried, Frank tried to recruit me and I interviewed at a few medium and larger sized firms. The interview at Wachtell, Lipton (about ten lawyers) made an impression. They asked me whether I would be happy working through my children's birthday parties. If not, this wasn't the firm for me. I told them I had no doubt they would make money, but I would choose my happiness another way. I decided to focus my search on small firms (ten lawyers and under) with strong partners and interesting practices. I thought I would learn faster, be exposed to clients more often, and in general be on a faster track. This was a very unusual choice for a *Harvard Law Review* student. The "safe" track was to go with a blue chip firm in an important city. I just didn't see myself fitting into the life patterns of the partners I met. The eight-year path to partner was well advertised as a grind. Hard work didn't scare me, but the idea of no fun certainly did. There were other factors as well. My father had taught me not to trust institutions as a source of security, but instead to trust yourself.

Mine was not the only interesting job search. Two of my *Law Review* friends followed unusual paths as well. Barry Forman went to his interviews with one question for the interviewers, "How much money do you make?" Somehow, that was not a popular question. Barry chose a mergers and acquisition oriented career path and today invests self-made money from Seattle. Jim Binns worked out the best answer I heard to the frequently asked question, "What kind of law do you want to practice?" Jim's answer, "Part time." Jim went on to have a major success in medical imaging businesses. When I told the Fried, Frank recruiter that I was serious about working at a small firm, his comment was, "You are out of your fucking mind." That comment never discouraged me from later hiring Fried, Frank as my lawyers.

I found a letter on file in the Harvard placement office that the firm of Janklow and Traum was looking for an associate, since a Harvard Law School alumnus had left them to join the short-lived Sargent Shriver campaign for Vice President in 1972. When I called, Mort Janklow and Jerry Traum were close to hiring an associate away from Davis, Polk, a large firm of excellent reputation. But they were busy enough that they really needed two people and I talked my way into starting in January at the same time as the other, more experienced associate. I didn't bother to inform Harvard Law School that I would be working in New York City four days a week in the second semester of my third year. No one seemed to notice.

Janklow and Traum immediately attracted me. Their practice was diverse: general counsel to the advertising agency McCaffrey and McCall, a radio station group, an active group of off-shore mutual funds, and various small underwriters. They had strong resumes and were entrepreneurial. Jerry Traum was determined to train me in his vision of a good lawyer. First to go was my typewriter. These were the days before word processing. Traum's view was that a lawyer should best learn to organize his thoughts verbally and that legal stenographic secretaries were paid to take dictation and free the lawyers to accomplish more work. That dictating discipline ultimately made my own word processing more efficient. I learned each matter from the ground up, since the curriculum at Harvard Law School had prepared me for just about none of the work I saw in the early months in the office.

I didn't bother to return to Cambridge for graduation from law school. However, one test I wanted to be certain to pass was the Bar Exam. In 1973, most Ivy League law graduates took a Practicing Law Institute refined preparation course. I was more interested in the practical approach of Joe Marino, whose classes were more Brooklyn Law than Ivy League. Marino promised that he would always give you questions you could expect to find on the exam. One day, the guest lecturer was Jacob Fuchsberg, Chief Judge of the New York Court of Appeals. Marino said, "Listen very carefully." Fuchsberg laid out a hypothetical problem and the answers. The Bar Exam has short answers and a few major essays. When I opened the essay section to find Fuchsberg's precise question, I understood why Marino had a good business, although I wondered if our exams would be thrown out (they weren't). I passed the exam and was admitted to the Bar. With the exam behind me, I was committed full time to Janklow and Traum.

It was quickly apparent that Janklow had lost much of his interest in being a lawyer before I arrived, perhaps long before, but much of the business which came in the door was due to some combination of his contacts and personality. Janklow and Bill Safire had been close since their college days at Syracuse. Janklow had been Safire's personal lawyer, which mostly meant handling the sale of Safire's public relations consulting business when he went to work for Nixon in 1969. Shortly after Nixon won his landslide reelection in 1972, Safire accepted an offer to become a columnist with the *New York Times*. He also planned to be the first Nixon insider to write a book and asked Janklow to represent him. Janklow offered to refer Safire to experienced book agents like Swifty Lazar, but Safire insisted on being represented by someone he knew and trusted.

Janklow arranged for a section of the manuscript to be read at our offices in the Seagram's building. Larry Hughes, then the publisher of William Morrow and Company, bought the book for an advance of $250,000, a lucrative deal at the time. Morrow was betting that a strong, positive, insider's book on Nixon would have the same success they had recently achieved with Margaret Truman's book about her father. Manuscript pages poured in. Favorable Morrow comments were received, including much praise for the description of Tricia Nixon's wedding at the White House. Then the scandal—Watergate emerged and a positive insider's book on Nixon seemed less of a good idea. Morrow rejected the manuscript and asked for their money back. Publishers at the time did not expect authors to put up a fight under these circumstances. The acceptability clause historically meant that the publisher could take or reject what it pleased. A public challenge by an author could compromise that writer's reputation. But Morrow had not encountered someone of Safire's toughness and resolve. Safire decided to fight, which meant an arbitration proceeding with Martin Garbus, a strong First Amendment litigator, representing Safire and Theodore White (of the *Making of the Presidents* books) prepared to testify that the manuscript Safire had written was wonderful.

The arbitrators refused to hear any expert testimony on the book and refused to read the manuscript. They also reached a Solomonic outcome favorable to Safire. The arbitrators concluded that Morrow could reject the book, but they let Safire keep the money he had received (about $85,000) and maintain ownership of the book without obligation to Morrow. The outcome of the arbitration called industry-wide attention to possible abuse of the acceptability clause, brought positive attention to Safire, and placed us in the role of aggressive author-advocate. It also taught me to avoid whenever possible an arbitration clause in contracts. In litigation, you have at least a chance at factually based dispositions and a right of appeal. With arbitration, you truly get an uncontrolled role of the dice. Janklow proceeded to sell Safire's manuscript for $25,000 to Doubleday. The book was published to excellent reviews and good sales. It was titled *Before the Fall.* Had Morrow gone forward with publication and taken a loss if necessary on the advance, their outcome would have been far better. They also might have been able to sign their author's next book.

While Safire could be a fierce enemy, he was a loyal and well connected friend. Over the next few years, he referred as clients Marvin and Bernard Kalb for their biography of Kissinger, William Colby when he exited the CIA, the journalist Dan Schorr, and John Ehrlichman from prison. Between 1973 and 1976, these assignments improved our publishing experience and profile as tough-minded independent representatives.

The Kalbs, who were then on-air correspondents for CBS, were under contract to W. W. Norton & Company for a biography of Kissinger. The opportunity to publish Kissinger's memoirs was considered to be the big prize of those years. Norton thought they had a shot at being that publisher. They felt that the Kalb manuscript was too critical of Kissinger and might cost them the opportunity to compete for Kissinger's book. Norton had paid an advance of $25,000 and made clear that they were unhappy with the manuscript. Janklow recommended that the Kalbs pay back the advance and that we would remarket the book. We offered the book for a $250,000 advance (our "going rate" after Safire) and Little, Brown and Company said yes. Little, Brown published the manuscript as submitted. The book received wide attention, including a front page review in the *New York Times Book Review* section which criticized the book as a fawning biography of Kissinger. Meanwhile, Little, Brown's foreign subrights and book club deals more than repaid their investment. Little, Brown also acquired the Kissinger memoirs. We never found out what Norton thought of their strategy.

Safire's most commercial referral was John Ehrlichman, his friend from the Nixon White House, who was still in prison for his role in the Watergate scandal. Ehrlichman's series of successful books helped turn us into literary agents. I had known Ehrlichman a little during my White House days. He was by far the kinder, gentler gatekeeper of the Ehrlichman-Haldeman team, whatever the public image. During the Watergate hearings, Ehrlichman decided to, and was permanently damaged by, coming on as a combative litigator. Ehrlichman wanted to write to make money to pay legal bills and to vent his anger with Nixon and his team.

Safire, meanwhile, decided to write a novel about a blind president. The premise was that the president was a philanderer who was blinded in an accident while committing adultery. This fact could not, of course, be disclosed. The novel was called *Full Disclosure* and Doubleday bought it for $25,000 because they had published *Before the Fall*. Then and now, Doubleday was under common ownership with the Literary Guild book club, which offered to take the book as a main selection. Safire had an approval by contract over any book club deal. We used the approval to create a bidding contest with Book of the Month Club over Doubleday's objection. Literary Guild bought the book for $250,000, about triple their initial offer. Word of the bidding war was all over the publishing community. While almost no one had actually read the manuscript, the paperback houses decided that if the clubs were fighting over it, they had to acquire the book. Ballantine won the auction for $1,300,000 (50 percent to the author), then a record price for a first book of fiction in paperback. Doubleday made money in spite of themselves.

The publicity surrounding this deal again helped us. This was one of the first big money deals for a *New York Times* journalist. There was envy, finally put to rest by a *Times* senior editor's comment of, "After all, it's 50 percent of $1.3 million, less commission, less taxes. How much can you hate a guy over $300,000." Ballantine proceeded to publish the book to the largest write-off (more than $1 million) then recorded by a paperback house. Very few people ever bought the book. I realized then that we were selling rights for money, not books in the marketplace. My share of that commission and others that followed from unearned advances never felt quite right. It seemed to me that selling books and building an author's career was what my work should be.

Janklow's strength as a literary agent was his own enthusiasm. He truly believed, at least for the moment, in what he was selling. Janklow was also a great storyteller, so he could enchant an editor with a verbal account which was often better than what the author had put on paper. Janklow also had a good sense of the need for the buyer to acquire. That's why he favored buyers who were recently appointed to their positions or who felt a need to prove themselves against their competition. Janklow later blurred some of the lines between buyer and seller by representing editors Michael Korda and Richard Snyder of Simon & Schuster on personal matters.

When I first met Janklow in 1973, he was about forty-two, disinterested in the practice of law and becoming risk averse from the difficulties of rescuing his work and investment in cable funding. I doubt that he had a clear professional plan in mind for the upcoming decade. Becoming a literary agent almost accidentally transformed Janklow professionally, and personally. Janklow had the drive to claim the mantel of the leading agent of his generation. He was an expert flatterer. Personal notes flowed from his office. To crack his social circle in the evening required much more than a professional relationship through work. Barbara Walters and Walter

Cronkite were friends. Editors, publishers, and authors were luncheon companions.

I worked closely with Janklow on all of our early book projects, but they were certainly "his." The first client of consequence who was mine was Daniel P. Moynihan, who was also coincidentally a friend of Safire's. I had kept in close touch with the Moynihans (Pat and his extraordinary wife, Liz) through my Harvard Law School years. Moynihan accepted an ambassadorship to India from President Ford and Checker Finn joined him there as a senior staffer. Checker became engaged to an Indian pathologist with two kids and planned a trip to India in 1974 for his Dayton, Ohio, parents to meet their daughter-in-law to be, Renu, and new grandchildren. Checker had arranged for a private railroad car to take a one-week expedition from Delhi to Bombay including stops at the amazing caves of Ellora and Ajanta. He invited me to stay in the embassy and join him, Renu, and his parents on the train. I understood that I was needed as a possible buffer, but the offer was irresistible.

While in India, Liz Moynihan arranged for me to corner Pat on a subject he would normally avoid, his personal representation. Moynihan planned to write books; he had until then represented himself, and Liz wanted him to be appropriately protected. In a steam bath in Delhi, Moynihan promised that I could consider him a client. He appreciated the significance to me that he would be my first client. As a primarily academic writer, Moynihan had not received a significant advance for a book. My goal was to get him a favorable advance. The editor keenest to publish Moynihan was Peter Davison of the Atlantic Monthly Press, which was affiliated with Little, Brown. We signed a two-book deal in 1974, but Moynihan accepted the job of Ambassador to the United Nations before the first book was even begun. Ultimately, that book would be *A Dangerous Place*, written with Suzanne Weaver. The photo of Moynihan with his arm raised in veto at the Security Council was the image on the cover. In the background of the photo is Len Garment, who came to the UN as Moynihan's deputy. As good as the manuscript was and as visible as Moynihan was at the United Nations, the book did not sell particularly well. I learned that not all good books sell even if the author is a notable figure.

Bill Josephson and I kept our political consulting company when I joined Janklow and Traum. Josephson once showed me a draft private-offering document outlining funding for a voter study company with a chief executive and substantial equity role for me. The problem with turning voting analysis into a career was exactly what Moynihan had warned against. Soon you would be working for the money, rather than to make a difference. I declined the full-scale business model. We did, however, do a voter study for Howard Samuels, a Democrat who, in 1973, appeared to be the favorite for governor of New York in 1974.

Samuels was a good man and a successful businessman. He had run the Off-Track Betting Corporation with distinction. The press had dubbed him "Howie the Horse." His campaign manager Ken Auletta (now a noted writer) was talented and focused. Another staffer, Amanda (Binky) Urban, went on to marry Ken and is now a prominent literary agent. I saw two problems with the overall campaign strategy. One was that Samuels had been denied the designation of the party in convention in 1970, and was determined at all costs to get it. The designation as a practical matter could avoid a primary fight only if no other candidate got 25 percent of the vote (or failed after that to get sufficient signatures to be on the ballot). The second was a fear of running as "Howie the Horse," since it seemed to be undignified in a race for Governor.

Congressman Hugh Carey ran unexpectedly, secured 25 percent of the vote at the convention (Samuels got the designation), and promptly defeated Howard Samuels, who had dissipated too much of his campaign war chest before the real race began. Howie the Horse never made an appearance either in the campaign or the winner's circle. In politics, the only ticket that pays is a winning ticket. You can't bet on place and show.

I came away from the Samuels experience convinced that you run on your background, never afraid of your prior experience, courting rather than fearing any playful way the press decides to address you.

Never assume early on who your competition is. The race often takes shape late in the game. Samuels was my last paid candidate political consulting assignment and the end of Josephson and Klebanoff as a business. Bill Josephson has remained one of my closest friends and, at all critical transitions for me, a very effective lawyer. I promised myself I would work only for friends when I was personally motivated, and if that meant sitting out electoral politics for years to come, so be it. No one could have realized at the time that Moynihan for Senate, Bradley for Senate and ultimately for President, and Schumer for Senate were in the cards.

Moynihan's tenure at the United Nations, and particularly his vocal opposition to the resolution declaring Zionism as a form of racism, started speculation that he would be a strong Democratic candidate for Senate in 1976 against the Republican conservative incumbent James Buckley. It was clear that former congresswoman Bella Abzug would run a formidable race for the nomination. But party leaders like Joe Crangle in Buffalo and Lane Kirkland of the AFL-CIO were eager to get Moynihan to run.

Moynihan was uncertain. At the time, I thought he wasn't sure that he wanted to be a senator. In retrospect, I think he was just afraid to run and lose. Moynihan resigned his United Nations appointment in February 1976, in time to protect his Harvard tenure for the fall semester. As someone who had grown up in Hell's Kitchen, he was not about to surrender tenure at Harvard until it was absolutely essential. There were limits at Harvard on leaves and Moynihan was about to exceed his. I arranged for Moynihan to lecture for money with the Harry Walker Agency. The several months between his tenure at the UN and the start of the Senate campaign were probably the only time in his career that Moynihan made any significant private money. Jewish groups throughout the country were clamoring to hear him.

The groups that sponsored his talks often wanted more of Moynihan that anyone should be asked to give. I got a call late one night the first week of the tour with a simple request from Moynihan: "Get me out of here." His host in Cleveland had insisted that Moynihan stay in his home. Moynihan was not only delivering a speech, but working for his dinner and his bedroom, too. We got hotels and drivers worked out after that.

By 1976, Steve Weisman had more senior reportorial responsibilities on the *Times,* frequently filing stories about the upcoming Senate race. Since Moynihan was not commenting, I became a background source. Moynihan never encouraged or discouraged what I was doing to promote a candidacy. Moynihan and I would meet frequently, to and from his public appearances, at a hockey game, in his suite at the Waldorf Towers. The topic was Moynihan's potential candidacy, and between the meetings I would give Steve Weisman background to the effect that Moynihan was thinking seriously about becoming a candidate. On the day Moynihan resigned from the UN, I was quoted on the front page of the *Times* saying that he would consider a Senate race. Moynihan called me and said, "That's twice I've put you on the front page of the *New York Times.*" That was the first and last time he ever talked to me about my resignation from his White House staff.

The night before Moynihan was to make the announcement of his candidacy, I visited with him and Liz. She was cutting his hair. After I read the text of the announcement, I strongly recommended that he include a line that he would support the Democratic nominee. Since I knew that he and Abzug despised each other and that liberal Democrats would try to bait him with his Nixon and Ford public service, this seemed to me a diplomatic opening position. Also, I felt that Abzug wouldn't promise the same. Moynihan had so backed into the decision to run that no fundraising had been authorized. A few core volunteers, led by Dick Blumenthal, were working from a room at the Biltmore Hotel with one telephone line. So Moynihan couldn't reach them and they, likewise, couldn't reach too many people.

The day after the announcement, Moynihan asked me to join him at the *New York Times,* since he couldn't get through to the Biltmore headquarters. He asked for the advertising unit. A *Times* employee looked absolutely flabbergasted as Moynihan provided the UN arm-raised photo, some text he had typed himself, and a request that the fellow make the ad "look good" in the Sunday "Week in Review" section. I at least had the presence of mind to ask for a coupon in the ad which people could return with donations. Within a few days, I joined Dick Blumenthal at a meeting with the group that hoped to raise money for Moynihan. There were long discussions about traditional constituencies of support, carving up targets, reaching out for more solicitors, and so on. At some point, Blumenthal interrupted and said, "This is all very interesting, but we have a hotel bill at the Biltmore of $1,500 and we can't check out. Does anyone have the money?"

In the early weeks, Moynihan was a terrible candidate. A mutual friend, the journalist Edward Jay Epstein, had arranged for Moynihan to have dinner in Easthampton with Steve Ross, the head of Warner, and his companion, Amanda Burden (William Paley's daughter). Ross was a very active Democratic fundraiser and an extremely competitive man. During drinks, Ross asked Moynihan a simple question, "Pat, why do you want to be Senator?" Moynihan's rather off-the-wall answer was, "Well, I don't actually want to be a Senator. Lane Kirkland, the head of the AFL-CIO, called and talked me into running." It was then I thought we might not get dinner. We did get dinner, but we certainly never got any special Ross efforts.

Moynihan finally became good at campaigning when he understood that he could actually lose. He even chose, over my heated objections, to go into personal debt. In the campaign's final stages, Abzug said in anger that she couldn't promise to support Moynihan if he won the primary. That may well have been the difference in the ten-thousand-vote spread in Moynihan's favor on primary night.

By three A.M. that night, Abzug had not conceded, and there was talk of a demand for a recount and possible litigation. I had a beer with Moynihan and he asked what we should do. I said to run straight ahead and dare the Board of Elections to run the election twice. This obviously wouldn't have worked in 2000, but it did in 1976. The following morning he was doing a superb job of handling Jim Buckley, who started by attacking Moynihan as an academic. Moynihan's retort was, "So he has called me a professor . . ." Moynihan was prepared to run on his resume. Moynihan decided to teach at Harvard to protect his tenure. The campaign staff reacted strongly to a candidate who would be out of state several days a week. The national and New York press proceeded to follow him around Cambridge. His coverage was probably better than if he had run around New York.

Moynihan beat Buckley easily. The night after the election, Pat, Liz, and I went to a celebration dinner at a French restaurant opposite the Carlyle Hotel. Who should walk in but Jim Buckley and his wife. There was no awkwardness, since they both were gentlemen. Perhaps Buckley didn't expect to win. That was certainly the way it felt watching the campaign. In January 1977, I met with Moynihan shortly after his swearing in. He told me that within the week he had been to his last meeting of the government faculty department at Harvard in which great minds wrestled with small questions, and to his first meetings in the Senate where small minds wrestled with great questions.

One of Moynihan's first appointees was Tim Russert, a young Buffalo lawyer protégé of Joe Crangle who had been helpful in the campaign. Moynihan had also hired his first press spokesperson. The staffer put out a press release in Moynihan's name (standard practice on the Hill) and promptly got fired since Moynihan was determined to write his own releases. During my time in the White House, the key piece of equipment was the typewriter that sat behind Moynihan's desk and which he took to the schoolhouse at his Oneonta farm where he wrote as well. Moynihan's words were his. I have heard Russert tell a wonderful story imitating Moynihan's speech, which begins with the firing of the press staffer. Moynihan turns to Russert and says, "You will be my new press secretary." Russert asks if he can ask a question of the Senator: "What do I need to know to be a good press secretary?" Moynihan says, "That's easy, one thing—good judgment." "And Senator," says Russert, "how do I go about acquiring good judgment?" Moynihan says, "There's only one way—experience." "And, Senator, if I can ask one more question," says Russert, "how can I gain experience?" Moynihan says, "Only one way—bad judgment."

Pat Moynihan had met his wife Liz Brennan during Averell Harriman's 1954 campaign for governor of New York, so he had a soft spot for campaign romance. The best personal reward for me from the Moynihan campaign was meeting my wife, Susan Hirschhorn, at a Moynihan fundraiser. Moynihan offered us an engagement toast at the Harvard Club during a book reception after his election. His publishing comment was, "Another of my books which will sell in the hundreds."

Fortunately, not all of the books we represented were selling in the hundreds. By 1976, the political books agented had announced a presence for us in the publishing community. In 1976, Janklow received a manuscript from Steve Krantz, a Hollywood producer, with the comment that a "friend" of his had written a novel and needed representation. The friend was his wife, Judith, and the novel was *Scruples.* Janklow submitted the manuscript to the editors he knew at Random House, Simon & Schuster, and Doubleday, all of whom rejected the book. I asked Janklow if I could submit *Scruples* to Larry Freundlich at Crown Publishers. Freundlich called me with a $50,000 advance offer for the book and a question about whether the author would be good at promoting herself (she was and is). Judith Krantz met with me to review and sign her first contract. One of the questions during the Rosetta litigation with Random House was what authors were thinking when they signed their agreements. In Judith Krantz's case, she was thinking about articles of hers that *Cosmopolitan* had rejected because they were too sexually revealing. Freundlich then proceeded to interest Warner Books almost before the ink was dry on our hardcover contract to preempt the paperback rights for $500,000. This was good news. Freundlich then went to London and conducted a successful six-figure auction of British rights. Crown's sensational jacket—a black background with a veiled woman—was later frequently imitated. The book took off upon publication and the $50,000 sale had established a career for Judith Krantz and commercial fiction credibility for us.

Krantz's next book, *Princess Daisy,* came to the rights marketplace at the peak of competition among the houses for top commercial projects. Crown put the rights up for auction and Bantam paid a then record $3.1 million for the paperback rights. The deal hit the front page of the *New York Times*. We bought the original of the *New Yorker* cartoon which shows someone at a book counter saying, "I'd like to buy a copy of that book they paid $3,200,000 for, whatever its title is." When we entertained Judith Krantz at the Four Seasons to celebrate her success, she signed the guest book, "I write for money." As time passed, she would write for respect and money. Her publishers, however, would keep an eye on the money. For example, there was an editorial suggestion for *Mistral's Daughter* to add one early sex scene for "character development." She thanked her editor for the suggestion and promptly followed it.

I was eager to handle my own projects. This meant looking for opportunities in which money was involved, but in which the work or personality of the client was not attractive to Janklow. One day in 1977, an older man with a raft of papers presented himself at our offices. Aaron Goldblatt was the "manager" for the astrologer Linda Goodman, whose book *Sun Signs*, published in 1968, had popularized astrology in the United States. Linda Goodman had been in and out of fights for nearly seven years with Taplinger (a small publishing house which was living off of the backlist life of *Sun Signs*) and other publishers over the rights to a nearly completed large manuscript called *Love Signs*. Harper & Row had made a new offer of $50,000, provided Linda Goodman could deliver clean rights. Like Zero Mostel in *The Producers*, Linda Goodman had also given others percentages of her revenue in the book totaling well over 100 percent. Some of the recipients had loaned her money, provided lodging, or were helping on one of her many other projects.

From a representation point of view, I could also call the project with the benefit of hindsight "Warning Signs." There had already been several nasty litigations. Linda Goodman had apparently camped out for days on the steps of St. Patrick's Cathedral trying to persuade Bantam to release moneys to her that by contract went to her hardcover publisher. Linda Goodman was convinced she was a direct descendant of Abraham Lincoln and could prove it with the help of a signed Lincoln photograph that had been passed through the generations in her family. She had "channeled" a nearly 1,000-page blank verse personal story on the theme of reincarnation. And she thought that I had returned from ancient Egypt to rescue her or, for a more modern incarnation, was somehow connected to Howard Hughes.

Nonetheless, I saw a major project if the mess could be resolved. With that in mind, I offered to negotiate and present a reorganization plan for Linda Goodman to accept or reject. Taplinger had a letter which had survived one litigation with Random House which promised Taplinger a 50 percent interest in *Love Signs* since Linda had refused to honor her contractual commitment to deliver the book to Taplinger. I got Taplinger to agree to a $250,000 buyout of that 50 percent interest with the argument that something substantial was better than a ten-year war over 50 percent of nothing.

I then persuaded Harper & Row to up their advance offer to $500,000, which comfortably funded the Taplinger buyout and left money to deal with the other percentage holders. One by one, I arranged to buy or freeze them out. The book was scheduled for Fall 1978. As soon as the date was locked in, Linda started to hound Harper & Row with demands for everything from design and type issues to jacket layout to a frontispiece letter to her daughter who might or might not be dead. To meet production deadlines, Linda released the final chapters one by one directly to the printer, and I found myself sitting in Harper's offices in New York confirming to her that her various creative demands had been met.

While the editorial process was an agony, the rights were headed to great financial success. British rights were auctioned for $275,000, more than the reported amounts for Kissinger's memoirs. Rights were sold throughout the world, including to publishers who planned to break the book up by sign and publish twelve volumes. The major opportunity was, of course, the paperback. Fawcett then a unit of CBS, ultimately acquired the rights for a record advance of $2.2 million (70 percent to the author). Linda also asked me to step in and help Taplinger negotiate a record ten-year $450,000 renewal advance with Bantam for the paperback rights to *Sun Signs*.

It looked like a triumph. But Linda Goodman was not easy to manage or keep happy. The more the money, the more she spent— starting with building a headquarters for a new religion in Cripple Creek, Colorado, all the way to a full-blown detective and advertising effort to locate her daughter. I sold another book for her to Harper. The *Star Signs* $450,000 advance was spent without the book being written. Ultimately, Linda Goodman filed for what apparently became the longest running personal bankruptcy in Colorado history. She went through several teams of representatives. The first team used threats of fraud against our agency to negotiate a fixed, capped fee of $100,000, instead of our ongoing commissions. Had we fought, the vagaries of bankruptcy law would have left us with the risk of getting nothing. At the end, the ongoing earning power of *Sun Signs* and *Love Signs* enabled all the creditors, including the agent, to be paid 100 cents on the dollar, undoubtedly another Linda Goodman first.

With a deadline of a major project and a difficult client, you get a chance to learn how far you will go to save a commission. Linda Goodman opened each section of *Love Signs* with a quote from *Peter Pan*. Since the book had more than 100 sections, the quotes used nearly half the text of *Peter Pan*. It is generally the author's responsibility to clear permissions, and Linda hadn't. Potentially, this could have posed a major problem, as the book was ready for the printer and Linda wouldn't agree to delete the quotes. Although Scribner claimed valid copyright on J. M. Barrie's book, I decided to research the question more deeply and discovered a record of a 1905 edition filed in the United States which would have placed *Peter Pan* in the public domain. We published without contacting Scribner. When their lawyers came screaming, they quickly agreed to a nominal permission fee and credit in the next printing, provided we didn't tell anyone else of our discovery. This deal bought Scribner another ten years in the marketplace with exclusive rights. It pays to do your homework.

One day, in 1979, our largest law client was visiting the office and overheard my side of a conversation with Linda Goodman. When the call was over, he said, "It sounds like you were talking to a crazy person." Jerry Traum asked me to estimate for him our agency commissions from Linda Goodman. I said, "Over time, about $500,000." He said, "I see, she's not crazy, she's eccentric." Perhaps, but serving eccentrics even for big fees is no easy task.

Linda Goodman had a pattern of publishing her major *Signs* books at ten-year intervals. In between, it frustrated her that publishers wanted only "brand" when she wanted to explore poetry and personal works about reincarnation. She believed that publishers would publish *Linda Goodman's Manure Signs* if she offered it and she may have been right.

Years later, Linda Goodman was finally interested in writing *Star Signs* and asked me to be her agent once again. *Star Signs* was intended to popularize numerology. This time around I insisted on a completed manuscript before I would start work and a full set of guidelines of what would be acceptable to her from a publisher. It wasn't easy, but I was absolutely firm that we would play by my rules or not at all. St. Martin's Press bought the book for a $450,000 advance and some of the headaches of handling a Linda Goodman title. *Star Signs* appeared in hardcover editions around the world in 1987 and in mass market editions a year later. The title has joined *Sun Signs* and *Love Signs* as backlist perennials. Even her channeled narrative poem was published successfully under the title *Gooberz*.

Linda Goodman also asked me to represent once again the backlist rights for *Sun Signs* and *Love Signs*. In 1988 and in 1998, *Sun Signs* was once again renewed for a ten-year paperback license with Bantam at an industry-record-level advance price of $450,000. *Love Signs* was to do even better. The initial $2.2 million record-setting advance for *Love Signs* had been one of the last large acquisitions in 1978 for Fawcett, then a unit of CBS. The overly large commitment for *Love Signs* was always assumed to be one of the reasons that CBS decided to sell Fawcett to S. I. Newhouse to be combined with the Ballantine Publishing Group as part of Random House. While the advance was too high, *Love Signs* sold well year in and year out, and by 1989 had earned back about half of its advance and sold more than 50,000 copies per year.

Harper & Row had by then become HarperCollins*Publishers* and was eager to develop its own paperback line. I had a call suggesting that Harper would license the renewal of *Love Signs* for an advance of $50,000. I asked if the rights had been offered to Fawcett. Harper suggested they didn't have to. I suggested that fiduciary responsibilities and an approvals clause would lead to a different conclusion. Fawcett bid aggressively. After many rounds, Harper prevailed with an advance of $750,000. That earned out with a millennium edition.

The brand of Linda Goodman's *Signs* books would even survive her death. Linda had written material for a computer generated "matching" analysis. Crystal Bush, who owns most of the Linda Goodman rights now, my deputy Lisa Edwards, and I figured out how to convert this material into *Linda Goodman's Relationship Signs,* which earned nearly $1 million in a series of worldwide editions. And the brand continued to carry the backlist. Linda Goodman titles are among the leading backlist titles of Bantam and HarperCollins in the United States and of Pan MacMillan, one of the largest paperback houses in the United Kingdom. And every now and then a foreign publisher translates one of the books, sometimes publishing in twelve volumes by sign. The only manure sign here is dollars.

By the end of 1977, Mort Janklow, Jerry Traum, and I now held the following sales records:

Paperback fiction—*Princess Daisy* by Judith Krantz
($3,200,000)
Paperback first fiction—*Full Disclosure* by William Safire
($1,400,000)
Paperback nonfiction—*Linda Goodman's Love Signs*
($2,200,000)
Paperback renewal nonfiction—*Linda Goodman's Sun Signs*
($450,000)

British sale—*Linda Goodman's Love Signs*
($350,000)

It might not have been my plan to become an agent, but accident was certainly starting to feel attractive—and remunerative. I was, in fact, not a bad advertising lawyer. I also had a broad range of corporate experience in small underwriting deals, workouts, and real estate transactions. However, if my goal was to become a good lawyer, I would need to specialize in something, and if I planned to be a successful lawyer, I would need to attract and serve my own clients. While I understood only it in part at the time, by 1977 my transition away from being a corporate lawyer and toward becoming a literary agent was nearly complete.

FIVE

....

Wrap it to Go

In 1978, when we moved into new offices, the name on the door read "Janklow, Traum & Klebanoff, Law Offices" and "Morton L. Janklow Associates, Inc., Literary Agents." While my name was now on the legal masthead, and our revenue was still, until 1982, disproportionately from legal billings, my energies were increasingly tied up in literary related matters. And for the next five years, Mort, Jerry, and I proceeded to build a major literary agency. Working on a book deal had moments that were hard to replicate in the practice of law, not that the practice of law was without its interesting moments.

Mort Janklow socialized with Pete Peterson, then cohead of Lehman Brothers and formerly Secretary of Commerce in Nixon's Cabinet. Peterson had been friends since business school with Generoso Pope, Jr., the owner of *The National Enquirer.* Pope was also one of Peterson's unpublicized clients who needed new lawyers. We were hired for corporate purposes (the business was privately held) and in turn hired Williams & Connolly for litigation. David Kendall, who was to gain more visibility for his client Bill Clinton during the impeachment proceedings, was assigned to libel readings as lead litigator. I took quite a few trips to the *Enquirer* offices in Lantana, Florida. Pope enjoyed having a Board of Directors and regular meetings, even though he owned 100 percent of the stock.

Gene Pope was one of the first to decide that the tabloid paper should have color photographs. With a nearly 6 million–copy weekly press run and no way to test the shift to color, Pope had to switch to color and increase the cover price in a single stroke. I remember the Board meeting in which some of the members said that Pope was "betting the company" on this move. It worked. Pope certainly had his idiosyncrasies. Some were just clever, like the handful of reporting accounts from which he could quickly judge the weekly sell-through of the paper at newsstands (very little of the circulation was by subscription). Others, like not trusting the printer with a contract, were just expensive. Pope loved secrecy, even from his own people. We once spent months negotiating a *National Enquirer* mass market book line with Pocket Books. The heart of the deal was distribution on racks which would hang from the checkout counter racks of the *Enquirer*. Pope never consulted his own staff until the tortured negotiations were completed. When his distribution team questioned the wisdom of having books at the racks possibly to conflict with the Enquirer itself, Pope withdrew his interest and our months of work collapsed.

The *Enquirer* was only the beginning of Peterson referrals. Peterson sat on the Board of Directors of the international oil company, Cities Service. Like many others, Cities Service had been caught making inappropriate foreign payments to secure or protect business interests abroad. The Board asked a committee of Peterson and Robert Lilly, the former chairman of AT&T, to investigate whether the company's efforts to deal with the problem were thorough enough. The committee hired AT&T's lead lawyer Lawrence Walsh (later the Independent Prosecutor in Reagan's second term for Iran-Contra) from its outside counsel Davis, Polk. Peterson got us hired to protect him independently. I made a few trips to Tulsa, Oklahoma, then the company's headquarters. On one trip, we learned that there was, in fact, an additional undisclosed payment. The payment was made public, nothing terrible happened, and Cities Service paid our bill. We had done our job to protect Peterson's independence and reputation. Walsh, who was a very formal person, reminded me of all the reasons I had chosen to work in a small law firm.

One of our assignments illustrated for me the appeal of a commission instead of a fee. With legal assignments, Janklow took a very conservative view of billings. We represented a team led editorially by Steve Birnbaum (whose ambition to become the Fodor's of his generation was cut short by his untimely death) on a travel magazine and book assignment. *Diversion Magazine for Physicians* had begun as a free magazine circulated to nearly 80,000 physicians by Johnson & Johnson, carrying only Johnson & Johnson advertising. The editorial content addressed leisure activities for doctors. The hope was that both the doctor and patient in the doctor's office would read the magazine and respond to the advertising. Johnson & Johnson decided that the magazine could be more effective with broader advertising and more editorial pages. With a promise of advertising support, they transferred rights to the magazine to a retiring executive. The investment effort was tightly budgeted (under $150,000). Our legal bill alone was more than $20,000. The group pleaded with Janklow to take an equity interest in the deal instead of the fee. Janklow dug in. We were paid.

Birnbaum built a book line with the same editorial content (*The Get 'Em and Go Guides*). With an independent survey showing that doctors and patients read and liked *Diversion Magazine* and indicating a surge in consumer advertising, the business plan worked. Several years later, the company was sold to Hearst for $25 million. Our commission would have been more than $1 million. I have never since had a problem trading modest certain fees for large uncertain commissions. And in this instance, pushing for the fee alienated the client team as well.

Whatever legal business I attracted didn't excite me. The playing field was simply too small, and billing by the hour began to run contrary to my feeling that I should be paid very well for a result or not at all. While my name was on the door of the law firm, my heart was increasingly in agency work. My objective, of course, was to land my own clients. While Bill Bradley thought that I was too inexperienced to represent him in 1974 for *Life on the Run,* his wonderful book on his life in basketball, he referred a friend to me in 1977. Frank McDonald, a charming, intelligent person, presents himself as a man of the world and someone with links to the intelligence community. He claims to have had a stint in a Cuban jail and a neatly arranged escape that led to an Irish farm near the home of Frederick Forsyth, the thriller writer.

When I met McDonald, he had been researching for some time the OSS files regarding recovery of stolen or confiscated art after World War II. At the time, these files were not publicly accessible. Now, of course, parts of the art world have been turned inside out due to the detailed exposures of the Nazi confiscations of that art. McDonald had focused upon reports in the files concerning the Wildenstein family, who had been prominent art dealers in New York and Paris then and now. The historical record concerning the Wildensteins has been the subject of recent litigation. McDonald didn't want to write the historical account. He wanted to use it as the starting point for a novel.

I helped McDonald refine an eighty-page proposal for a novel called *Provenance,* loosely based on an investigator who uncovers an art dealer who collaborated with the Nazis and hid important paintings in a cave. There was interest from several publishers. Peter Davison (Moynihan's editor) at Atlantic Monthly Press finally convinced his partners at Little, Brown to commit $100,000 for this unwritten first novel, a sum at the time that led Dick Snyder of Simon & Schuster, the underbidder, to scream at Janklow that we were destroying publishing. McDonald completed quite a good manuscript. The paperback houses chased the rights, and we found ourselves in negotiation with Avon Books (then owned by Hearst) to preempt the rights by making a bid that would discourage any need for an auction.

A preemptive price offers a hard decision for the rights-holder (no one knows if the price is higher or lower than an auction would bring). When both we and Atlantic Monthly Press thought the price was right at $750,000, we talked to McDonald, who asked what we would do in his shoes. Janklow's answer on the conference call was that Frank had 90 percent of our action. He voted to go ahead, which proved to be the right call, since the book did modest business both in hardcover and paperback editions. McDonald produced no other work and committed to no other contracts. I learned that good clients who went the distance were not easy to find.

Bill Bradley's decision to run against Clifford Case in New Jersey for the U.S. Senate brought me back to politics, but this time, as with Moynihan two years before, motivated to help a friend. While Bill was only a few years older than I was, he was already a national figure when I met him in 1971, with a reputation as a scholar-athlete with sound values from a modest Midwestern background. His A&E biography years later would be a moving show that ended with his election to the Senate as man of thirty-five. In the time we spent together during the Missouri voter study days, I grew to admire him and I certainly enjoyed his company. If we needed to talk about the study (I was at Harvard Law School while preparing it), Bill would send player's tickets to a Knicks-Celtics game and we would have a working dinner afterward. Some of the meetings were in his apartment on Eighth Avenue in Manhattan, just up the street from Madison Square Garden. On one cab ride together passing the Garden, Bill commented, "There's the office."

Crystal City, Missouri, was where Bill grew up and part of the definition of his character. Anyone who traveled with him during the 2000 presidential race would hear its stories probably more times than they cared to. But in 1971–1972, Missouri became for Bill too small a playing field, particularly since the open race to try was state auditor. He passed. And passed again on a series of opportunities to run for Congress from a variety of jurisdictions. Somewhere along the path, Bill realized that electoral politics was risky and that if he was going to take the risk, it might as well be for a chance to win a serious reward, like a seat in the United States Senate.

I was the volunteer member of a small group that helped Bill organize the 1978 race for Senate. Doug Berman, who would ultimately run Bill's 2000 presidential race, built a voter study for New Jersey. Susan Thomases, who was very close to Hillary Clinton (and now is managing partner of the New York law firm Willkie, Farr & Gallagher), was the manager. And Marcia Aronoff, who went on to run Bill's Senate staff for many years, ran issues. My contribution was to be a bit of a contrarian. The first assumption was that Bill would get the support of the Democratic Governor Richard Hughes and perhaps foreclose a primary. I didn't have a crystal ball, but I did warn against the assumption. Hughes instead backed another candidate and Bill faced the primary without his support.

The second assumption was that the race should be positioned against the Republican incumbent Clifford Case, who, while elderly, had carefully cultivated a moderate image in a moderate state. Case had a young conservative primary opponent, Jeffrey Bell. Having seen a few unusual electoral developments before, I urged caution and no assumption that Case would win the primary. Indeed, like many moderate Republicans before (Lindsay) and since (John McCain), Case lost the Republican primary. Bill beat Bell comfortably in the general election.

Bill had none of Moynihan's early problems as a candidate. Bill knew why he was running, and was a disciplined and hard working as any staff could hope for. The same work ethic that had made him a successful basketball player went to work in the political arena. Bill said to me early in the process, "I understand running for office. It is a bit like a basketball game. They blow the whistle, you run like hell, and when they blow the final whistle, you add up the score." As a ball player, Bill was known for throwing more than the occasional elbow and, of course, fouls could sink your team. In politics there are no referees, and, over time, even Bill's most ardent supporters would wish that his standards for public life would permit more of the elbow throwing of his game.

One of the key positioning decisions for the race was how to deal with Bill's basketball career. As a legendary Princeton player who had carried his team all the way to the NCAA final four and a New York Knick who had played a key role on two championship teams, Bill's basketball resume was certainly in front of New Jersey's voters. As with "Howie the Horse," there was some debate about the dignity of the basketball resume in the context of a race for the Senate. Mine was not the only voice urging that Bill run straight ahead on his resume. Ultimately, there was a wonderful television commercial (produced by Michael Kaye): Bradley speaks from behind a desk about running around in drafty arenas in short pants learning teamwork, leadership, and so on. At the close of the commercial, he crumples a piece of paper and sinks it into the wastebasket. I suspect Bill didn't need extra takes to make that work.

When Bill first decided to run, I arranged for him to be invited for dinner at Liz and Pat Moynihan's Washington home. I told Moynihan that Bill was precisely the kind of senator he wanted to join him in Washington, that they should get to know each other and that Moynihan should help in the campaign. That happened in a good way for them both. On general election night in 1978, I was in Bill's suite in a Meadowlands hotel. I had arranged for Moynihan, who was at his Oneonta, New York, farm (later the scene of the launch of another Senate campaign by Hillary Clinton) to be available for a congratulatory telephone call. Once the results were clear, I grabbed Bill and put him on the phone with Moynihan. I heard Bill say, "Thank you, and, Senator, I am counting on your support for my application to the Finance Committee." Bill handed the phone back to me and Moynihan said, "So, Klebanoff, I see you have two Senators now." Bill got on the Finance Committee. While I stayed in touch with Bill and his wonderful wife, Ernestine, during his Senate years, it was to be more than fifteen years later before our roles changed again, and, among other things, I landed him as a book client.

Politics, of course, was a hobby. Janklow and Traum encouraged good hobbies (and sane working hours), one of the reasons I enjoyed our work. Meanwhile, the agency started to get into more commercial fiction. With Judith Krantz branded, our goal was to add more. Barbara Taylor Bradford had scored a great international success with her romance novel *A Woman of Substance*. Her husband, Bob, was deeply involved in the management of her career, as Steve Krantz was with Judy's. The Bradfords had lost confidence in their agent Paul Gitlin (ironically Bill Bradley's agent as well) for a number of reasons, particularly in foreign rights negotiations.

Most agents work through a network of subagents market by market around the world. Some of these agents work in piles of paper from home; others have serious enterprises representing many agents and publishers. When these agents represent large numbers of projects, there is a temptation to use the best projects to force buyers to take a variety of other titles in a group. The buyer will tend in the process to reduce his or her offer for the best title. *A Woman of Substance* had scored big in many markets, particularly the United Kingdom and France, where its numbers were said to rival *Gone with the Wind*. Bob Bradford was undoubtedly one of the few author's representatives ever to conduct a "world tour" to see how the subagents were doing. He was not impressed.

Barbara Taylor Bradford wrote long romances. It seemed to me that Barbara spent long days at the typewriter, took a break to walk the dog, and worked some more. Meanwhile, Bob made certain that her work realized the greatest commercial potential. We sold a package of three Bradford books for more than $5 million for North American rights and proceeded to make major deals in Britain, France, and other foreign markets as well without using subagents. The Bradfords not only happily paid our new 15 percent commission, but when the contracts were signed they sent the three of us engraved Cartier pens. I have carried that pen since to remind me every day what I like about the agency business.

Several other romance writer gave us the chance to see both the values of backlists and the problems an unrepresented writer can have. Harlequin then and now was the leading international brand in formula romances. Their North American book clubs alone could send six titles a month to hundreds of thousands of subscribers.

When Harlequin fired Pocket Books as its United States distributor, Dick Snyder, who headed the parent company Simon & Schuster, responded by forming Silhouette Books and going into competition. Simon & Schuster had all of the detailed account information on where these formula romances were racked and sold, and planned to use their distribution muscle and give Harlequin a run for their money. They needed authors.

Some authors of formula romances are incredibly prolific. Dick Snyder referred to us two of Harlequin's productive authors—Anne Hampson, who had written more than one hundred books, and Roberta Leigh, who could write one of these books in a weekend and had written nearly fifty. We promptly made major deals for these writers with Silhouette, in Anne Hampson's case a deal for more than twenty books and $1 million. Ultimately, the Silhouette-Harlequin war was settled by Harlequin buying Silhouette and reappointing Pocket Books as a distributor.

I began to review the Anne Hampson backlist and was shocked by what I saw. Mills & Boon, a London-based subsidiary of Harlequin, would sign unrepresented writers to worldwide contracts. The true romance was between the Boon brothers and mostly British authors capable of writing the formula books. The UK subsidiary would license North American rights for a fifty-fifty split to the Canadian parent, which would, in turn, license U.S. rights for a further fifty-fifty split to an American subsidiary. This meant that any royalty offered was, in fact, reduced by 75 percent for the largest market. At least in the Anne Hampson case, none of this had been disclosed or explained to the author. Since the standing North American press run for book club and retail distribution of a Harlequin title was about 750,000 units, the difference between a full royalty and a one-quarter royalty times one hundred titles was considerable.

I pushed Harlequin for an audit. They quickly realized that a purchase of one hundred copyrights from one author was much more protective of their business than risking audits from many authors over this royalty practice. Harlequin finally agreed to meet with us substantively on price, but only in London, to protect themselves, they hoped, from jurisdiction in the United States. Janklow and I flew over to find that the Harlequin representatives had "misunderstood" our earlier conversations. The meeting was over in no time, as were the flights back on the Concorde. When we later achieved a seven-figure sale back to Harlequin of past published copyrights, Anne Hampson was happy. By purchasing the backlist, Harlequin avoided the accounting issue and the risk that other authors would focus on these practices.

While our work for Barbara Taylor Bradford was a big step forward, our major opportunity came when Janklow was able to pitch Sidney Sheldon for representation. Sheldon had long been a world-wide success. He had used a business adviser rather than a literary agent for his multibook contract, which at the time had been a top deal when signed several years earlier. Sheldon was published in hardcover by Morrow (then owned by Hearst) and in paperback by Warner. Morrow and Warner had a joint venture specifically for publishing Sheldon. Crown and Bantam had a similar arrangement for publishing Krantz. This pattern of joint hard- and softcover publication, either by related publishing subsidiaries or outside joint ventures, had become typical for major fiction authors. The hardcover and paperback houses could spread the risk of advances and share the rewards. They could also better coordinate promotion and timing of the appearance of the editions.

A "hard/soft deal" simply meant that the author committed both hardcover and paperback rights simultaneously and in exchange received a "full paperback royalty," instead of a share of the royalty. If you sold in the millions of copies like Sheldon, this was a big difference. Sheldon was in the middle of his multititle book contract. With a multiple book contract, publishers try to protect themselves against failure of any one title with a royalty "basket," so that the total advance is charged against all of the books, not divided by title and charged book by book. This is referred to as "joint accounting."

We offered to review, at our expense, all of Sheldon's contracts and royalty statements and make certain recommendations about what improvements might be discussed with his publishers. I did the research and wrote the detailed report that found that Sheldon was a victim of his own success. His titles were out-earning the contemplated advances by a significant margin, but cash was being withheld against the arithmetically impossible event that the future books would fail to earn out their now relatively low levels. We asked for a chance to renegotiate his cash flow. In effect, we were starting our representation with the backlist and happy to wait as long as it took to work on the frontlist.

There are good reasons for publishers to keep major authors happy. The negotiations I conducted were prolonged. Morrow and Warner finally agreed to accelerate Sheldon's cash flow (they were simply giving him money he had already earned in sales). When payments were slow to arrive at the appointed date, I called to inquire. The royalty manager said that we would have to wait since they processed royalties in alphabetical order and his name started with S. I said that as a courtesy I would not repeat that remark to Sheldon if they hand-delivered the seven-figure check we were owed. The check arrived.

We had to wait several years to be able to negotiate Sheldon's new contract. When there was one option book left on Sheldon's contract, we offered Morrow and Warner a new three-book deal with a sum total North American advance of $10 million—then a top of industry deal. During the contractual process, which I handled, we essentially used Sheldon's success as leverage to rework every provision of the standard publisher's contract we had learned to be concerned about. Warner's lawyer was Robert Stein. At a recent publishing seminar at the Association of the Bar of New York City, Stein and I were both speakers in my case about RosettaBooks. He told me that night that the process of negotiating the Sheldon contracts with me was a critical learning point for him. Completing that contract was a very proud moment for me. It also symbolically completed my education with standard book deals. There would be more to sell, but not that much more to learn about negotiating and contracting for them. Sheldon sent each of the three of us a case of Dom Perignon champagne. It was typical of the man—a classy and live-for-now gesture.

We had dealt directly for Sheldon overseas, more than tripling his German and British deals and bringing him better deals throughout the world. Sheldon came to reflect the international power of a top American commercial fiction writer. Like music, films, and television, the top commercial fiction writer could now start to realize between twenty-five and forty percent of his or her copyright values overseas. Bestseller lists throughout the world, particularly in fiction, are sprinkled with American titles (rarely reciprocated here for works in translation).

Sheldon also helped us break into the Japanese market in an impressive way. Typically, a deal for an American title into Japanese was no more than a $10,000 advance (Sidney Sheldon included). The Japanese market buys more books per capita than any in the world, but the Japanese taste for American clothes, music, and film rarely extends to books. There are significant problems with the translations. Western names do not translate well. Many of the translations read in a stilted way in Japanese. The more skilled translators have their own following and get cover billing on the books. To keep the characters straight, fiction often requires a character list in the front of the book. Nonfiction, particularly by international personalities perceived as having some impact on Japan's future, sells better. Fiction is harder to sell.

Soon after 1980, I received a fax in broken English from a Japanese publisher who wished to commission Sheldon to create a short ten-part story suitable for teaching Japanese students English. The fee offered was $100,000. Intrigued, Sheldon delivered the story. The publisher sold primarily door to door rather than through bookstores, since its primary business was English as a second language. After the success of the initial project, the Japanese publisher asked, even though they were not a bookstore publisher, if they could try to publish Sheldon's new novel. Their offer was $500,000, proving that sometimes there is a better way.

Sheldon also helped us address the role of book clubs in launching major titles. The William Safire experience made us aware of book club practices. Clubs paid an effective royalty rate of about 7 percent of retail which was split fifty-fifty with the publisher. So, for a twenty dollar book, the book club royalty to the author was about seventy cents per unit versus a hardcover royalty of three dollars (15 percent of retail). It always seemed to us that the major author was helping out the club, rather than the other way around. Publishers tended to value the club advertising, even if most of that advertising offered to give the book away for free for club membership.

Both the Book-of-the-Month Club (owned by Time Warner) and the Literary Guild (owned by Doubleday) use a "negative option" strategy—to refuse the main selection of the month you have to send back a card affirmatively rejecting it. The clubs could gain sales by saving very popular titles as alternates, since their members would order those titles from affirmative interest. As a result, Sheldon's titles had typically been alternate selections of the Literary Guild. We took the rather simple position that if the title was not a main selection, we would hold it back from the clubs entirely. Main selection it was, and is. Today, of course, the clubs are jointly managed by Bertelsmann and face significant competition from electronic sellers.

Sheldon knew how to use his power, albeit in gracious ways. He would offer hotels the chance to be "plugged" in his book in exchange for a suite while in town. When his manuscripts were completed, he would invite his editors as guests to his California home, have them read under his watchful eye, and ask their reaction. Of course, they would say they loved it. For the three-book contract, the publishers needed to know what the books would be about. Sheldon didn't know. We pointed out that the publishers would be successful with any book called "Sidney Sheldon's New Novel." A compromise was a one-sentence description before Sheldon started work on a book.

Judith Krantz, Barbara Taylor Bradford, Sidney Sheldon all had in common one thing: the growing power of "brand" in publishing. The publishers were selling the name of the author, not nearly as much the title or content of the particular book. The authors themselves became personalities, more like a movie star or a political candidate than the traditional vision of the secluded author at work on manuscripts. Of course, the traditional vision was not entirely accurate. Hemingway's public personality and writing were closely entangled. Jacqueline Susann and her husband, Irving Mansfield, had long before shown what promotion could mean to branding a writer of commercial fiction. The difference for us as agents was that we were beginning to line up several major authors under one representation roof at a time when the distribution of hardcover books was beginning to explode.

We and our authors benefited significantly from several multihour miniseries seen by millions to drive attention and sales for the book *Scruples* and other titles by Judith Krantz, most Sidney Sheldon novels, and many Barbara Taylor Bradford titles. Soon, the historian David McCullough recognized the value of the media potential. Most of our book-into-film packaging was handled by Creative Artists. The author would either work through us, or as is frequently the case, directly through a Hollywood relationship. Both Steve Krantz and Bob Bradford became extremely active in this area. Our titles became one of the major "feeders" of long-form miniseries.

Meanwhile, not all contracts came out on a linear path. Some manuscripts end up never existing at all. Marvin Kalb and Ted Koppel partnered on a novel with a character who bears some resemblance to Henry Kissinger. They decided not to write the manuscript for a second work of fiction. Of course, they returned the advance. The highest ranking Soviet defector Arkady Shevchenko came up short for us and Simon & Schuster. In between meetings at safe houses and the like, the CIA promised not to interfere and to help with any needed clearances. We sold the concept to Dick Snyder at Simon & Schuster, who promptly took the outline to the Frankfurt Book Fair and sold hundreds of thousands of dollars in rights sales (despite one German publisher who was very interested until he learned that this was not the Russian poet Yevgeny Yevtushenko). The problem was that Arkady Shevchenko didn't write the manuscript and withdrew from the contract. Even worse, he surfaced later with a new agent, Random House as his publisher, and a debut appearance on *60 Minutes*.

You can't publish a book without a manuscript. This seems like a rather simple idea, but publishers contract all the time to buy unstarted or unfinished manuscripts, and for one reason or another the manuscripts never come in. Our record was better than average. Our most interesting no manuscript story involved David McCullough, the wonderful writer of history. Janklow had a chance to work with McCullough just as *Path Between the Seas,* his book on the building of the Panama Canal, became a surprise best-seller. McCullough had delivered the manuscript several years late, but right into the Carter negotiations to extend the Panama Canal treaties. It was definitely the peak for public interest about the canal in a long time, and the book reaped the benefit. McCullough's work had been first-rate for a long time—wonderful books on the Johnstown Flood, the building of the Brooklyn Bridge, and a biography of the young Teddy Roosevelt and his family. But wonderful books and commercial sales are not the same thing. McCullough now had a chance for both.

We handled some PBS hosting deals for McCullough, appearances which raised his profile through television. The big question was his next book. Janklow was very close to Arnold Glimcher, the owner of Pace Gallery. Glimcher represented Jean Dubuffet, whose work Janklow collected. Glimcher landed the representation of the Picasso estate and Janklow saw an opportunity for a fabulous Picasso biography. Glimcher promised to cooperate. McCullough was very excited, since art history had been his passion at school and Picasso was perhaps his favorite artist. Janklow quickly negotiated from Simon & Schuster, McCullough's publisher, a $500,000 advance, a multiple of his prior advances because his recent book had done well and the subject matter was highly visible and international.

As a general rule, the commercial prospects for writers of nonfiction are heavily influenced by choice of subject matter and sometimes by fickle public response to subject matter. For example, John McPhee always writes well, but his book on Alaska became a bestseller while others did not. Scott Berg wrote an excellent biography of Louis B. Mayer, a titan of Hollywood, and achieved modest sales, but was invited as a result to write a biography of Lindbergh, which became a best-seller. For McCullough, subject matter was key to commercial prospects.

About six months after the Picasso contracts were signed, McCullough stunned us with a call that he didn't plan to write the book. He explained that every book he had written involved characters he admired, that he had to live with these characters for several years to create his manuscripts. McCullough's research to date had revealed Picasso to be a despicable human being and there was no way he was going forward with the biography. Out of this development, Janklow turned to Arianna Stassinopoulos Huffington, an author who was excited to take on the project. Her biography of Maria Callas had done well commercially. Simon & Schuster was happy with the substitution. Peter Matson, her agent, saw no reason to share a commission with us, so Dick Snyder of Simon & Schuster compensated Janklow for the initiating the project. The Huffington book on Picasso went on to be an international best-seller.

Meanwhile, we had to find a substitute project for McCullough. He decided that his next project would be a book on the 1950s. Since this didn't sound as internationally commercial as the book on Picasso, we had to negotiate a reduced advance with Simon & Schuster. Years later, working from this initial idea, McCullough wrote *Truman,* which became a major best-seller. All of which illustrates that real writers should stick to what they believe and that publishers should have the patience to wait for the effort.

Nearly twenty years later, I was invited to advise Michael Steinhardt, the legendary Wall Street hedge-fund investor. He had been working on a book for almost three years. The only problem was that all there was to show for the effort was a question-and-answer transcript. My assignment quickly became finding the framework of the book within the assembled materials and recruiting an appropriate collaborator (which took several tries). My mantra to Steinhardt and his advisers has been "no manuscript, no book." *No Bull,* the real book and a good book, appeared in fall 2001.

By 1982, my interests were beginning to range beyond agency work. The chance to change a long-standing antiauthor publishing practice attracted me to help create and represent an insurance product. With Linda Goodman's *Love Signs*, I had seen firsthand the unfairness of the standard author's warranty and indemnity to the publisher. A family mentioned in *Love Signs* sued, upset with their playful portrayal in a few lines of the book. The case went nowhere, but Linda Goodman's account was ultimately charged several hundred thousand dollars in legal expenses. The standard author's agreement includes a warranty and indemnification agreement. In substance it says that the author is responsible for issues like plagiarism, libel, and the like, and that if any third party sues the publisher for such issues, the author will indemnify the publisher for the publisher's expenses. Of course, the typical author has limited financial resources (unlike Linda Goodman's royalty stream) and the typical publisher is the "deep pocket" of any litigation. Publishers usually insured themselves, but not their authors, against these risks. In the early 1980s, such insurance coverage was rarely available to individual authors, or, if so, it was very expensive. Publishers would basically not negotiate on altering these indemnification provisions.

I recruited a friend, active in the insurance business who saw an opportunity to correct this inequity. We thought it would be simple to construct a policy that covered both publishers and authors on a zero-deductible full cost of defense basis. The insurer favored this approach since a few test cases actively litigated would hopefully discourage contingency lawyers from seeing publishers as an easy target. The cost of the policy could be charged back to authors per title at costs likely to be less than five hundred dollars. There was a recent precedent for charging back certain freight expenses (a practice known as "freight pass through") so this seemed like a realistic approach. The publisher could spread the costs to authors in such a way that their own cost of insurance coverage was significantly reduced or even free. Authors would finally have the threat of crippling litigation off their backs. The policy was written and reinsured by Lloyd's of London.

I began a series of presentations to general counsels of publishers to explain what we had in mind. There was a lot of curiosity. The immediate response was to talk with their carrier. When those carriers focused, they realized what I had argued was true. The party at economic risk was the publisher. The economic commitment of the author was not valuable. Employer's Reinsurance proceeded to offer a rider to their basic policy covering all of a publisher's authors for a modest additional premium. The deductible was substantial, but the publisher could now cover its authors if they wished. Viking Press figured out that the first publisher to act would get favorable attention in the author community. Indeed, their *New York Times* story was very flattering. Many publishers followed, each with slight variations of how authors were to contribute to the deductible. Today, almost all major publishers offer warranty and indemnification insurance to authors as an extension of the publisher's own coverage.

My effort had the intended substantive result. Before I started, no author had insurance and afterward most authors did. As the instigator, I found the experience exciting, but I had also intended to make money. That didn't happen, since we never sold one publisher on our policy and pricing approach. Neither did we get any credit, private or public, for changing industry practice. I learned that deals can work, but not necessarily for you. I redoubled my efforts to turn ideas and initiatives into concrete and recognized results.

With no particular plan 1983 became my breakaway year. The agency was focused on big-name authors of commercial fiction. We had added Jackie Collins as a client. I helped place a series of her previously published British titles in paperback as originals to complement a plan for new hardcover titles. It would be the year when agency revenues exceeded legal billings, although not by much. The futures in the commissions already on the books were several times our current annual revenue, and growing. I realized that the significant event for an agent was the signing of a major retainer agreement. The odds were then very good indeed that project contracts would follow. By that standard, our future looked bright indeed.

Early in 1983, Janklow was approached by Marvin Josephson, who controlled ICM, a successful publicly held entertainment agency. He convinced Janklow that ICM was keenly interested in acquiring our agency, that the price would be very generous, and that Janklow would be an even bigger star after the acquisition. With Janklow's backing, we went through the full process of exploring a sale. Josephson saw all of our key contracts, which I believe was one of his purposes. Of course, if we were acquired, ICM could try to package our clients' books through the ICM television and film divisions, helping ICM and hurt Creative Artists. ICM's book division charged the same ten percent commission as its motion picture and television division. We charged fifteen percent, which was increasingly typical for independent agents. By acquiring us, ICM might be able to raise their existing literary commission structure.

As the ICM discussions were getting underway, Janklow received a call from Louis Blau, a prominent West Coast entertainment attorney. He was calling on behalf of his client Danielle Steel, who was looking for new representation. Three agents were being invited to compete for her business. The only ground rule was that the commission rate would be ten percent and the agents would have to fly to California to present their case in person. There was an amusing fact: Janklow had never heard of Danielle Steel.

In 1983, Danielle Steel was an author with almost twenty mass market and trade paperback titles to her credit. Her sales, frontlist and backlist, were nearly forty percent of the revenues of her publisher Dell Publishing, one of the leading paperback houses. Steel was prolific. New titles typically appeared at least twice a year. I had heard of Danielle Steel and promptly did as much research as I could from public sources. I also read several of her books to try and understand her popularity. The books all involved a woman of independence who suffers a loss in love, lives alone wondering if love will ever return, and finally finds true love again.

Danielle Steel was married to a very wealthy man. She was motivated to become a hardcover "star" author. Her publisher had discouraged this idea and urged her to keep writing paperback bestsellers. Her agent made the fatal mistake of agreeing with the publisher. Now her lawyer was recruiting a new agent. We were competing against Lynn Nesbit of ICM and Scott Meredith's agents. Our last competition had not been successful. In 1980, Lloyd Cutler, a prominent Washington lawyer, had invited us to compete for Jimmy Carter's memoir. The most pressing question was, "How much do you think it's worth?" Our answer: not much more than $500,000. Cutler heard what he or Carter wanted from other agents that the book would go for $1 million. Lynn Nesbit got the assignment. Bantam got the book for $500,000.

For Danielle Steel, the issues were straightforward. Any publisher in town would happily publish her in hardcover and risk a lot of money for the privilege. All one needed to do was ask. The question was how to look thoughtful and responsible for the presentation to Steel. We would never have "shopped around" the possibility of publishing Danielle Steel without her permission. Yet that was what Scott Meredith did, arriving with a $3 million per title offer from Simon & Schuster. After I bought his agency ten years later, I developed a better insight into his practices.

I focused on Danielle Steel's backlist as part of our strategy. I guessed that Danielle Steel did not have top of the market royalty rates for her older titles, since the books had been delivered over a ten-year span, most before she became a star author. Improving those rates, of course, meant year-in, year-out money for Steel without doing any work. This backlist strategy was well received. We were retained. Dell and its sister company, Delacorte, realized that they needed to hold onto Danielle Steel at practically any price. The first contract mandated hardcover publication for several new titles and raised the backlist royalty rates. The hardcover launch was extremely successful, and Danielle Steel was soon a name that few would have trouble recognizing.

Meanwhile, I realized that I had no interest in joining ICM. I had spent the first ten years of my career happily far away from institutions. Also, I realized that this was a rare moment of choice to decide my future. I had a stock certificate to show for my minority interest in the agency. ICM was offering largely cash, so I thought I could exit cleanly with the buyer's money. The ICM offer also placed a value on my minority interest in the agency. Janklow, Traum, and I had no buy-sell agreement, so the outside offer was crucial for defining my values. The key thought process was whether I would be happy in a role that felt like Janklow's permanent protégé. I was thirty-five years old. My first son was six months old. I had just purchased a country house in Litchfield County, Connecticut, the first real estate I had ever owned. If I was ever to make a move as my own person, I felt that this was the time, whatever the risks.

Janklow was surprised when I announced that I would not work for ICM after the deal closed, and that I would leave the agency and withdraw as a law partner whatever happened to the ICM sale. I turned down an increase in my percentage participation in the agency. I tried to focus on positive issues, but Janklow obviously didn't like the idea that I had, in effect, resigned as his protégé. The deal ultimately fell apart over tax issues on our end (how to get a capital gain) and on ICM's (how to amortize the large amount of good will in the high priced deal). With the collapse of the sale, I would have to negotiate my own exiting arrangements.

It took months of on-again, off-again discussions to nail down an agreement for the sale of my interest in the partnership and the agency. It was a bit like a divorce in which neither side moves out of the house. Each day I came to the office, tension was everywhere. After several months, the letterheads and the sign on the door dropped my name. I was determined whatever the temptations to avoid litigation or a permanently fractured relationship. A public fight could only hurt me, no matter how much damage I could inflict along the way. I was tempted to take my chances with the clients, but didn't. Finally, with Bill Josephson's help and counsel, we reached agreement on a ten-year royalty payout for the projects under contract and a tight two-year noncompete for the fiction clients. There was a stilted going-away party.

During these months, I had time to think through some of what I would do on my own. Almost everything that happened later was not anticipated. My father counseled during the negotiations that some people are well suited to be in business for themselves, and some can survive only when working for other people. I have always felt that he was trying to tell me that I was the second. While my ten-year royalty would include a participation in the first Danielle Steel commissions, one legacy would be the creative use of backlists. The backlist is the profit backbone of any mature publisher. For an author, the opportunity to get more exposure and revenue from work already done is hard to resist. An agent can make himself popular with writers by suggesting ways to do better with existing work. I made it my business to think of the backlist opportunities first. Much of what I later achieved related in one way or another to the backlist.

While the negotiations over dividing commissions from the agency had been arduous, issues surrounding withdrawal from a law partnership are usually pretty straightforward. Thanks to an unusual turn in my final year, the law firm discussions took on a business implication as well. Our client Jean d'Hennery controlled companies which had owned garden-style apartment complexes, mostly in Texas. When these apartments were sold, the companies had taken back so-called "wraparound mortgages." The buyer built up his purchase price for purposes of depreciation but did not have to address meeting the payments for many years into the future. Also, payments on the wraparound mortgages were largely interest for many years and therefore tax deductible. The terms of the wraparound mortgage were probably more favorable than a bank would have offered for the same mortgage balance. This compounded the tax advantages for the buyer. The phrase "wraparound" probably emerged because the first mortgagee did not have to give permission unless their instrument specifically said so. For older mortgages at favorable interest rates with high payments of amortization, this was particularly advantageous to buyers.

The seller hoped that the properties would stay sound long into the future and that ultimately the so-called "balloon" payments would be made after the underlying mortgage had been paid off. There was a catch, which was that for many years the wraparound mortgage created so-called "phantom income." Taxable interest income came in, but nondeductible first mortgage amortization payments went out. Since the cash spread was very small, the reportable tax would be larger than the cash available and the condition would get worse year by year until the underlying first mortgage was paid off. For example, as a first mortgage neared maturity, annual payments might be $100,000, of which $80,000 was amortization, while the wraparound mortgage might have paid $105,000, of which $100,000 was interest. This example creates $80,000 of taxable income ($100,000 of interest income minus the $20,000 of tax deduction). In a 50 percent bracket, that means $40,000 of taxes to be paid and only $5,000 available from the wraparound to pay them with. The $35,000 gap is referred to as "phantom income," or taxable income for which there is no cash available to pay the tax.

We needed to find a way to help d'Hennery's companies deal with this phantom income or the companies would be forced to surrender their mortgages and lose the valuable down-the-road backend. The solution I found was a partnership with a nonprofit institution, which could absorb (most of) the phantom income during the "bad" years, since it paid no tax in exchange for a (modest) share of the cash in the down the road "good" years. We interested Columbia University, where Janklow had gone to law school. I negotiated and structured the deal. Jerry Traum handled his client d'Hennery. Janklow made the introduction to Columbia. When the deal closed, d'Hennery promised us a fair percentage of the down-the-road cash for which we and Columbia would have to wait nearly ten years. Columbia had no risk in the partnership and a solid chance of hundreds of thousands of dollars of cash flows. D'Hennery's companies stood to save hundreds of thousands of dollars in taxes, hang on the healthy wraparound mortgages, and realize their healthy cash flow years later.

When I withdrew from the law firm, this was the only significant item where I was promised my share of down-the-road payments. I also negotiated the right to re-create this deal structure with Columbia with other holders of wraparound mortgages in exchange for cutting Janklow and Traum in for a modest percentage of what I would make. I was very proud of what I had structured. I thought at the time that other holders of wraparound mortgages must have the same problems and that perhaps I had discovered a license to print money. I was wrong.

When I set up on my own, I did a considerable amount of work with Columbia University and Fried, Frank to make generic the deal formula which had worked for Jean d'Hennery's situation. My goal was to create a business in wraparound mortgage joint ventures with Columbia as the charitable partner. Had I succeeded on any reasonable scale, the fees and backend participations would have been enormous. I had the cooperation of a preeminent not-for-profit partner. I had a joint venture formula that had already been successfully implemented and improved for new participants. I was missing new business partners who had similar tax oriented needs with their wraparound mortgages.

Through a variety of contacts, I went on the road to try and interest holders of wraparound mortgages in this transaction. What I quickly learned was that the typical holder of a wraparound mortgage was not too worried about the Internal Revenue Service. Some had depreciation losses to offset the phantom income. Others just figured that IRS would never figure out the complicated structures. None were too inclined to share their backend returns for the advantage I had to offer. I was never able to convince a single holder of a wraparound mortgage to work with Columbia. What should have been obvious was the wisdom of testing the marketplace before putting too much energy into the product or service. Marketing also requires a major time commitment. Presenting author insurance to a handful of publishers I already knew was one thing. Seeking out holders of wraparound mortgages for an unfamiliar transaction was quite another.

Years later I learned that Columbia Law School had named a chair for Mort Janklow. D'Hennery had died in the interim. Traum and Janklow had separated in a bitterly litigated fight. Lynn Nesbit sat in my old office, and the name on the door was Janklow & Nesbit. Over the years, Columbia's share of the wraparound money became several hundred thousand dollars. My share of the revenue was paid out for at least as long a period as the agency commissions. The first deal worked. The extensions didn't. Always read the market first.

SIX

··

The Agent for the Situation

My assistant at Janklow, Mary Jo Valko, was even a happier risk taker than I was. She immediately agreed to join me. We located at 10 East 53rd Street in a sublet from the new and growing law firm of Howard, Darby & Levin. It wouldn't be long until their needs propelled us to our own office at 250 West 57th Street. In 1983, an office, assistant, phones, computer, letterheads, and the like was quickly an $85,000 to $100,000 annual commitment. If I wanted to duplicate my compensation at the time, I would need to generate about $225,000 in annual fees. In hindsight, I hit those numbers my first few years while building valuable future commissions, but week to week and month to month it was never too clear where the fees were going to come from. I did business under my own name as a professional corporation.

I was retained by my first private law client even before my departure negotiations with Janklow and Traum were completed. At a $500 per person cocktail fundraiser for Bill Bradley's 1984 reelection effort at the home of Nina Rosenwald, a prominent Democrat I had met during the Moynihan campaign, I bumped into Bill Lilley. When he saw that Bill Bradley and I were friends and was reminded of my relationship with Moynihan, he asked to see me about a professional assignment. Lilley had left Yale for government and journalism, and then left journalism for the private sector, starting as the government affairs chief for American Express in Washington. He had been head-hunted to perform the same function for CBS and had recently been promoted and transferred to New York to take over the entire corporate communications function, reporting directly to Tom Wyman, the CEO.

Lilley's major undertaking (joined by the other networks) was to try and achieve the repeal of the so-called financial interest syndication rules. These rules, put in place during the Nixon years by the Federal Communications Commission (FCC) (and said by some to be a punishment of the networks), forbade the networks to own an interest in the valuable syndication rights—local station rebroadcasts—to the shows they aired. Naturally, the studios and other providers of the network shows liked these rules. They were profiting from the regulation, then splitting up as much as $1 billion dollars annually. In the book business, this would be as though publishers were forbidden by law to participate in the revenues of paperback editions of hardcover books.

Lilley believed in the power of reason over pure politics. He had commissioned a series of studies which documented that the rules no longer had their intended purposes, that with cable breaking down the dominance of the networks, the networks were not a threat to the suppliers of programming, and that the program suppliers were themselves large businesses fully capable of protecting themselves in negotiation. In other words, the fight was just over money and lots of it. The network argument had already been endorsed by several federal agencies. The FCC was nearing its final review. Now, however, CBS needed all of the political support it could get. I had no more set out to be a lobbyist than a literary agent. CBS was an attractive client. Their point of view was persuasive and Bill Lilley as a point person was fine by me. I signed on for hourly billings consistent with a lawyer's rate. Then I set out to earn my keep.

It seemed to me that relaxation of the rules would lead to greater television production in New York, where the networks were headquartered. If that were the case (it has turned out years later to be true), then the New York congressional delegation should be interested, as well as the New York City and State Film and Television offices. I invited Chuck Schumer, by then a four-term Congressman, to join Bill Lilley and me on the executive floor at CBS. Bill Paley, CBS's founder, had left behind quite an impressive floor. Only about half a dozen executives worked on the floor, each with his own conference room/dining room. The art collection was effectively interchangeable with the Museum of Modern Art.

Schumer talked strategy for a while and offered to circulate a letter for the New York City delegation to sign. When it came back with a fair number of signatures, my credibility increased, particularly with George Vradenburg, the CBS general counsel (later the general counsel for AOL). The city and state film offices were also responsive. The state office asked for commentary from the studios. The studios' point person, Ed Bleier of Warner Brothers, was a close friend of Janklow's. I heard from Janklow that I was ruining Bleier's evenings as he was busy working on responses to my activities.

I urged a public strategy. The networks had virtually no positive press on their side of the issue. Ken Auletta was by then a well read columnist for the *Daily News*. I briefed Ken in full, gave him the opportunity to hear the studio side, and read with pleasure the first full column that came down on the network side of the issue. At the corporate level, CBS had not courted key elected officials, and most of its relationships were with Democrats. The Republicans had gained control of the Senate and an outreach strategy was vital. Lilley and I were on the same wavelength. New York Senator Al d'Amato was happy to accept an invitation and try to do battle for CBS, his constituent. New York City Mayor Ed Koch was a long overdue visitor.

Lilley called throughout Capitol Hill on senior Republican Senators, who listened sympathetically.

The big question was still the FCC and its upcoming vote. Moynihan's intervention could make a difference. I took Moynihan to dinner, tried to drink significantly less than he did to stay sober for my question, and asked him as a personal favor to me to help CBS. I brought Lilley to meet Moynihan in his office and Moynihan wrote Mark Fowler, Chairman of the FCC, urging him to get on with a vote, which was for practical purposes a pro network position. When studio executives and lobbyists tried to challenge Moynihan for his action, he explained that it had been "personal." My stock at CBS went higher still.

As the battle within the FCC and in Senate subcommittees escalated, CBS strategy teams grew larger. At one retreat, all of the involved lobbyists heard a presentation on the future competitive inroads of cable. The theory was that the threat of cable reduced the threat of the networks. When the presentation was over, I took Lilley aside and said that the CBS business problem was really not the rules, it was cable. In Washington, the lobby team met for expensive catered dinners (better and better as the showdown loomed) sometimes with the sounds of the theme song from the movie *Rocky* piped in. At the end, it was politics that decided the issue. Lew Wasserman, long time head of MCA and close friend of Ronald Reagan, called in a chit and Reagan shut the network position down cold. The FCC was simply ordered to reverse its position to date. That account was confirmed to me years later by Reed Hundt as he finished his stint as Chairman of the FCC. I felt that I had done a good job, but I had not developed a positive feeling about the role of a professional lobbyist.

My assignment for CBS was visible in New York and Washington. My personal links to Moynihan were also known. A reasonable inference was that I was politically comfortable with people loosely labeled "neoconservative." The group in charge of CBS by contrast looked more liberal. At the same time I was working on Lilley's assignment, CBS's most visible litigation was the libel lawsuit launched by General William Westmoreland against a CBS documentary on the

Vietnam War. The litigation was funded by conservative interests and Westmoreland's lead counsel was Richard Burt. CBS was defended by its lead outside counsel Cravath, Swaine & Moore and their star litigator, David Boies (most recently the FTC's counsel in the Microsoft case and Al Gore's in Florida for the outcome of the 2000 presidential election).

Burt called offering to talk to me and only to me as a possible intermediary for settling the Westmoreland litigation. This led to a series of meetings at CBS with Boies, Vradenburg, their public relations adviser, John Scanlon, and others. Burt and Westmoreland did not want money. They did not even want an explicit apology. But they did want a statement which would permit both sides to claim victory. CBS had already spent a small fortune on the litigation. I had a number of meetings with Burt, who had sole authority to think through options. We exchanged a number of draft statements. I thought we were very close to a workable formula, then CBS backed away. I think their concern was that somehow they would look weak in this fight. The case was settled as the trial began with essentially the same language I had worked out earlier. Since they were in court and Westmoreland appeared to be the one "suing for peace," CBS could claim a more publicly credible victory.

Bill Lilley was happy enough with my new career as a lobbyist to refer me in 1984 to a friend, Richard Blewitt, who handled corporate communications for Velsicol. Velsicol made a termiticide called chlordane, which, after DDT, had been one of Rachel Carson's favorite targets in her book *Silent Spring*. Chlordane had been banned years before for use with crop dusting animal feed. In 1984, chlordane was the leading termiticide in New York State.

One FDA study concluded that mice injected with large amounts of chlordane may or may not have developed cancer. The scientific data of these tests was open to debate. Whatever the science, exterminators didn't help the image of the product by their behavior. A proper application involved drilling holes around the house and injecting a mixture of chlordane under pressure. If you were careless, the chlordane was injected into the basement.

What triggered Velsicol's problem was guilt by association, when a New Yorker's house had been irreparably damaged by exterminators applying a termiticide (not chlordane, but it didn't matter). The irate homeowner called in television cameras and a wrecking ball, and demolished his home for the six o'clock news. Velsicol was hard at work with the state Environmental Protection Agency. With one telephone call, I was able to find out that their real problem was with David Axelrod, the State Commissioner of Health, who was given broad authority by Governor Mario Cuomo to implement his own judgment in any case in which health interests might be involved. Axelrod was not friendly to a business point of view. In simple terms, Axelrod aimed to give Velsicol a fair trial and then hang them, which is what he did.

Of course, New Yorkers still needed to kill termites. Dupont manufactured another termiticide called Durasban. They had an insignificant market share, but they did have a favorable EPA report. Why? Because the product was so toxic that the mice died before they had a chance to develop cancer. The product itself was toxic enough that the human applicators needed to have their blood tested at intervals. No one ever said that regulation led to fair results, but participating in this process certainly made me more cynical. Velsicol was to be my last lobbying assignment for money, and happily so.

My name in the lobbying arena must still have carried some weight because, years later, a representative of casino interests in Las Vegas called and said he understood I could be very effective with Senator Moynihan on legislative issues. Moynihan by then was chairman of the Finance Committee, and there was easily a six-figure retainer just for saying "yes." No one except me would ever have known what I could, in fact, deliver or not. That was enough. I thanked the caller, said I was unlikely to be effective (true), and I ended my career as lobbyist.

Of course, one of my prime purposes in setting up on my own was to seek out creative ways to explore deal-making in the publishing business, particularly business that related to backlists or had the potential to create projects with long-term values. Publishing is often as much about channels of distribution as it is about content. While still with Janklow in 1982, an unlikely phone call led to representing Easton Press, today the leading leather-bound publisher and my largest client. When the call came, Easton Press was a small competitor of the Franklin Library, and the call was not about leather-bound books.

The call was from Robert Lewin, the highly energetic owner of Mill Pond Press, a leading publisher of nature lithographs. Lewin called because Mill Pond controlled exclusive licensing rights to certain images created by his friend and leading artist, Roger Tory Peterson, and both Mill Pond and Peterson needed representation in a licensing deal with American Express. Peterson, of course, was already a publishing legend for his *Field Guide to the Birds* series with Houghton Mifflin. The 1980 revised edition of his *Guide to Eastern Birds* had sold more than 1 million copies. Peterson was unrepresented in his publishing dealings. Through Bob Lewin, I hoped to do business with Peterson.

Lewin was a fierce protector of his artists' interests and an excellent businessman. He also was the kind of client who knew how to back up an agent. I knew little about the art business, but I knew enough about rights for money and contracts. Peterson had created a series of paintings of songbirds which Mill Pond had published as signed limited edition prints. These images lent themselves to use as decals on porcelain products. Both American Express and the Danbury Mint were interested in a set of porcelain plates. American Express at the time was experimenting with its own marketing of collectibles. They had up to that point provided the marketing for other people's products.

American Express bid a more attractive royalty and won the right to reproduce the Peterson images on plates. We had some interesting approvals problems. Getting the right color red in the cardinal meant using color with traces of lead in it. Our Food and Drug Administration would not let these plates into the American market from France, where they were fired with a trace amount of lead. Even though these plates were for collectors, the FDA referenced a case of one consumer who left food on a plate for weeks in a refrigerator and got ill when he ate it. The cardinal, after quite a lot of wrangling with the decal maker, came out a bit orange.

American Express sold $2.5 million or so of the plates, which was a solid performance but well below their projections. They learned from this and other efforts at the time that it was strategically better for them to make marketing partnerships than to go into the business themselves. This opened the door for us to license the songbird images to the others. Ultimately, we would execute many Roger Tory Peterson licenses in a broad range of product categories.

For Mill Pond and Peterson these deals meant royalties in the $100,000 range per deal and a commission of $15,000 or so, not much compared to the $1 million commission from Sidney Sheldon. Since I was handling the client and the economics were modest, I was able to take the client with me when I left Janklow. I saw in Bob Lewin and the Peterson world a path to an entirely different form of selling—direct marketing—which I felt had powerful implications for literary properties. The Franklin Mint had already made the leather-bound Franklin Library a success. I knew that Bill Safire had been asked to sign more than 30,000 books as part of their first edition program. The Danbury Mint's sister company, Easton Press, was Franklin Library's main competitor. Also, Bob Lewin represented many artists whose work was suitable for decal porcelain licensing. I couldn't tell exactly how or when, but I felt that with and through Lewin and Peterson, I was bound to find them a valuable client.

Our next deal for Mill Pond and Roger Tory Peterson licensed songbird imagery to the Danbury Mint for a set of porcelain vases. They sold more than 20,000 vases at one hundred dollars each. MBI is the privately held parent of the Danbury Mint, the Postal Commemorative Society, and the Easton Press. Formed in 1969 with a collector's medallion to commemorate the moon walk, MBI was the brainchild of Theodore Stanley, a true direct marketing genius. In the early 1980s, the strongest license for the company was Norman Rockwell. The book division published the "100 Greatest Books" in leather-bound editions. Ted Stanley built his company by careful testing each offer and aggressively marketing those that worked.

The Franklin Mint was and is the prime competitor of MBI. Franklin approached Peterson in 1983 to create a five hundred dollar porcelain figurine, a product category which the Danbury Mint didn't sell. I spent several months negotiating a license for the figurine. When the contract was set, Franklin invited Roger Tory Peterson, his wife, Virginia, and me to Philadelphia to meet the key executives and inspect their finest bird figurines as examples of the quality that could be achieved. I rented a limousine for the occasion. We arrived for lunch. The table was set with half a dozen bird figurines. Peterson, in his typically low-key way, proceeded to pick apart each image ("wrong color; wrong foliage; wrong branch; wrong body proportion"—just wrong). As Peterson talked, the executives started to seethe and I already knew that the deal was dead.

Back in the limo, Peterson was able to enjoy the ride on the New Jersey Turnpike for its combination of wildflowers and birds. I thought it was a rare gift to be able to enjoy the New Jersey Turnpike. Peterson felt that I might be angry with him, since I was out a few months' work and a limousine ride. That wasn't a crazy assumption, but even in adversity I look for opportunity, particularly with serious people, rather than push them away. Instead of venting, I asked what was on his upcoming schedule. He mentioned casually that the Smithsonian was giving him a show on the upcoming occasion of the fiftieth anniversary of the publication of the *Field Guide to the Birds of the Eastern United States,* a book the New York Public Library would later name one of the one hundred most important books of the century.

I saw immediately that the Smithsonian show might help recruit Easton to try a leather-bound collection of the then thirty-five field guide title line. I asked Peterson if he would autograph books and provide a frontispiece of original art and help gain marketing cooperation from the National Audubon Society and the National Wildlife Federation. He agreed. I convinced Easton, Houghton Mifflin, Audubon, and NWF to participate. My cobbled together commission (from Peterson, Easton, and Houghton Mifflin) was probably half of a fair commission, but I was the "agent for the situation" and just starting out in my own business. Also, I now had a direct relationship with Roger Tory Peterson and his wife, Virginia. The Peterson program was a great hit. Seventeen years later it is running strong, with total sales more than 1.2 million copies at $30-plus. The annual marketing budget has consistently been higher than what Houghton Mifflin can budget for the trade editions. Easton was now in the category book business, ready to set its sights on Franklin Library. And I was in the process of securing my most important client, Easton Press itself. Houghton Mifflin cut me out of my commission when the deal was renewed seven years later. By then, Easton was my largest client.

I would eventually represent Peterson personally, then his estate after his death in 1995 at age 87, his wife's estate after her death in 2001, then Mill Pond Press, which published Peterson lithographs, and Easton Press, which published Peterson in leather-bound editions. I would later sit on the Board of Trustees and briefly serve as President of the not-for-profit Roger Tory Peterson Institute for Natural History. There were many different roles, requiring a balance of responsibilities. At Harvard Law School, someone told the story of an exchange at the Senate confirmation proceedings of the nominee Louis Brandeis to the Supreme Court. The proceedings were very contentious. Brandeis was charged with unethical behavior in a particular bankruptcy proceeding in which he appeared to be professionally involved with more than one party. When a senator asked, "Who was your client?" Brandeis retorted, "I was the lawyer for the situation." With appropriate disclosure, I have never been afraid to be the "agent for the situation."

Chuck Schumer referred my first serious book clients in my new business. Sheila Lukins and Julee Rosso had offered Workman Publishing *The Silver Palate Cookbook* in 1979 to promote their small New York City takeout food establishment and growing national specialty-food line. The book exploded. Workman's promotional line for Lukins and Rosso was that "they changed the way America eats." In 1983, Lukins and Rosso were thinking about another book. They also had some concerns about their contract, which had been handled without an agent. Sheila's husband, Richard, was Chuck Schumer's campaign treasurer. We had all discussed financing Chuck's first race for Congress in the Lukins' Dakota living room. When Chuck heard that Sheila and Julee were considering hiring an agent, he said, "Arthur has just gone out on his own; call him."

Lukins and Rosso walked into my new offices just barely after my arrival. At the time, *The Silver Palate Cookbook* had sold more than 250,000 copies and was selling at the rate of more than 100,000 copies per year. The women wanted to know if this was good. I said this was very good, second only perhaps to books like *The Joy of Cooking*. We worked on what they wanted to achieve with their new book and what needed to be adjusted in their current contract. We all agreed that Workman had done a great marketing job and, of course, was the only one who could improve the existing contract and leverage the backlist title. Again, I was applying a backlist strategy similar to what we had used to interest Danielle Steel. It worked.

In 1983, Peter Workman ran a team of perhaps thirty people. They worked informally and irreverently. It was like a summer camp dedicated to promoting books. I had met Workman some time before when Lisa Birnbach, one of the authors of *The Official Preppy Handbook*, had issues to discuss. I found that Workman made sense, was highly creative, and, most important, owned his own company so that I could deal with the sole decision maker. We had no problems working out arrangements for what became *The Silver Palate Goodtimes Cookbook*. In its first year, that title sold as many copies as the first book did in its first three years. Lukins and Rosso, meanwhile, had ever-increasing corporate difficulties with the company they had founded, and ultimately they and their investors sold the company and the Silver Palate trademark to an entrepreneur. I represented the women during the sale. Ultimately, the books' value was comparable to the business. The women and Workman held the continuing right to market the two books.

The question was what would happen to future publishing efforts. Lukins and Rosso wanted to create a basic cookbook, almost the length of the two books combined, which would summarize their new sensibilities for lighter, easier to prepare food. The book was to be published in 1989 as *The New Basics* in a season with the simultaneous release of Julia Child's *Way to Cook* from Knopf and a revised edition of the *Better Homes and Garden Cookbook* from Hearst. We were all nervous, Workman especially so since the 350,000 first printing of a twenty dollar trade paperback was the largest printer's purchase order he had ever signed. All three books triumphed. Newspapers throughout the country wrote long glowing pieces about the three titles. The transition away from the Silver Palate store and books was a success.

The "brand" Silver Palate was, and is, a publishing phenomenon. Nearly 90 percent of its sales have been achieved since my first meeting with Lukins and Rosso. But *The New Basics* created a brand all its own and now sells more copies annually than *The Siver Palate Cookbook,* even though it is much more expensive. Each of the three books is among the top ten best-selling cookbooks ever published.

Soon after I started working with Lukins and Rosso, Walter Anderson, the longtime editor of *Parade* magazine, proposed they write a monthly column for *Parade.* Anderson is a fierce friend, a former Marine with a strong sense of dedication and mission. He is personally committed to literacy causes. Unusual for any company in publishing, *Parade* has retained its senior editorial team for decades, thanks to Anderson. His editorial vision had helped to build the magazine from a modest advertising-supported Sunday supplement into one of the strongest profit centers in the Newhouse empire. Anderson worked with writers such as Norman Mailer and Carl Sagan. I had met Anderson during my Janklow days when some of our clients became contributors.

I liked Walter Anderson and I liked the idea of big circulation. The weekly printing was then more than 30 million copies and still growing. A cover story landed in most American homes at a predictable date. Some writers and agents found *Parade* a lowbrow option and gave Anderson a hard time. My view was that the articles might be short and simply edited, but the authors could present themselves in a favorable light. Anderson was assembling "star" editor contributors, and his writers convinced the major personalities of the day to be interviewed for cover stories. Also, *Parade* paid double or triple the going magazine rates for stories from established writers, and was generous with expenses.

Julia Child had been the food editor of *Parade* and planned to resign. Anderson had his choice of personalities in the cooking world to replace Julia Child. He had selected Lukins and Rosso to take the column in new directions. We immediately recognized the importance of the opportunity. I quickly negotiated a multiyear once a month column deal that included a few appearances a year with *Parade* advertisers. The exposure to food advertisers would prove to be useful over the years. The monthly column would accumulate an archive of recipes that could be put to other uses. Part of the deal was that Lukins and Rosso got to work with top flight food photographers and stylists. The first contract was the beginning of one of the financially largest continuing arrangements in the magazine business. The contract also helped to transform Lukins and Rosso from book authors into personalities.

The chance to appear with *Parade*'s advertisers helped to stimulate corporate tie-in deals for Lukins and Rosso. The dessert portions of the *Silver Palate Cookbook*s became a pamphlet you could earn by purchasing Yuban Coffee. The *Silver Palate Cookbook*s were offered on both Post Grape Nuts cereal and Quaker's Natural Cereal (10 million boxes each) in promotions. Lukins and Rosso's diabetic-safe recipes were packed on Becton Dickinson syringes. Barbecue recipes were in wrapped Lea & Perrins Worcestershire sauce bottles. None of these were endorsement deals (no product preference was stated). All involved large circulation. All moved books and paid money. And one led to another.

Easton's success with the Peterson Field Guide series demonstrated that its opportunity was bigger than the "100 Greatest Books." In 1985, Ted Stanley, the owner of the parent company MBI, decided that Easton Press should test a series of leather-bound presidential biographies highlighted by autographed copies of the memoirs of Presidents Carter, Ford, and Nixon. David Ward, the publisher of Easton, challenged me with an assignment. Fail and earn nothing, succeed in securing the rights to the autographed memoirs and earn substantial fees based on Easton's ultimate marketing success. This was my chance to land Easton as a client.

Warner had published Nixon's memoir, *RN*. My first (and key) decision was that each president would be offered a "most favored nations" deal. The president who got the best deal would determine what the other two received. My gamble was that no one would ask for more when offered a responsible deal on this most favored nations basis. We needed a commitment from each to autograph up to 15,000 copies of his book. Nixon was the first president to answer that he would cooperate. Ford was the next to say yes. Carter said yes, provided as the most recent president his book could be scheduled first in the series.

When Ford and Carter had agreed to their contracts, I got word that Nixon had changed his mind and wouldn't sign. I tried to talk Easton into a two presidents program. That didn't work. I then went to work on getting Nixon to change his mind again. I called Len Garment, a Washington lawyer close to Nixon, for advice. Garment hypothesized that Nixon hated any activity that presented him parallel to Carter and Ford; Nixon must have assumed that Carter and Ford would have declined to participate. Garment suggested that I talk to Ray Price, a former Nixon speechwriter who was still close to him.

Price had arranged to place a protégé, John Taylor, in Nixon's office as chief of staff. Price introduced me to Taylor and we began a series of conversations to see what might entice Nixon to participate. I made progress with Taylor, but not with Nixon. Then our luck changed. Someone at the Danbury Mint, the sister company to Easton Press, noticed that Nixon had purchased dolls for his granddaughters. I arranged for Ted Stanley to send a "president to president" package to Nixon with a four-color mock-up of the direct mail selling piece with the strong pitch that "your name and face belong here." Nixon agreed to sign, with the proviso that his book be scheduled last. He realized that the later the title was published, the fewer the sheets he would have to sign (due to attrition in the program) and the longer he would have to sign them, which was fine by him. Nixon donated his fees to the Nixon Library.

As a reward for signing the three living former presidents, I was invited to secure the rights to publish biographies of each of the other presidents. Working on the forty volumes helped me develop a relationship with the Easton team. The subscriber base for Library of the Presidents exceeded Easton's highest expectations. The program ultimately had revenues more than $25 million and is successfully offered today. There were moments of tension with Ford, Nixon, and Carter. Carter at first balked, then calmed down, when the 15,000 sheets arrived in his office for autographing (15,000 sheets is quite a pile). Ford at one point refused to approve a new set of marketing materials, as his staff pointed out that Nixon and Carter each had one photograph more in the spreads than did Ford. We added a Ford photo. Nixon waited until the last moment to deliver his sheets. With the program more than two years old, two dozen–plus presidential biographies shipped and more than 10,000 subscribers, Easton began to get very nervous about whether they would get a flood of refund requests if the Nixon book was not forthcoming. Easton wanted to explore life insurance on Nixon, which would have required both his permission and a physical. I nursed Easton and John Taylor in Nixon's office until Nixon delivered in full.

Years later, Easton tried and tried to interest Ronald Reagan in signing a leather-bound edition of his memoir. We managed to get sample books to Reagan's desk in the White House. Reagan personally called David Ward to thank him for the books, but the call didn't get us the autographing commitment. As part of the major Simon & Schuster effort for the publication of Reagan's memoir, they organized a very expensive campaign to sell several different editions of deluxe and signed copies of the book. The most expensive included a signed leather-bound book and a set of Reagan recorded speeches in a wood presentation box with the presidential seal. Simon & Schuster's own direct marketing efforts for the deluxe editions were not successful. They had more than 1,000 of these boxes, manufactured at a cost of one hundred dollars each, in their warehouse. Internally, the boxes were referred to as "the coffins." I arranged for Easton to buy the boxes, the signed books, and the audios, and sell them successfully for $250 to their subscribers, so that at least some of the Library of the Presidents subscribers could enjoy Reagan, too.

The Library of the Presidents was the first of many so-called "continuity" offers I helped arrange for Easton: Masterpieces of Science Fiction, the Library of American History, Great Lives, Books That Changed the World and Military History, Signed Science Fiction, and Signed First Editons, among others. Easton also acquired other sets of books to offer each month to their subscribers. The deal that confirmed Easton's ascendancy over the Franklin Library was the right to publish a complete nineteen-volume set of the works of Ernest Hemingway. It took me more than a year to negotiate the arrangement. At the end, Scribner chose Easton's offer over a slightly higher offer from Franklin. Easton's marketing efforts and results proved that decision correct several times over.

Of course, you learn in the publishing business and in the direct response business that not all offers work even if the deal is elegant. In 1988, for the twenty-fifth anniversary of the Kennedy assassination, Easton wanted to offer a video set based on the historic footage. Tim Russert had by then left Moynihan and was number two to Larry Grossman in news at NBC in New York. I approached Russert and pitched the project. While NBC had never explored a third party marketing offer, they were willing to explore this one since the footage was being cut for a documentary in any event. John Chancellor recorded introductions and closings ("tops and tails"). NBC insisted on controlling the advertising. David Ward offered the Solomonic solution of two ads, one created by Easton, the other by NBC. Easton would run whichever ad tested better. The Easton ad outperformed the NBC ad about three to one. There was just one hitch. The Easton ad itself cost more than the orders it produced. While we had a wonderful offer with exclusivity from NBC, there were many other offers in the marketplace with comparable footage. The offer failed.

Several years later, Easton had a giant success with a public domain video offer of NASA documentaries prepared after each space flight. Since copies of the masters were hard to locate and Easton improved the masters with lab work and donated copies back to NASA, as a practical matter they had an exclusive. When I finally saw a competitive ad in Smithsonian, the Easton team explained why they weren't concerned. As a large direct response advertiser, they got favorable rates from Smithsonian. The competitor, a small advertiser, did not. Easton knew the offer would be uneconomic for the other company. They were right. I learned that exclusivity has many different meanings beyond a phrase in a contract.

SEVEN

....

Here, Take the Pope

By bringing to the Vatican Library in 1984 an opportunity to license a collectibles program with the Danbury Mint and the Easton Press, I became their licensing agent for about five years. My contact and partner for the project was Alfred Bloch. Bloch came from a prominent Polish Jewish family. His Ph.D. in political science was from the University of Warsaw. While there he met Karol Woytila (later Pope John Paul II), and translated one of Woytila's early books, *Toward a Philosophy of Praxis,* from Polish into English. Bloch had made many friends in the Roman Catholic Church during his university days in Warsaw and also found himself studying with some of the future leaders of the Solidarity movement. He met as well a range of officials of the Polish government.

Bloch believed that large quantities of Judaica confiscated by the Nazis throughout Eastern Europe were hidden in Poland. Bloch's dream was to rescue the hidden Judaica and in the process make some money for himself. By the early 1980s, to accomplish anything in Poland you needed the cooperation of the government (and President Wojciech Jaruzelski), Solidarity (and its leader Lech Walesa), and the Roman Catholic Church. Bloch was able to negotiate a formal three-party agreement to search for, catalog, and ultimately return the confiscated Jewish-owned art hidden in Poland. To close the contract protocols, he interested Sargent Shriver in his cause. Shriver visited Poland with Bloch and helped persuade the parties to sign. My introduction to Bloch was through Bill Josephson, protégé and partner of Shriver.

I didn't see how I could help Bloch immediately with his ultimate objective, but I was very interested to see if Bloch thought it was feasible to use his relationships to interest the Vatican in commercial ventures. We decided to explore some possibilities. First, I asked Easton Press and the Danbury Mint what would most interest them if rights could be secured in the Vatican. The Danbury Mint, which had a major business selling Christmas ornament collections, wanted "The First Vatican Ornament Collection." I convinced the Danbury Mint, which normally was conservative with advance guarantees and certainly so before testing a program, to commit a $100,000 advance on signing of a suitable contract. Easton Press was excited about a Bible they could market as "The Pope's Personal Bible."

The Bible project turned out to be wild goose chase. Bloch knew that Jaruzelski, the President of Poland, had presented the Pope with a single facsimile copy of the Bible of Gneizno on the occasion of the Pope's recent pilgrimage. The Bible of Gneizno is a fabulously illustrated thirteenth-century book that symbolizes the joining together of Eastern and Western European wings of Catholicism. Since the facsimile Bible had been prepared, the Polish publisher had production materials to make the book. Bloch and I set out for Warsaw and Rome. It was soon apparent that "The Pope's Personal Bible" was not a doable project. The publisher in Poland surprised us by announcing that they were unwilling to license the production materials. Nonetheless, if we could borrow the Pope's presentation copy, film could be created from the book itself. We later discovered that the Pope was so offended that the Polish government had touched this holy book that he left the only presentation copy behind in a hotel room Poland. More than ten years later, Turner Publishing Company made an arrangement with the Vatican Library to create an extraordinary Bible, illustrated with a range of images collected from manuscripts in the collection. I successfully negotiated for Easton a leather-bound edition of that Bible, which sold for five hundred dollars. So that project showed up ten years late in another form, as did my commission.

We were much more successful landing the rights for the ornament collection. In Rome, we met with Church officials and with Jerzy Kluger, a Jewish childhood friend of the Pope's who claimed that he could be useful to us. Everyone we met recommended that we try to work with the Vatican Library as a licensing partner. The Vatican Library could enter licensing agreements without involved processes. We learned that a former prefect of the Library had gone to the Pope and asked for funds. The Pope had answered, "We have no money, but here is a pen, find your own funds." So, within limits, the Library could enter its own agreements. The Library had a wide range of holdings that could be transformed into Christmas ornaments. In 1984, the prefect of the Vatican Library was Archbishop (later Cardinal) Alfons Stickler. Stickler was Austrian, an ecclesiastical lawyer fluent in seven languages and committed with purpose and humor to bringing the Library into the twentieth century.

Kluger arranged my first meeting with Stickler to discuss the Danbury Mint offer. I had with me a proposed licensing agreement, which I proceeded to review line by line with Stickler. Kluger was aghast, since he thought that somehow I was challenging a man of the cloth. In fact, I was probably more in need of a lawyer than Stickler, who jovially walked through the contract. One clause authorized the use of the Pope's image in advertising the ornaments offer. Stickler pointed out that the Library was in no position to make such a commitment. The Danbury Mint, of course, envisioned advertising with a central photographic image of the Pope. Stickler pointed out that we could buy images of the Pope and no one would be in a position to complain.

The next step was to see Arturo Mari, who was the Pope's personal photographer. His offices were part of the official Vatican newspaper, *Osservatore Romano,* which was published daily in five languages. On Wednesdays after the Pope's public audiences, those in the front rows rushed to Mari's office to buy images that had captured the Pope at the balcony and an identifiable image of themselves in the crowd. Mari traveled with the Pope on pilgrimages and had broad access to the Pope in Rome. The photographic archive was overwhelming. Any image purchased from Mari was so stamped on the reverse. That stamp constituted permission to publish, so we had a range of Papal images. One problem solved.

The Danbury Mint wanted the first ornament collection to be an assemblage of crosses. The Vatican Library held an extraordinary assemblage of crosses from many centuries. None of the senior people working on the project for the Danbury Mint were Catholic and, of course, Bloch and I were Jewish. No one noticed that Christmas trees don't tend to hang decorations of a cross. The simple explanation is that Christmas celebrates Christ's birth, hence the manger, the Wise Men, and so forth. The cross signifying the crucifixion, then, was the least suitable image for Christmas. As a careful direct response marketer, the Danbury Mint tests new offers with limited placements of advertising or direct mail packages. The results guide them to where, or if, further marketing investments should follow. Though elegantly produced, the First Vatican Ornament Collection, a series of crosses, didn't test particularly well. The initial test revealed as well that an informal image of a smiling Pope performed much better than the formal stern image of the Pope. Also, the Catholic media (Church newspapers) were more successful advertising venues than the general media.

For another marketing test, the Danbury Mint created an splendid looking frame with a two-dimensional art image appropriate for Christmas (manger scenes, the Wise Men, Mary, and so on). This program tested far better and justified a marketing effort in the specifically Catholic media that could reach about 6 million people.

However, the Danbury Mint thought of themselves as a broad-based marketing company and backed away from the program and their investment when the general market testing numbers were not persuasive. In the midst of these dealings, I arranged through Jerzy Kluger for Bob Capria of the Danbury Mint and his wife to get an audience with the Pope (I thought it was far more important for the buyers than for me to see the Pope). The Danbury Mint had marketed without any rights a papal figurine. Of course, unofficial Vatican memorabilia was available all over the streets of Rome and marketed in a variety of ways in the United States. During his audience, Capria presented the Pope with the figurine. Without missing a beat, the Pope turned to his secretary and said with a smile, "Here, take the Pope."

Stickler, Bloch, Kluger, and I celebrated the signing of the Danbury Mint license on Yom Kippur at Passetto's, a fine Rome restaurant in 1984. While my cooperation on the project was always ecumenical, I have always felt something was amiss with the decision to have Catholic-Jewish business success celebrated on a High Holiday of the Jews. The celebration was the beginning of a change in my relationship with the Library. Soon Stickler called for a private audience and discussed whether I could bring projects to the Library as I had brought the Danbury Mint. I said to do so, I would need to be retained as the Library's representative. Stickler said that was not a problem. I suggested a 35 percent commission, not atypical for licensing agents. Stickler proposed instead a 50 percent joint venture arrangement, citing arrangements he had with other publishing licenses and the recognition that I would have considerable expenses. Stickler also probably realized, more than I did, how difficult this assignment was likely to be. Stickler went to his typewriter, typed out the retainer on Vatican Library letterhead, signed it, and handed it to me.

We had several interests in the Library. First, its holdings were more than diverse enough for a wide range of potential offers. Second, the Library name included the word "Vatican" and its seal was one of the official Vatican seals. Third, the ornate display hall adjoining the Vatican Museum offered a range of opportunities for promotional photography or visits. Fourth, and most important, Stickler could sign any license agreements on his own authority.

The Vatican Library had recently celebrated its 500th birthday. The Library holds more than 100,000 handwritten manuscripts, many of them lavishly illustrated. An extraordinary collection of maps and the repository of gifts to the Popes over the centuries are housed there. Its holdings are deep in Judaica and Islamic material. The limited access to the Library in prior years and the rumors about holdings which were not publicly confirmed (like artifacts from the destruction of the Second Temple in Jerusalem) gave the place an air of mystery. Stickler once hosted me on a private preview of a Library show. The objects were in their cases, often without explanatory cards. Stickler explained some of the constraints he worked under. When he first became prefect in the early 1960s, the philosophy of public display was that the same handful of books were in cases open to the same page at all times. Stickler suggested rotating the books on display. This was rejected as unnecessary. He next pointed out that by leaving the manuscripts open to the same page, the light would yellow the pages. Could he at least turn the pages? Permission to turn the pages was the beginning of opening the Vatican Library to broader public view.

Stickler picked up a vellum page as we toured and explained that it was an original page of Virgil. One of these pages had been part of the Vatican exhibition at the 1964 world's fair. The page was so valuable and insurance so expensive, that Stickler had hand-carried the page to New York. Stickler told me that a Sotheby's representative had been to visit the Library the year before. Stickler asked what a page of Virgil would be worth in the auction market. The response was a reserve price of at least $2 million. Stickler said that he had more than forty pages of Virgil in the back, but policies forbade deaccessioning anything so his fundraising would need another focus.

I was able to close some licenses promptly. Reproducta is the leading Catholic paper products company in the United States. Many of its clients use greeting cards as part of their fundraising appeals. The cards are sent free with an appeal for money. Reproducta owns outright an extensive archive of art suitable for its business purposes, but the Jewish Schulhof family, who owns the privately held company, was willing to entertain a Vatican Library image license for royalty payments. The Schulhofs and their expert Paul Murphy were knowledgeable about the Library's holdings and planned to collect transparencies from a particular series of manuscripts on their first trip to Rome. As the priceless items were being wheeled to their table, a wheel fell off the cart which sent the manuscripts flying. The Schulhofs were horrified. The attendant said, "These books have survived for five hundred years. They will make another five hundred."

Reproducta produced a variety of well designed cards, mass cards, bookmarks, and the like, using images from the Vatican Library collections. They presented the seal of the Library to convey the official endorsement of the program and background information assembled by Paul Murphy. In its first few years, the license produced nearly $50,000 in royalties, which was, at least, a beginning.

Collector plates were a natural use of the Library's images. The Bradford Exchange in the early 1980s was the largest marketer of collectibles porcelain plates. Bradford was based in Chicago but had marketing subsidiaries in many countries outside the United States. I interested Bradford in a series of plates on the life of Jesus selected from a single spectacular fifteenth century manuscript. That program was marketed successfully in Europe. My goal was to get the program marketed in the United States, the larger market. Bradford tested the program with the marketing headline "Illuminations from the Vatican Library." The test didn't go well. Test respondents didn't seem to understand the word "illumination." When I suggested that Bradford call the program "Bible Art from the Vatican Library," they held rigidly to their first view and the program never appeared in the United States. The European efforts did produce another $50,000 over time.

We organized television commercial tests for a Vatican cross with a direct response company. Early sales never justified a full marketing investment, but this was one way to explore the potential for jewelry. We came close to organizing a travel program that would have included a private visit to the Vatican Library to view manuscripts related to family trees. A delegation of publishing (Harry N. Abrams, Inc., a leading visual publisher), academic (a Jewish theological seminary scholar), and auction representatives (Sotheby's) was organized to study what commercial applications might emerge from the Library. Nothing concrete came of the exchange except good will. We explored a documentary option, but couldn't find a way to make it commercially viable.

My hopes for a major licensing campaign never materialized. When Leonard Boyle succeeded Cardinal Stickler as prefect of the Library our efforts started to wind down. Boyle later generated several million dollars from an investing group in transactions, an act which led (many scholars felt unfairly) to his dismissal and litigation for the Library. A recent attempt to license the Library as a brand has met with only modest success. When someone offers you a higher fee than you ask for, the chances are that they know something about your odds of success that you don't. Ten years later, the Franklin Library and the Vatican Museum developed a very successful collectibles program and the Danbury Mint was back calling me to see if I could revive the Vatican project. For an institution with a 2,000-year history and horizon, we hadn't missed by too many years, but it was enough.

I had landed the Vatican Library as a client by much the same technique by which I landed Easton Press: bringing in a project as a buyer and ultimately becoming the buyer's agent. When I turned toward studying the Pope's writings and ways in which he might be more broadly published, I truly found myself as an "agent for the situation," and in this case situation that became messy. All of the Pope's writings had been published in *Osservatore Romano,* the official Vatican newspaper. The newspaper contents were technically in the public domain, but in reality the Vatican controlled republication rights by their ability to denounce anyone who proceeded in an objectionable manner. In effect, you could reprint, but then suffer the consequences. The Pope's writings were voluminous and ranged from esoteric theological subjects to general interest. Bloch was very familiar with the Pope's writings over the years. I tried to conceptualize some projects we could get done editorially with commercial support initially in the United States. In each case, we needed official support in Rome from one or more Cardinals for the particular project.

One straightforward opportunity was to explore a commemorative photographic book, timed to coincide with the Pope's pilgrimage to the United States in 1987. I made the publishing deal with Jonathan Wells, a book packager formerly from *Rolling Stone,* who arranged distribution for the book with Crown. The photography was supplied by Arturo Mari. Bloch edited appropriate writings by the Pope. Cardinal Joseph Bernardin of Chicago provided an introduction and the "imprimatur" that supported the reprinting of the Pope's words. Some of the proceeds went to Arturo Mari and some to the Vatican Library. The book sold a modest 35,000 copies, but it was the first example of a book by the Pope published by the trade in the United States.

A second opportunity was to collect writings of the Pope in one or more trade books. If Bloch edited these books from the most accessible of the Pope's writings, their potential audience could have been large. In 1985, CBS owned two Catholic publishing houses, one based in London and the other in Minnesota. The editors of the two publications had never met. Thanks to my relationship with Bill Lilley and my lobbying work for CBS, the CBS team flew representatives of both publishers to New York to meet Bloch and me to discuss how they might jointly publish the Pope. Bloch and I presented as best we could the material that was available and how we thought it might be crafted into book form. We were prepared for a range of questions about our level of authorization. Instead, we were floored to hear, "I wouldn't publish this Pope under any circumstances." These liberal Catholic editors had spoken against publishing this conservative Catholic Pope.

The most commercial opportunity we could execute to publish the Pope's existing work came about in a curious way. The oceanographic explorer Robert Ballard was organizing the expedition which would find the *Titanic,* but he was short of funding and his creative

Canadian lawyer Michael Levine was looking for ways to finance the project. Levine called to ask if I would solicit interest in the United States from newspaper syndicates. The offer was exclusive pictures of the *Titanic* from the ocean floor, paying nothing if Ballard didn't find it and a large amount if he did. All the media players I contacted said, in effect, call us when the *Titanic* is found. Rick Newcombe, who ran News America Syndicate, then owned by Rupert Murdoch, said, "Well, what you would have are pictures of bodies coming out of water. The closest analogy is the body of Natalie Wood coming out of the water. The Syndicate grossed only $35,000 for those pictures, so this is not worth a special deal."

That statement should have been a warning, but I went on and told Newcombe about other activities including the Pope's writings. He immediately flipped over the notion of a newspaper column by the Pope. Finally, we had a buyer for the Pope's words. Bloch edited about twenty columns emphasizing the Pope's secular writings. News America set a few columns in type so that we could show them around Rome. We were guided by our increasing circle of cardinals and archbishops on how to handle the project. The Vatican Library would split the proceeds with us. We worked out a contract with News America. One critical element in the deal was the public characterization of the arrangement. It had to be clear that Murdoch was reprinting the Pope's writings and not publishing original work. The other critical element was international. Many European cities had both Catholic-owned and secular newspapers. We were advised by our clergy friends to make certain that the secular press did not outbid the Catholic press for the column, even if it meant fewer financial proceeds.

From the presentation kit and column title *Observations* by Pope John Paul II, News America lined up several hundred American newspaper subscribers and started the process of selling internationally. The public project got off to a bad start, when a Murdoch spokesman strayed from the approved press release and left the impression that the column would be original work ("We are delighted that the Pope will be going to his typewriter. . . ."). Bloch and I had to work hard explaining to our friends in Rome to tone down an initially negative comment from the Vatican press office. Also, Murdoch himself could not have been too happy. The public coverage of the negative comments from the Vatican occurred the week of the 200th birthday party of the *Times of London*, which he owned.

Next came the fatal error. News America got active bids for the column from both the Catholic paper and the secular paper in Madrid, Spain. Contrary to their instructions, New America accepted the bid of the secular paper. As the launch date approached, the Catholic paper stole the text of the first column from its competitors and ran it on the front page under the headline, "The Pope's words are free. The Pope's words are for all." The Pope's personal press spokesman, Navarro Valls, was originally a journalist at the Madrid Catholic paper. It took only moments for a brutal denunciation of Murdoch to be issued by the Vatican press office. This release came several days before Murdoch was to be sworn in as an American citizen. Once again, he was seriously upset.

Rick Newcombe had no intention of explaining to Murdoch that he and his team had screwed up twice, so they blamed the mess on me. Fred Bloch was referred to in London papers as the "Holy Ghost." A series of *New York Times* reports tried to be fair, but inevitably left me with a mess on my hands. With everything public, my options were limited. I received a letter from Murdoch's lawyers accusing me of fraud and breaking the contract. Meanwhile, after some talks with Murdoch's people, Archbishop John Foley, an American in the Vatican communications office, appeared on the *Today* show and announced that of course the columns would be published. The twenty columns Bloch had edited were published as prepared. To this day, I have no idea what happened to the fees paid by the subscribing newspapers. Foley's appointed editor shifted the column to religious and philosophical subjects, newspapers canceled, and the column slowly died.

Thanks to Rick Newcombe's handling of the project, the seat between Murdoch and the Vatican was not a comfortable one for me. My only option involved suing Murdoch, requiring witnesses from the clergy and a long, drawn out battle. By law, I had six years to decide, so I put Murdoch on notice and set the issue aside. Murdoch proceeded to sell News America to Hearst to combine with King Features. Several years later, I had a meeting with the editor-in-chief of King Features on other matters. I arrived to find a Hearst lawyer sitting in. He was there to find out if I planned to sue. A friend later asked why I hadn't asked for my money then. The answer, I think, is that we truly were acting for the Vatican Library, not simply for ourselves.

Rick Newcombe started his own syndicate with Ann Landers as his main client. As a postscript to publishing the Pope, Robert Ballard, of course, found the *Titanic*. The first pictures from the ocean floor were stolen from the open satellite feed and no one paid for the privilege to reproduce them worldwide. Michael Levine made a photographic book deal for Ballard that sold more than 750,000 copies worldwide at fifty dollars. So much for Newcombe's predictions about the value of pictures from underwater.

The home run publishing project with the Vatican, of course, was a book "by John Paul II." Fred Bloch and I presented a variety of ways such a project could be executed consistent with Vatican concerns and standards. I would like to think we got close to approvals, but I don't think I will ever truly know. Years later, Mondadori organized a project with a journalist interviewing the Pope which became the enormously successful book *Crossing the Threshold of Hope*. Mort Janklow represented the book in the United States without having to spend months on the Warsaw-Rome shuttle. Fifteen years later, Fred Bloch is still at work on his definitive presentation of the best of the Pope's writings. Somehow, I feel like I already gave this my best shot.

The Vatican deal which was to prove the most visible was neither licensing nor publishing. During my first trips to Rome with Bloch, he would present and explain my background to Polish-speaking members of the clergy. As our discussions proceeded, the Vatican became more interested in my relationship with CBS. At some point they questioned me about American television. They explained that they had been unable to find a dignified approach to American television. They felt perhaps I might bring them the senior level attention they needed to structure something appropriate. We again agreed that any rights payments would benefit the Vatican Library or other designated papal causes.

With this in mind, I went to Bill Lilley and told him that I could potentially deliver the Vatican to American television. He set up a meeting for me with Tom Wyman, the CEO of CBS. Wyman listened carefully to the presentation of my Vatican relationship. He offered the full cooperation of CBS as a company and said that they would do "whatever it takes" to be the network that makes the Vatican team happy in the United States.

Within a day or two, I had a distraught call from Lilley. Wyman had briefed Gene Jankowski, the legendary chief of the broadcast division of CBS. Jankowski had, in effect, dismissed my presentation and virtually characterized me as a fraud. His argument was that if the Vatican wanted to talk about television with CBS, the Pope would have called him or Dan Rather. He refused absolutely to cooperate or even speak with me. Wyman was apparently powerless to deal with his division chief, so the broadcast option was dead. I immediately asked to be relieved of any fiduciary obligation to deal with CBS. That was not a problem.

My next call was to Tim Russert, who was just under Larry Grossman, the chief of NBC News. Russert had joined NBC after working for Mario Cuomo, the Governor of New York. He had joined Cuomo after his years with Moynihan. I explained my circumstances and told Tim I needed two things from NBC, a list of Vatican projects of interest and a check for $100,000 which I would return if no projects were realized. After a brief meeting with Grossman and Russert, I had the list and the check. At the head of the list was an interview for Tom Brokaw with the Pope. That was not too likely to happen. When I was already in Rome, NBC added the idea of broadcasting the *Today* show from Rome for a week. The *Today* show was trailing the CBS Morning Show in the ratings, but had recently enjoyed some success taking the show out of the studio into the field.

My feeling was that Russert and Grossman didn't think I had much chance of success. I later learned they had not even briefed the NBC Rome bureau chief. Russert knew me well enough to know that if I failed, I would bring NBC's money back. Archbishop Foley in Rome promptly issued a letter to NBC inviting them to bring the *Today* show. My next call was from Russert in London saying that he was on his way to Rome to take over the project and was calling as a courtesy. In effect, my success prompted NBC to assume direct control of the process and cut me out of the middle. Bill Josephson was ultimately able to persuade the NBC lawyers that a good chunk of the $100,000 was mine for expenses, and Russert did confirm publicly my role in bringing the parties together. My goal of attaining rights fees for the Vatican Library wasn't realized, but the project was.

The week itself was grand television for NBC. The *Today* show ratings soared, badly hurting CBS and its entire morning schedule. Russert's career took off at NBC. We could claim a success. The broadcast created jealousies within the press corps that covered the Vatican. I had become friendly with E. J. Dionne, at the time the *New York Times* bureau chief in Rome. Our paths had crossed earlier in politics during Lindsay voter data days. One of the *Today* show interviews was with Cardinal Casseroli, the Secretary of State of the Vatican and, next to the Pope, the most powerful man at the Vatican. Journalists, try as they might, could rarely if ever get the Cardinal to speak to them. E. J. Dionne of the *New York Times* was at the broadcast in the hope of covering what Casseroli said and getting him for a few words on the side. No luck. The on-air interview began. Time was tight and NBC cut off the interview for a commercial, never to return to Casseroli. But the shot of the Coliseum in the background certainly looked good.

The *Today* show in Rome was a ratings triumph. NBC trumpeted its success in a wave of advertising. The ratings gains carried well beyond the week and reestablished the *Today* show as the leader in daytime television. Tim Russert's outdoor picture with the Pope was ubiquitous, and soon enough he was given a chance in Washington to try his hand on camera. The big loser was CBS and its morning show. While I didn't gain from the CBS loss, this story has helped my credibility in many other business rooms since.

There was one other more substantive encounter with Dionne. In 1985, the Vatican did not have diplomatic relations with the state of Israel. Jewish groups had been pressing for some time to get the Vatican to recognize Israel as a state. Since Pope John Paul II was clearly interested in Catholic-Jewish relations, there was hope that this would occur sooner rather than later. As part of our commercial efforts in Rome, Bloch and I were inevitably drawn into other concerns for those who were helping us. One of our patrons was Archbishop (later Cardinal) Andrzej Deskur, a Pole very close to the Pope who was responsible, among other things, for all Vatican communications. Deskur was interested in floating a trial balloon about the Vatican's interest in recognizing Israel and enlisted us to do his bidding.

The American ambassador to the Vatican was Bill Wilson, a friend of Ronald Reagan's, who was not highly regarded inside the Vatican because his appointment was not seen as a substantive gesture. No Vatican official had chosen to speak with Wilson since his arrival, an unmistakable message of what they thought of the quality of the appointment. Deskur wanted to have a private meeting with Wilson and asked us to be the intermediaries. The subject of the meeting was to be the recognition of Israel. Deskur realized that Wilson would file a long written report to the State Department. Deskur was confident that we could get a journalist to uncover that report to protect him and the Pope from having to talk on the record.

I knew Marvin Kalb, then covering State Department issues for NBC, from my Janklow days. So part of our dealings with NBC involved the offer of the news story. Kalb promptly got the gist of the memo and went with a story that the Vatican was contemplating recognizing Israel. E. J. Dionne tried confirming the story through me ("a source close to the discussions"). In the end, recognition was deferred for several years, but the balloon had been floated.

I was, of course, never the Pope's personal agent. But Bloch and I did have more commercial licensed activity with the Vatican to reach the United States than anyone during the mid-1980s. We also had our share of near misses. Basically, we were too early to persuade a very conservative institution to do what was necessary to transact. Plans we outlined in detail for a book by the Pope surfaced in another form to enormous success almost ten years later. Plans we proposed to use the archives of Vatican Radio for recordings are projects of Sony today. I certainly satisfied my sense of adventure on the project.

What I needed was a record of the story of my Vatican experience, so that I could claim the successes and protect my role in instances where it could be misconstrued. One of my close friends from Yale was Paul Goldberger, then the architecture critic of the *New York Times*. One of his friends from the *Times*, who had become a freelance journalist, was Charles Kaiser. Kaiser was interested in doing a piece which he placed in *Manhattan, Inc.*, a magazine that for a while competed with *New York* magazine. The good news was the article put my side of the story on the record. It also gave me a favorable hearing on the *Today* show project and a summary of the licensed deals we had completed. The title "The Pope's Agent" was a bit of hyperbole. I also thought I learned how not to get your photograph taken for an article. At the photo shoot, the camera was set up perhaps a foot off the floor, and the photographer asked me to hold a telephone. The resulting shot looked like I was talking to the sky and the caption read, "Pope's agent talks to God."

Fifteen years later, Inside.com profiled me as "the Accidental Crusader" after Random House sued RosettaBooks. Inside.com was merged with *Brill's Content* soon after the piece ran (my profiles don't seem to be lucky for magazines). When the photographer visited my apartment, I told the story of the *Manhattan, Inc.*, photo shoot and expressed relief that I was in the hands of a business photographer. They showed me test shots in various locations in the apartment. I posed. One of the pictures purposely cut off my head and showed me from the neck down. The editors ran the photo. Next time perhaps *I* will supply the photos.

The combination of my collectibles experience and the Vatican Library trials and errors brought me into the midst of the licensing world. I was not, in fact, a licensing agent. Those professionals work on trademarks in hundreds of category deals. But I was not strictly speaking a literary agent either. I would maintain a commitment to both licensing and agenting activities. The difference was that, in publishing, I could initiate a wide range of projects, while in licensing I had to pick my projects carefully.

EIGHT

....

Haldeman and Nixon

The reprise of my White House experience twenty years later was to change my business career. In 1989, Richard Nixon was seventy-six years old. He had resigned the presidency almost fifteen years earlier and rarely made public appearances, yet he was probably one of the single best known and most controversial personalities in the world. Nixon had entered public life before I was born. Almost everyone had a strong opinion about him. Enough of those who supported him bought his books, so, by 1989, he had authored seven *New York Times* best-sellers. Nixon had used many different publishers, starting with Doubleday for *Six Crises,* Warner for his presidential memoir *RN,* and, most recently, Simon & Schuster for *1999: Victory Without War.* His agent for *RN* and the books that followed was Swifty Lazar.

A rarely known fact was that Nixon had written more nonfiction

New York Times best-sellers than any author of his generation. Of course, the New York publishing community was largely liberal and had a relatively hard time dealing with his publishing success. And likewise, Nixon generally had contempt for the publishing community.

In continuing my work for Easton, I kept in touch with John Taylor, Richard Nixon's chief of staff. In 1988, Taylor called and asked, "Do you represent individuals?" Nixon, he said, was contemplating a change of agents away from Swifty Lazar. Nixon had recently moved his offices to New Jersey from downtown Manhattan. When Taylor offered a meeting, I was extremely interested. Nixon was a tenant in a building owned by Perillo, the largest Italian tour packager. A replica of Michelangelo's *David* was in front of the building. The entrance hall was decorated with impressionist style paintings by New Jersey artists. Nixon's office space was utilitarian.

Taylor warned me before the meeting began that I might have no more than fifteen minutes and that Nixon might not respond to my presentation, but I shouldn't take that as a negative sign. I had prepared for the meeting by studying each of Nixon's books. The books were very hard to locate. Nixon's library in Yorba Linda, California, the only presidential library privately funded and outside the National Archives presidential library network, was scheduled to open in 1990. By protocol, the opening of the library would attract all of the living presidents. The opening would be a major Nixon press event, which offered certain tie-in publishing opportunities. The library was projected to attract more than 300,000 annual visitors, presenting an opportunity to sell books in the gift shop.

Taylor had shared with me Nixon's next book plan, a memoir of his post-presidential years. A "personal" Nixon book was automatically more valuable for publishing rights than a foreign policy book. In fact, Nixon had even self-published *Leaders,* a very good foreign policy book, before Little, Brown bought the rights and republished it as a trade best-seller. I had decided before the meeting to start with the old books, much as I had earlier advised Janklow for both Sidney Sheldon and Danielle Steel. My experience with Easton had taught me the value of uniform editions. My thought was to create "Nixon Library" uniform trade paperback editions of the prior books with new introductions by Nixon and to require the publisher of the new memoir to reissue these books as well. Using the rights skills I had sharpened for Easton, I would clear the rights from the original publishers as a courtesy. Since these already had agents of record, I would have to look for my commission from the new title. In effect, this would create a valuable backlist project out of moribund books.

Before the meeting, I reminded Taylor that I had quit the White House staff over the Cambodia incursion. I didn't want to hide that public record issue and wondered if it would be a problem. Taylor smiled and said, "If we had to rule out doing business with everyone who ever had a disagreement with Richard Nixon, we could never do business with anyone." That was comforting, but I later saw examples when Nixon did not quickly turn the other cheek.

Meeting someone as famous as Richard Nixon was simply different than being presented to other accomplished or powerful people. The face and the voice forced you at all times to recognize that you were talking with a figure of history. I started my presentation emphasizing the historic importance of Nixon's earlier books and the opportunity the library opening presented for a tie-in. I must have gotten his attention, because the fifteen minutes stretched into two hours with plenty of commentary from Nixon. Nixon clearly was unhappy with publishers in general. He perceived the community as generally liberal and hostile to him and his work. He was also galled that Book of the Month Club had generally snubbed his books, even though they were best-sellers.

Nixon and Taylor had a ten minute discussion as though I wasn't present about the firing of Swifty Lazar. Nixon ran through the various ways Lazar could get the news. Taylor could call him. Nixon could write him. They could explain that the work on the Nixon Library set of rights would be too time-consuming for him. They could explain that a former White House staffer would be handling the work. The exchange reminded me of some of the better known

Nixon tapes as Nixon and staffers were exploring options. The exchange also reminded me that my time of dismissal, more likely as not, would arrive, too. The bottom line of the meeting was that Taylor would speak with Lazar and get back to me.

Simon & Schuster was extremely keen on keeping Nixon as an author. Michael Korda, who was very close to Swifty Lazar, had a $750,000 offer on the table for two books, the post-presidential memoir and a foreign policy book. Taylor told Lazar that Nixon planned to replace him and that part of the logic was a wish to explore a Nixon Library set of his prior books. Lazar called Korda to try and save his position. Korda called Taylor to say that he never got in the middle of agent and client issues, but that he wanted Nixon to know that Simon & Schuster would publish the library set. Taylor called me to report these developments. Of course, I was now at risk that my plan would simply be Swifty Lazar's to enjoy. My comment to Taylor was, "At least we know that my strategy will work." Taylor laughed. I guess Nixon laughed. Lazar was fired and I was retained.

I began the process in complete secrecy. I read the partial manuscript on site in New Jersey. We worked out a confidentiality agreement before any publisher would get to see the pages. I asked Nixon for a complete list of his complaints from prior publishing experience so that I could get him what he wanted up front in the negotiation process. Nixon wanted a contract clause that he was not obligated to promote the book. In fact, Nixon always had made several television appearances to promote his books, but he wanted no constraints on his options. Nixon also wanted to make life difficult for Book of the Month Club. He would offer the book as a main selection or not at all.

Michael Korda quickly revised Simon & Schuster's offer. The package would now be for one book, the post-presidential memoir, and the advance would be $1 million. The rights package for the Nixon Library set would carry its own advance and a promise of a 25,000 per title printing. In my opinion, I thought we had a serious offer. I also felt confident that other publishers were unlikely to compete at anywhere near these levels to publish Nixon.

When I reported the offer to Taylor, Nixon called me and said that he wanted to take the book to auction. I thought there was a chance we would end up with a smaller offer from Simon & Schuster, but Nixon had made up his mind. I arranged for a number of other publishers to review the package in confidence. Random House had originally been singled out by Nixon as a house so liberal that he would not consider being published by them. Len Garment, who had been so helpful to me in the beginning of my Easton assignment for Nixon, called and asked to get the book to Random House. Garment represented S. I. Newhouse, the owner of Random House, and wanted the political editor Peter Osnos to see the book. I told Garment to convince Nixon and then I would make the submission. I got the okay. Random House got the package and promptly said, "Why would we publish Richard Nixon?"

A day before the scheduled auction, Michael Korda submitted a three-page letter detailing all of the reasons he personally, and Simon & Schuster corporately, wanted to publish Richard Nixon. The letter also raised their one-book offer to $1.5 million. No other publisher bid at any level. I heard from Taylor that Nixon was walking around the office reading Korda's letter aloud. The letter, and the improved offer, certainly had the desired effect. Nixon stayed a Simon & Schuster author.

Part of the deal was a commitment by Nixon to record a four-hour "books on tape" version of the manuscript. This was during the early days of coordinating the release of audiotapes with books. The audiotape market was small. Ten thousand units was considered a good sale. Simon & Schuster convinced Nixon to let a television camera record him in the studio reading the text. The video footage was "Nixon on tape." When the book, *In the Arena,* was published, the release of the video footage became a publicity bonanza. The book did well on the best-seller list. The audiotape was a major best-seller. Foreign rights were quite strong. Nixon supported the book with several television interviews. The author's account didn't earn back nearly $1.5 million, but Simon & Schuster staked itself to a major work of nonfiction.

I did have to deal throughout the project with Nixon idiosyn-crasies. After I worked in complete secrecy at their instruction, Tay-lor called me in the midst of the auction preparations to ask whether placing an item in gossip columns would help. I thought it might make Simon & Schuster nervous if their bidding level was in plain view. No item was placed. After the contracts were signed, Korda called me to ask one favor. Dick Snyder, the publisher of Simon & Schuster, and Korda wanted to take Nixon to a celebra-tory lunch either at their office with Snyder's chef cooking or at the restaurant of Nixon's choice. Nixon refused to go, putting me in an awkward position. Nixon did subsequently invite Korda to a dinner at his home. Korda has written about that dinner in his own book *Another Life*. What he didn't write about was Nixon's signal that Korda, not Snyder, was his man and that Richard Nixon didn't "do lunch."

I did get one extraordinary opportunity to observe the public Nixon and to see how he used his position to his advantage. Nixon had a longstanding policy against taking fees for public speaking. In 1989, *Time* magazine set up its Man of the Year issue with American Express as the sole advertiser. *Time* promised American Express a small dinner with the Man of the Year, to which key advertisers could be invited. Then *Time* selected Gorbachev, who was not exactly avail-able in New York. *Time* decided that Nixon was a worthy substitute. Let's say that it was a coincidence that *In the Arena* ended up on the cover of *Time*. Also, when the guest list arrived in New Jersey, Nixon informed *Time* that its editor Carl Bernstein, one of the authors of *All the Presidents Men,* should be uninvited or Nixon would not be there. Bernstein wasn't there. I wrangled an invitation to the Morgan Li-brary for the event. Nixon spoke without notes for nearly an hour. It was an astonishing performance about the state of the world. He mes-merized an unfriendly audience. This public Nixon was worlds apart from the stiff, sweating presence television conveyed.

I managed to get Easton Press to publish a leather-bound set of all of Nixon's books. I tried a number of times to set up other Nixon deals. If they involved a television appearance—for example, a live feed to college campuses, then Nixon simply wouldn't say yes even with seven-figure income prospects on the table. I quickly realized that personal appearances were not going to happen.

The most tantalizing publishing issue involved the diaries Nixon had kept from his vice presidential days forward. It was never clear to me how many years these diaries covered and to what extent they had already been mined for *Six Crises* and *RN*, but I certainly tried to get the material reviewed for publishing opportunity, though without success. Nixon had at one point told me about the material as a possible publishing resource. I wrote him long memos explaining how the material might be utilized with a trusted editor to interlineate context comments. For awhile, I thought I had made some progress when a British author, Jonathan Aitken, was given some access to the material. Aitken produced a good one-volume biography of Nixon. Nixon never gave me or anyone else the chance to review the underlying material for publishing potential.

I also began to work with John Taylor personally. Taylor had published a novel on the premise that a president not unlike Nixon had fought impeachment proceedings and won. The book had been published by Wyndham, a small press owned by Norman Vincent Peale's foundation. To negotiate a movie option, I had to unscramble some rights issues with the publisher. In the same season Wyndham listed John Taylor, another writer was about to debut with a small press run. His name was John Grisham and the title was *A Time to Kill*. Unfortunately my only contact with John Grisham has been as a reader.

That two-hour meeting with Nixon was my last in-person meeting, but not my last contact. Typically John Taylor was the intermediary, but sometimes Nixon called himself. When it was time to offer Nixon's next book, a foreign policy work that became *Seize the Moment*, I got instructions that Nixon would be happy with an advance between $150,000 and $200,000. When I negotiated a $400,000 advance, Nixon called to congratulate me. The book again was a solid *New York Times* best-seller. The deal for *Seize the Moment* called for Nixon to record an audio version of the book. When the time came, Nixon said that his voice was not in good shape and he didn't want to go forward with the recording. Simon & Schuster wanted to reduce the advance package by the $25,000 allocated to the audio. Nixon was unhappy and I got instructions to make sure that Simon & Schuster paid the advance anyway. This seemed to me out of line, since Nixon wasn't going to deliver what had been promised. Simon & Schuster offered half of the advance as a compromise. When I relayed this, Nixon had his personal lawyer write a scathing letter to Martin Davis, the CEO of Simon & Schuster's parent company, asserting that he was being mistreated. Simon & Schuster paid the extra money, but I knew in my gut that I now didn't look tough enough for Nixon anymore.

My firing in 1991 was by a polite note from John Taylor's successor as chief of staff. Nixon's agent for his final book was Mort Janklow, and his publisher Random House. Nixon was the only author to work with Swifty Lazar, Mort Janklow, and me. As with much else, his true personal opinions of the three of us as literary agents are probably buried with him. My own sense is that he was well served three times. In any event, I have my autographed copy of one of his manuscripts inscribed, "To a great agent."

In less than two years "Nixon was back," although for me in the persona of H. R. ("Bob") Haldeman, Nixon's chief of staff who had served a prison sentence after Watergate. He had written a best-seller after prison and then more or less disappeared to a quiet business life in Santa Barbara, California. At the introduction of Ray Price, Haldeman arrived accompanied by Scott Klososky, an intense, bright young man. Over dinner, Haldeman informed me that he had kept a diary during his Nixon White House years, some handwritten and some on tape. Transcribed, the content would run to more than two thousand book pages. The diary had been kept in a safe in the White House. When all of his papers were seized the day Nixon fired him in 1973, the papers had been collected and shipped to the National Archives. Amazingly, no one on the Watergate prosecution team had discovered the existence of the diary during the investigation or trials. Its disclosure at the time would have been a bombshell, second only to the Nixon tapes themselves. While Haldeman didn't comment, my guess is that he was never asked if he had a diary, he didn't have access to it, and no one at the National Archives shared what was there with the investigators.

For years after his prison sentence, Haldeman had tried hard to get the diary back from the National Archives on the grounds that it was personal intellectual property. They were undoubtedly nervous about returning anything to a prominent Watergate figure. The compromise was a contract awarding Haldeman a copy of the diary and exclusive access and publication rights during his lifetime. The National Archives held the original, would hold all rights upon his death, and the diary would become publicly accessible and be in the public domain for purposes of publication.

Klososky was helping Haldeman with the task of transcribing and organizing the diary. Haldeman insisted that the diary would need to be made public in full or he wouldn't release it at all. For a publisher, this would mean a three- or four-volume effort. In the emerging technology of CD-ROMs, it was no problem to capture the content on a single disk. Klososky had already recruited Sony as a partner to work on the CD-ROM. Sony wanted to use the diaries to demonstrate their emerging multimedia technology. They felt they could get a lot of visibility working with Haldeman. The content lent itself to blending video, audio, and print sources. The length of the diaries alone and the search engines of the CD-ROM would demonstrate the technology.

Sony was prepared to have the product ready for launch at the same time as the book version, so that marketing budgets and public relations efforts could be coordinated with the book publisher. This would be an industry first; the simultaneous release of a multimedia CD-ROM and a book was intended to be a best-seller.

There was one difficulty. Haldeman had seen Mort Janklow, who had told him that the book would never succeed in the trade book marketplace. I politely disagreed and pointed out that Janklow was now representing Nixon and if Nixon would prefer the diaries not be published, this was one way to pass a message to Haldeman. I couldn't read Haldeman's reaction. When Haldeman expressed interest in hiring me as the agent for the project, we discussed the presentation I would need for publishers. Haldeman and Klososky had worked on the earliest section of the diaries, which covered the first six months starting in January 1969. I wanted to show the unabridged version with the proposed cuts highlighted, so the publisher could see what the edited book could achieve. The early material was low key, while interesting. The overtly commercial material would come later when the timeline overlapped Watergate. Haldeman was not prepared to show that material to me or publishers at that time.

When I circulated the presentation, Putnam made the most aggressive response: "Show us the Watergate material and we will tell you in twenty-four hours what we are willing to do." Haldeman produced the material and Putnam bid $200,000, which turned out to be the highest offer. As we went through the details of a contract, Klososky called to tell me that Haldeman was ill and would probably die soon. Compounding problems, Haldeman was a Christian Scientist and would not see a physician and the family didn't want the media to know of his illness. So I was to tell the publisher nothing.

Haldeman died with the contract unsigned. Technically, the diaries were now in the public domain, but only we and an archivist at the National Archives knew, so we could still gamble on publication. As a practical matter, the diaries became available only to scholars on site at the National Archives years later. Putnam was convinced that Haldeman's death depreciated their rights. They had been counting on the traditional author tour. I pointed out that Haldeman on tour would have positioned the diaries as pro-Nixon documents and hindered their sale. Haldeman's interest was in vindication, not in unit sales. I also pointed out that with Haldeman's death, Nixon critics and defenders could actively discuss the book, so that it was arguably even more valuable. We finally agreed to reduce the advance. Klososky had to go through a long series of meetings with the family to convince them to do what Haldeman had wanted, and authorize publication of the book.

Sony managed to interest Ted Koppel in doing two forty-five minute shows over consecutive nights on *Nightline* on the book during Sweeps Week. Haldeman's own voice from the tapes was laced through the pieces, as were scrolled excerpts from the diaries and historic footage. Some of that footage was shot by Haldeman himself and had been incorporated into the CD-ROM. The *Nightline* pieces beat the *Tonight Show* and Letterman for the first time in memory. Sony also tried to get Putnam excited about the CD-ROM. There were some problems. Not a single computer at Putnam is offices could even play a CD-ROM. The editor-in-chief's comment was, "I hope to be retired before this technology has any significance." He isn't, and it does. For key members of the press, like Bill Safire, Sony technicians arranged demonstrations.

The book, titled *The Haldeman Diaries,* exploded onto the best-seller list. Despite its very friendly introduction by the best-selling historian Stephen Ambrose, it was basically a magnet for anti-Nixon views. The CD-ROM reached a very narrow marketplace, but won numerous awards for Sony for its multimedia production values. Nixon published his final book with Random House at about the same time and died shortly after it was published. For a number of weeks, both books were on the best-seller list. If Haldeman had wanted revenge against Nixon (which I suspect he didn't), he probably had achieved some. If Haldeman wanted a page in history, the diaries were of some help, but not entirely, I am sure, in the way he intended. Negative language about Jews and Blacks and the general hardball political language of the book was not calculated to rehabilitate his reputation. Richard Reeves, currently working on a serious book about Richard Nixon, works each day with the relevant front page of the *New York Times* and the Haldeman diary entry to ground his chronology.

I felt that we had all worked on something extraordinary. Not only for me, but for the industry, I could always say that I helped put together the first simultaneous CD-ROM/book best-seller package. I had helped put a public domain book with a dead author on the best-seller list. The chance to do this was precisely why I was working on my own. And my experiences with Scott Klososky in the electronic world were just beginning.

NINE

....

Sports Agency Acquires Julian Bach

In 1989, the question for me was, "What next?" I was restless for a new challenge. The call that simplified my search came from a headhunter for International Management Group, privately held by Mark McCormack. McCormack was one of the great agent success stories and had long since moved beyond agentry. By 1989, IMG was a thirty-country enterprise with nearly two thousand employees. While its public image was focused on its star athletes (Arnold Palmer, Wayne Gretzky, Joe Montana, Monica Seles, Kristi Yamaguchi, and four hundred more—today led by Tiger Woods), the financial backbone of IMG was an intricate web of event ownership and management, broadcasting, and licensing. For example, IMG handled the international broadcast rights for the Wimbledon tennis tournament, the licensing of Wimbledon-endorsed products, the corporate hospitality and sponsorship arrangements for the tournament, and so on.

146

The broadcast division of IMG was one of the largest nonnetwork packagers of television programs in the world. Since its work was mainly sports and the interest was international, IMG's reach in broadcast was also fully international. The licensing divisions of IMG when aggregated (the golf unit selling golf-related items, tennis the tennis items, central corporate unit more general licensing) was larger than Time Warner's Licensing Corporation of America. Whether ice skating or motor sports, there were few enterprises IMG entered into in which its objective or reality was to be anything other than number one or two in the world. The corporate sponsorship groups, both centrally and from the divisions, sold hundreds of millions of dollars of sponsorship arrangements to corporations throughout the world. IMG did not stop with sports. McCormack had recently moved into classical music representation and event business, and was on the path by acquisition and growth to becoming one of the top two such enterprises in the world. So IMG would package tours in Australia for Kiri Tikanawa or stadium concerts in Europe for Jose Carreras.

I knew enough about IMG and Mark McCormack to identify the company from the headhunter's call and to know that I would be interested in their publishing operation. IMG had tried a number of approaches to publishing in the 1970s and 1980s and none had worked out satisfactorily from a corporate point of view. A talented packager, John Boswell, had worked awhile at the company, but his major contribution upon leaving was to dream up Mark McCormack's book, *What They Didn't Teach You at Harvard Business School*. Boswell's share of that and another book set up his business. After Boswell, a team of agents had concluded mostly smaller deals. Before I was interviewed, several people had started the job and left soon thereafter. There was actually an office pool on how long I would last.

McCormack had asked Barry Frank, the longtime head of the broadcast division and one of his most powerful lieutenants, to oversee a new approach to publishing. McCormack also enlisted Ray Cave, a former *Time* editor close to him, to work with Frank and study what was needed. Frank and Cave offered releases to almost all of the publishing clients since the projects then underway didn't fit with any other IMG activity. The publishing unit, other than Mc-Cormack's personal activity and a proposal to negotiate a license for Mayo Clinic, was, in effect, a blank slate. That was both a problem and an opportunity.

Barry Frank and Ray Cave interviewed me at some length. I shared with them the tax return for Arthur M. Klebanoff, P.C., to point out that as far as I could tell I was doing better at the commission business alone than they had done with a small army. I also pointed out that the backlist publishing commission values created at IMG in the past decade wouldn't cover the overhead of a secretary. I tried to convince them to be a client, even going so far as to suggest that they could put their sign on my door, since they seemed to like offices. They ended up making me an offer I couldn't refuse, with a two-year commitment and the right to operate and retain nearly all the commissions from my own business. My cash flow would more than double instantly.

Mark McCormack needed to meet me before the deal was sealed. He gave me the allotted eight minutes or so. I don't remember what we discussed, except that he had talked with Mort Janklow who had said good things about me. There was at least one return on a bridge not burned. McCormack was in New York for the U.S. Open, an annual tennis engagement among many on his multicontinent schedule. Traditionally, there was a meeting during the tournament of the so-called "dinner committee." The team who had been with McCormack pretty much from the beginning of IMG sat as a group and discussed strategy and big picture business issues.

The dinner committee invited me to make a brief presentation. I brought props. One was the twelve-inch by seventeen-inch leather-bound Roger Tory Peterson *Field Guide* Art book, a $350 signed edition for the Eastern and Western volumes. The other was a tiny pamphlet for Sheila Lukins called *New Barbecue Basics,* which had been wrapped around 2 million bottles of Lea & Perrins Worcestershire sauce. I pointed out that these were forms of publishing, too, and that with IMG's interdivisional help, perhaps we could together make some serious money in publishing.

In deciding to join IMG, I had a number of objectives in mind: Their stellar client base could refer book projects, their licensing and corporate sponsorship activities could exploit promotional publishing, publishing could play a more important role with IMG's institutional clients or major new representation opportunities, and IMG could produce new projects and licenses for my clients. Deals I had put together for Sheila Lukins and Julee Rosso, for example, could be far more lucrative at IMG. If you represent only the talent, you make a commission on the talent fee. If you represent the premium or tie-in project, you make a commission or mark-up on the entire project cost. This could be the difference between a commission on $25,000 and a commission on $1 million or more. I also thought I could learn something. IMG was, in effect, an international corporate marketing finishing school.

Barry Frank was my boss. Ray Cave usually sat in on key meetings. For broadcast work over the years on behalf of the International Olympics Committee, Barry Frank was known in a number of quarters as "Mister Olympics." Paul Goldberger was nice enough to place a good announcement of my appointment in the *New York Times*. My new office was in IMG's wonderful townhouse on East 71st Street. My landlord eventually settled my broken lease. I set up to work January 1, 1990. There was plenty of action soon enough.

One of my immediate challenges was to save IMG from a potential seven-figure publishing loss. The 1987 America's Cup race had taken place in Australia. Along with a wide variety of other successful licenses, IMG had self-published a book on the race that had netted several million dollars. A combination of high priced advertising and a big deal for newsstand distribution had been the keys to the outcome. IMG wanted to repeat that success for the 1992 sailing races in San Diego and sent me there to investigate the progress their partner was making.

There was indeed a plan for a beautiful self-published book. The best sailing photographers had been signed, one a specialist on land, one from the water, one in the air, and so on. Terrific text writers were also standing by. A first-rate designer was ready to turn the book around quickly since the idea was to have most of the book about past races and the final section about the upcoming race. There was a problem, however, the revenue structure for the book was not realistic. The assumptions looked good. The local volunteers would sell tens of thousands of fifty dollar books door to door, local businesses would flock to be sponsors, and so on.

What I saw was an expensive plan without predictable revenue. The loss exposure was between 1 and 2 million dollars. Once back in New York, I recommended that the project be terminated. This was not well received, so I recommended a $50,000 ninety-day evaluation with both partners splitting the costs. If we could demonstrate profitability, fine, make the books. If not, decide which loss you wanted, the $50,000 or the estimate of loss which would be incurred by going forward. We presented a plan to break even. The costs of the book would be reduced by cutting its trim size and page count. The book would make money if successfully bundled with overall corporate sponsorships of the America's Cup. When published, the book received a number of prominent industry awards. The overall corporate sponsors, who were not our responsibility to recruit, never materialized. My budget would most certainly have reflected a large loss with any other approach, but I didn't get credit for profits by saving a seven-figure loss. Chris Capen, our packaging partner, later formed Tehabi Books to publish a line of successful visual books tied to high-visibility partners. At the 2001 Tehabi booth at BEA, the display walls included jackets of future titles with the Vatican Library. Small world.

My second immediate opportunity was the chance to help Mark McCormack recruit the representation of Margaret Thatcher, who had recently resigned as Britain's Prime Minister. McCormack had been working for months on the representation, probably one of the largest in trade publishing in recent years. IMG had a major presence in England and McCormack spent a lot of time there. He and a few others were invited to submit a written proposal, following which Thatcher and her advisers would select finalists for personal interviews. I asked for the assignment of trying a first draft. Later, I learned that no other senior executive was in a hurry to work on a personal McCormack project for fear of retribution if the client recruitment failed.

My twenty-page draft was a guide through the range of open commercial opportunities, coupled with the need to protect Thatcher's reputation and image at all costs. The draft also emphasized Thatcher's worldwide visibility and IMG's ability to serve her completely through its more than thirty offices. McCormack shared the draft with some of his closest friends outside IMG. Word got back to me that he thought it was the best presentation document he could remember IMG ever submitting. Since it would go under his signature, I assumed this was a positive development for me.

McCormack invited me to his home in Orlando to meet Margaret Thatcher's son Mark, who would be involved in the selection process. Mark Thatcher had been talking with Robert Maxwell, the owner of Macmillan Publishers, and others and had convinced himself that his mother's books could break every record set thus far in advances for a memoir. Since the American market was the backbone of this pricing theory and the fact was that Margaret Thatcher was not that dominant a figure here, I rather doubted his view. I brought to the dinner a set of Easton's signed, leather-bound Nixon, Ford, and Carter memoirs as a gift for his mother, which seemed to be well received.

Next was our invitation to meet Margaret Thatcher in London, with the assurance that ours was the only personal meeting. In other words, the opportunity was now ours to lose. McCormack decided that I would handle the book part of the presentation and he would captain the meeting. The meeting was set as an all-day affair at IMG's London offices over Easter weekend. This scheduling was supposed to preserve secrecy for the meeting. Margaret Thatcher arrived accompanied by her son Mark and a financial adviser. She was an active participant throughout the meeting, except for a brief time when very specific money issues were discussed. She then stepped out and thanked the staff for working on a holiday. Margaret Thatcher was impressive and clearly in command of herself. But for me she was not an overpowering celebrity.

At a session the night before, McCormack had made clear how the meeting would go and that we would win or lose based upon how he personally wanted to play the meeting. McCormack opened the meeting with nearly an hour long review of IMG's reach, but mostly focused on opportunities he knew could be secured in Japan. He had made confidential inquiries before the meeting and reported on Japanese personal appearance opportunities. Mark Thatcher jumped in to point out they had a G7 jet available for their use whenever they liked and could make their own Japanese or other market arrangements whenever they liked. I am not even sure that Thatcher wanted to hear anything about what she could earn by making appearances in Japan.

As for my part, I had worked hard on my presentation. What Mark Thatcher wanted to hear was, "Don't worry, we will get you at least a $15 million advance for the book," which was perhaps triple a rational number. What McCormack wanted me to say was, "Don't worry, we will get you at least a $10 million advance for the book." What I wanted to do was illustrate how the values of a book offer could be built.

For example, the American publisher typically acquires North American rights and distributes in Canada through an overall distribution arrangement. The Canadian royalty to the author is based on receipts and perhaps one-third, in unit terms, of the American royalty. Since Canada is only about 10 percent the size of the American market and the typical, even successful, American author cannot command an aggressive independent Canadian publication, the standard arrangement is rarely challenged. When Janklow and I worked on *Lace* for Shirley Conran, we were able to challenge these assumptions, since Conran's prior nonfiction book had been a number one best-seller in Canada. Clearly, Margaret Thatcher would attract a major commitment from a leading Canadian publisher whatever the American publisher thought of the arrangement.

The UK publisher typically acquires exclusive rights to the British Commonwealth and nonexclusive rights in English to "open market" territories throughout the world. Open market territories include Europe, Asia, South America, the Caribbean, among others. The author receives a royalty based on receipts, which is significantly less than the "full" royalty from sales in England. In Margaret Thatcher's case, she could command top dollar, market by market, in English language territorial deals throughout the world. This was not true for any American political personality, since their visibility and popularity would not be strong enough throughout the English-speaking world to support this range of efforts. Therefore, the theme of my presentation was that building the licensing of the Thatcher book might involve seventy-five to one hundred separately negotiated licenses. The more the rights were split up, the more the advances and royalties were maximized and the greater the premium on an international agent. The presentation satisfied McCormack, but ducked the question of how much the rights might bring.

Contrary to the Thatcher assurance, their team had also invited Marvin Josephson of ICM to make a presentation that weekend. My guess is that his pitch was straightforward and focused on the book itself. He personally handled only Henry Kissinger and Barbara Walters, who had arranged the meeting and would personally make certain that the Thatcher book was handled appropriately. In other words, Josephson used flattery and the commitment of his personal attention, while McCormack presented expertise and a much more corporate pitch. The next thing we knew our "secret" meeting was in the British press. Margaret Thatcher's husband, Dennis, was known to enjoy golf and the press pieces speculated that any IMG arrangement would do something special for his golfing interest. My guess is that the leak came from the Thatcher team. Within a few days Josephson got the business. McCormack called me with the one sentence news, "We lost."

The gift of leather-bound books paid off later for Easton. Josephson sold the book to HarperCollins (Murdoch, not Maxwell) for much less money than the fantasy deals the Thatcher team expected. Margaret Thatcher graciously agreed to autograph sheets for Easton for both volumes of her memoirs, an offer so successful that it sold out to Easton's subscribers from one advance letter mailing.

I was able to help McCormack better the next time around. IMG had a long, close relationship with the International Olympics Committee, and Barry Frank had advised the committee on many of their international broadcast arrangements. IMG had also handled very lucrative corporate hospitality arrangements. Tying down IMG's role for future Olympics was of the highest corporate priority and profitability. Publishing would play a part.

McCormack invited me to join a large IMG delegation that had been invited to present to an IOC committee a variety of representation issues for the upcoming games. IMG's focus, of course, was on broadcast and corporate hospitality, where the big money was. My presentation focused on the role the IOC could play in reaching young people around the world through publishing in the Olympic spirit. McCormack realized that my presentation would pull on the heartstrings of the IOC committee. McCormack wasn't interested in whether the publishing business was awarded. His guess was that the IOC felt too entangled with IMG in any event, so any new assignment was unlikely. He wanted my presentation to set the stage for the big stakes commercial issues by emphasizing IMG's commitment to the Olympic spirit and mission.

When McCormack asked me at dinner to take the lead in the presentation the next day, I could see that the more senior people were very unhappy. I did what I was asked, and IMG received a variety of very valuable assignments. I had done my part in supporting the effort by participating in the key presentations, while, again, it would not appear in my unit's budget. I did visit Lausanne several times to try and work out a book on the 100th anniversary of the Olympics in 1996. The IOC was not willing to give that assignment to IMG, either.

I did get a chance to get a glimpse of the insular world of the IOC. IOC members were treated like local gods. The member from Mexico, a talented architect, had built the IOC headquarters (and later the Olympic museum in Lausanne as well). In the large lobby was an electronic board with the photograph of each IOC member from around the world. Even the halls of Congress wait for members to die before providing this treatment. In the archive itself, the photography collection was overwhelmingly "President Samaranch on tour." Arturo Mari's collection of papal photographs was almost modest by comparison. Nothing I read about years later about the IOC and its practices surprised me based upon these behind-the-scenes visits.

Of course, the most obvious IMG publishing opportunities involved their star personalities. Generally speaking, star personalities have the opportunity to write only one successful personal book. Major IMG stars like Martina Navratilova, Chris Evert, Joe Montana, and Wayne Gretzky had already been authors. The football broadcaster John Madden, whose books depended upon humor rather than a memoir, had been the author of several titles, but the earlier books had done best. Sometimes a star can couple a personal book with an instructional book, particularly for the golfers. I tried to persuade Monica Seles to write a book while she was recuperating from being stabbed by a fan. She did a book several years later. I tried to match the high offers for a Bob Costas book with the $1 million that Barry Frank thought was the right number. No deal. I tried to get John Madden to take a new direction with his books. No interest. I tried to persuade Itzhak Perlman. No interest. I learned that the golfers were typically represented directly from their division when they were ready to consider a book.

The issue was simple. Each IMG superstar had an agent dedicated to his or her affairs. The income opportunities were directly connected with their sports and indirectly, and often more lucratively, endorsement deals. Endorsement deals required very little of an athlete's time and carried guaranteed favorable exposure and fat fees. Book deals required a lot of time, and if not well executed and promoted, could hurt an image and probably net much less money than a good endorsement deal. Also, corporately, the star's agent had to split the commission credit with the publishing division for any book project. In short, there may have been four hundred clients, but there were very few candidates for books.

It was also not easy to attract new clients to "the world's largest sports marketing agency." Authors in search of an agent were not likely to make this their first stop. The largest fee client of the division was Mark McCormack himself, who chose to dedicate his royalty and lecture fee income to the division. I was never invited to join the ten-person group that met regularly to review his personal business options. I decided not to fight for a seat at that table. I was busy enough and they seemed to have a big enough committee.

While Arnold Palmer wouldn't consider a memoir until years later, he did authorize Thomas Hauser to interview him at length for a photographic book on his career. Again with Hauser as author, Neil Leifer as photographer, and Walter Bernard as designer, we created a wonderful book on Muhammad Ali for Rizzoli. Neither of these books produced signficant commissions, but the experience with photographic books was extremely useful for me.

There were always possible clients. I was invited by Mark McCormack to spend an afternoon discussing publishing options with Rudy Giuliani, the former U.S. attorney who was contemplating a 1993 race for Mayor of New York. We first discussed nonfiction books. Giuliani expressed great concern about what he could write within the ethical constraints he felt as a former prosecutor. Giuliani was also considering writing fiction with a dashing U.S. attorney as the central character. This struck me as more suitable for someone who did not plan to run for public office. We didn't end up with any literary representation, but Giuliani didn't write a book either until after two terms as mayor.

Another possibility was a book by George Steinbrenner, the high-profile owner of the New York Yankees. IMG was cultivating Steinbrenner as a potential financial backer of projects in Europe. Steinbrenner had made a deal with Gulf & Western for ten years of cable coverage of the New York Yankees, which was the largest contract of its kind in the world of sports. As part of the deal, Martin Davis, the CEO of Gulf & Western, ordered Dick Snyder of Simon & Schuster to prepare a $1 million book advance contract for Steinbrenner. The only problem was that Steinbrenner didn't want to write a book.

My meeting with Steinbrenner was several years after that contract had been offered. He was no more certain about writing a book now, but my IMG colleagues wanted to keep open the possibilities and Steinbrenner seemed willing enough to talk with me. We had a series of meetings. In Tampa, I traded a set of Roger Tory Peterson *Field Guide* art books (Steinbrenner is an avid birder) for an armful of Yankee stuff for my children. I heard tales of Steinbrenner's youth. The most memorable involved his relationship with his father, who was, by George's description, at least as controlling as the worst of the media images of George.

Steinbrenner's father was a very successful man in Ohio who owned a family barge business. He made his son work for everything, principally by gathering chicken eggs from their farm outside Cleveland. Young George finally scraped enough money together to buy a secondhand car. Father and son commuted in that car every day to work. When George married into a wealthy Ohio family, he traded the secondhand car and bought himself something more suitable. Within days, George's father had bought the secondhand car back from the dealer and insisted on driving George to the office in the old car.

Steinbrenner had varied interests. As a skilled conductor of John Philip Sousa and similar American band music, he regularly made himself available for fund-raising pops concerts and donated his fees. He flew his own jet to make speeches for fees that were donated to young people's projects. Extremely active in the U.S. Olympic movement, he personally sponsored some talented gymnasts. He made major gifts to Williams College, his alma mater. His purposes seemed to me to be genuine, not personally aggrandizing. My only problem with Steinbrenner was that he wasn't serious about writing a book. I couldn't quite replicate the $1 million offer, but doubt that he would have actually done the project even with that offer in hand. An agent needs a client to make book deals happen, but first you need a *willing* client. Steinbrenner has his string of World Series championships but still hasn't done a book.

I worked on the second floor of the beautiful IMG East 71st Street townhouse. The broadcast group worked on the third and fourth floors. I was eager to interest them in projects for my clients. Sheila

Lukins and Roger Tory Peterson were stars in their own worlds. Why couldn't IMG help package them for television? Every time I pushed I got the same answer, "We can get on television anything a sponsor will pay for."

Finally, I had a chance to test the television group when Roger Tory Peterson developed a license deal for bird trading cards. The marketer also handled a very successful IMG program for John Madden football trading cards. My IMG colleagues were more than a little surprised to see their licensing customer shopping for bird images on the second floor. The marketer also wanted to get one-minute excerpts about birds onto television and produced some sample footage. The broadcast group never had their heart in the project. I asked why. They said because no one on the floor knew who Roger Tory Peterson was. I said that he was the "Audubon of the twentieth century." My contact polled the floor again and reported that most had never heard of John James Audubon, either.

Licensing didn't work out much better, either. When IMG controlled a major property, such as Dennis the Menace or Raggedy Ann and Andy, the publishing rights were usually already spoken for. When we jointly explored expanding a relationship with *Playboy*, I got a box of books from Christie Hefner after a two-day licensing strategy meeting, but nothing happened. A tie-in book for a documentary on the 100th anniversary of the Nobel Foundation was underway when I arrived. I helped support the broadcasting group in an effort to do a year by year, one hundred–hour news special on the close of the century, but the overall deal collapsed. IMG corporate sponsors seemed to be interested in everything but books.

IMG meetings didn't help the process. Forty senior North American executives, myself included, would travel periodically to Cleveland for rather formal sessions with McCormack. The four hundred most senior worldwide executives gathered once every two years in Cleveland. I addressed the group on publishing issues, hoping to motivate client referrals. Not much happened.

IMG had built its classical music business by acquiring established agencies. McCormack saw in classical music a chance to merge the

IMG strengths in events, corporate sponsorships, and broadcasting. Publishing offered few of these attractions. How would John Grisham fill a stadium? When I presented a plan for acquiring literary agencies so that IMG Publishing could compete on its own with the top tier agencies, Barry Frank and McCormack simply weren't interested as a corporate priority. When I suggested in the alternative that the publishing unit become a service unit (like legal or corporate marketing) to IMG divisions so that agents would be more motivated to complete deals (100 percent of the commissions would be credited to their account), the answer was also no, presumably since McCormack enjoyed treating his personal activity as a profit-and-loss division of the company.

At Barry Frank's initiative, IMG did pursue one agency acquisition, the Julian Bach Literary Agency. Julian, an elderly, elegant man, had one great client, Pat Conroy, who had been with him since his first book. Julian tells a charming story of discussing Houghton Mifflin's first offer with Pat Conroy. After explaining the small advance, Julian was surprised to hear Conroy say, "I would love to go forward, but I don't have that kind of money." After Julian explained that the publisher paid the author rather than the other way around, the deal closed.

I didn't think it made sense to buy only one agency and went to McCormack to object. McCormack asked me if I thought he could lose money on the acquisition deal as presented. I said no. McCormack responded that he would always buy an agency from which he was reasonably assured of making money. Indeed, Pat Conroy's *Beach Music* paid for the acquisition a few times over. But my strategic point was correct. Spin the deal as we could, *Publishers Weekly* reported, "Sports Agency Buys Julian Bach."

Mark McCormack was very effective recruiting clients. In 1993, the Hertz Corporation celebrated its 75th anniversary. Mark McCormack was very close to Frank Olson, the longtime Hertz CEO, and IMG had done a wide range of business with Hertz. Arnold Palmer had been a Hertz spokesperson. When Olson said that he was thinking of a commemorative book, McCormack asked me to see him. Hertz headquarters are in an office park in northern New Jersey. Olson met me alone. His first thought would have David Halberstam write the corporate history of Hertz, as he had of the car makers. I told Olson that this was unlikely to happen for many reasons. We discussed a visually pleasing book that could be distributed, for instance, to the Hertz "family." Olson asked if I would do a survey of his executives as a consulting project to see if this was doable. I asked instead for Olson to convene a meeting of senior executives to see whether they would buy in for a minimum press run of 25,000 copies.

After my presentation, the European chief who normally offered premiums to platinum card members was interested in substituting the book for last year's key chain. Hertz was to be host in its anniversary year to a major industry gathering. Several thousand books could be gifts to attendees. Editorial content would be useful for trade publications to which Hertz was already committed for twenty-five-page sections. Hertz had already scheduled a large banquet to celebrate the anniversary. In the budget was several hundred thousand dollars for a short video to be shown only at the banquet. Janet Smythe, who was in charge of the event and all Hertz advertising, asked to shift that budget from the video to the book.

When the meeting was over, we had nearly a $1 million budget to make an award-winning corporate anniversary book. Janet Smythe was in charge for Hertz. IMG's fee would be an advertising style mark-up on the total project costs. This fee would help my IMG divisional budget. In a competition, we chose a young designer named Christopher Johnson. He and the team delivered a first-rate project that did win awards. The editorial and graphics developed for the project made their way from book to magazine to countercard use. The imagery developed for the book has been used repeatedly in Hertz marketing and advertising projects. Christopher Johnson finished the project with Hertz as his own marketing client. I finished the project with a new understanding of corporate and branded book publishing and a relationship with a design genius who would later become my partner and design alterego. You can find O. J. Simpson, a Hertz spokesperson, on some of the pages. Fortunately, the book was first distributed before Simpson's better known problems. Later, distribution of the book was another one of O. J.'s victims.

Mark McCormack came back with business even when he visited the doctor, which in his case was an annual physical at Mayo Clinic. IMG already represented the Nobel Foundation and McCormack felt that Mayo Clinic could become an extraordinary international broadcast client with medical information in a wide variety of video formats. Mayo Clinic was formed with an entrepreneurial spirit. While a not-for-profit, its operations were intended to yield significant net operating income for research and education. Its large endowment reinforced this commitment.

Mayo Clinic is simultaneously a conservative institution very much in touch with the constantly changing modern world. It has always been at the cutting edge of technology, both as a developer and an early adopter. To help focus the institution on commercial opportunities, yet preserve its mission, Mayo Clinic had formed a rather unique unit called Mayo Medical Ventures, staffed by a combination of very talented lay people and senior physicians on loan from the institution. Mayo decided early on that it would create all of its own editorial product, a tremendous commitment but one consistent with the standards of the organization. Many other institutions engaged outsiders to package their editorial product or, indeed, just endorsed product prepared by others.

The *Mayo Clinic Health Letter* was one of the most successful of its type with nearly 750,000 subscribers and an annual promotion effort of 15 million pieces of direct mail. The success of the newsletter encouraged Mayo in 1988 to publish its first book, *The Family Health Book,* a large, extensively illustrated A-to-Z disease book. While sales started out modestly, they quickly accelerated to hundreds of thousands of copies. In addition to the newsletter subscribers, Mayo had more than 20,000 employees, nearly as many alumni physicians from the largest medical training program in the United States and the ability to communicate with more than 2 million patients. They had not originally contemplated selling *The Family*

Health Book through the mail, but when they did, they had sold more than 150,000 copies. Since this was their first experience selling by direct response to the "Mayo family," they had no idea whether the numbers were good or not.

The video efforts never materialized. My assignment was to focus on publishing opportunities. For about a year, we went through a process which resulted in a restructured and improved license for their next two titles, a pregnancy and baby care book and a heart book, with Morrow, the publisher who had handled *The Family Health Book*. Each trip to Rochester had its own revelation. The Mayo brothers had encouraged clinic physicians to travel the world to learn more about medicine. While traveling, they were encouraged to return with fine editions of medical books. The private library in Rochester is one of the best of its kind in the world. The Mayo brothers had recruited one of the great medical illustrators of the day to establish their medical illustration group. Today, more than seventy-five people work in the group with state of the art equipment. Their collection of illustrations has more than 10 million images. The better 100,000 images have been catalogued and digitized and are truly amazing.

The celebration dinner in Rochester for the signing of the new-two book deal was one of my proudest moments in publishing. Negotiating the arrangements had merged my experience dealing with large institutions, my publishing skills, and my growing experience in direct response marketing. It was also a banner commission for IMG.

While Hertz joined the Mayo Clinic as significant revenue producers, there were two other intriguing near client recruitment misses. As Dan Quayle was leaving the official Vice Presidential Naval Observatory home after his general election loss in 1992, Barry Frank of IMG gave us a chance to represent his book and other activity through an IMG golf client who was close to Quayle. Our references were probably better for golf skills than general representation, but we did get an afternoon meeting with Dan and Marilyn Quayle. Dan Quayle was very personable and more than smart enough for purposes of our discussions. His wife was even more focused and obviously in the business of protecting him. A major book would be an important step in his future plans. I had prepared for the meeting by thinking through how to make a Dan Quayle book an important project. The negatives were obvious. He was the butt of many jokes. The combination of his conservative views and apparent lack of intellectual depth would meet a very skeptical publishing community.

I decided that the strongest book approach should bridge Quayle's strong support from the religious right and a traditional political trade book. Religious publishing was one of the strongest publishing areas. Advances and returns were lower and margins were higher than in trade publishing. Robert Schuller, Billy Graham, and a host of others had demonstrated that big numbers could be achieved. Murdoch's NewsCorp owned both HarperCollins and Zondervan, a leading evangelical publisher. Several authors had been published simultaneously by both houses, most recently Tom Landry, the coach of the Dallas Cowboys, and before that auto builder John Delorean, whose well publicized legal problems gave him the chance to cite Scriptures.

We discussed strategy for the Quayle meeting and decided that it was better to share our idea and risk not being hired than simply present credentials and hope for the best. The open presentation strategy was usually my preference. With Nixon, it had worked even though Swifty Lazar had, in effect, adopted my strategy as his own. The Quayles listened closely to everything we had to say. We did get signed vice presidential golf balls as a memento of the visit. We didn't get hired. And Bob Barnett, the Quayles' lawyer (later to represent both Clintons), negotiated a seven-figure deal with HarperCollins and Zondervan. It did very well in both the trade and religious marketplaces when published. Hopefully, Barry Frank was thanked.

My last new client opportunity at IMG was of my own making. Len Garment put me in touch with Ken Lerer, Michael Milken's publicist. Milken was the wealthy figure in the Wall Street insider trading cases. He was concerned about the upcoming release of James B. Stewart's book *Den of Thieves*. In particular, he and his team wanted to call attention to a British book friendly to Milken. I recommended that they get their lawyer, Alan Dershowitz, to write an introduction to the British book and become its spokesperson here at the same time the Stewart book was to be published. While this didn't stop the Stewart book from climbing the best-seller lists, it did give the Milken point of view considerable exposure.

Milken was still in prison, scheduled to go to a halfway house in several months. Collect telephone calls for me from Milken created quite a stir at IMG's townhouse. Milken and I talked at some length about his views of capital formation in the United States over a hundred year span and the typically ineffectual or counterproductive behavior of the government to foster capital formation. I was informed enough to know that I was talking with someone of extraordinary range and intelligence. While it was never stated, I think part of his interest in me was that I had worked successfully with Richard Nixon on what might be called redemption publishing. Milken's problems were obviously different, but he was also much more interested in redemption than in money.

Milken and I met at his Los Angeles office during a break from his halfway house (I later learned that this was the weekend he first learned of his prostate cancer condition). He had thought a lot about publishing, probably too much, and was already well along in meetings with William Novack, the most commercial collaborator of the day (Lee Iacocca, Tip O'Neill, Nancy Reagan, among others). I argued strongly that Milken should write a substantive book—for example, a book about capital formation, perhaps even called *Junk Bond,* that would build on all of Milken's obvious strengths.

I told him that a personal book could only have two points of view: "I'm sorry," since Americans love apologia (he didn't smile), or "I was screwed by the U.S. Attorney and the SEC," which wouldn't work for him or the marketplace. My guess was that Milken would never permit the release of such a manuscript in any event. Milken also hired Bob Barnett, explaining that he still had a large credit with Williams and Connolly from the criminal case. I had probably helped talk my way out of the assignment, but my analysis was correct. Milken drafted a personal manuscript with Novack and then bought the rights back from the publisher. No book has yet appeared. Recently, Milken surfaced in the editorial pages of the *Wall Street Journal* with a piece that was mostly about capital formation. The byline identified him as an "investor and financier," the same line my father had used to identify himself to me.

For some time after the initial meeting, I stayed in regular touch with Milken's communications representative Loraine Spurge. When Milken backed a publishing company, I was invited to hear one of the authors speak. His pitch was that service businesses work on the "80/20" rule, that your best business is from your few top clients while your bottom clients consume most of your time. In fact, if you can give your bottom clients to a competitor, you win twice—by freeing your time and chaining theirs. The moment the talk was over, I "fired" Milken as a client, felt free, and went on with my business. My philosophy of maintaining a connection with interesting people didn't change.

TEN

··

Scott Meredith

Jerry Traum called me in May 1993 and opened with the line that I was the only one of Janklow, Traum & Klebanoff who was still working on my freedom money and that he had the opportunity to change that. By "freedom money," the three of us had meant the amount of money you needed to accumulate before you no longer felt compelled to work. Scott Meredith, the literary agent, had died some months before without leaving a succession plan. The three senior agents had left to form their own agency, and clients were leaving in droves. the agency was in free fall, and his widow, Helen Meredith, and her advisers had approached Traum for advice. He said they should sell quickly to a literary agent who could stabilize the agency.

I had long thought about acquiring older literary agencies for the values of their backlists and the potential improvements in operating margins by consolidating overhead. Literary agencies are not easily transferable assets. Clients tend to be loyal to their individual agents, who can go their own ways. The agencies take specialized skills to run. Employees probably don't have the money to buy out an owner. The only hard assets are the commission flows from books in which the agency is "agent of record." Once in business more than thirty years, backlist commissions are somewhat predictable. Badly run agencies can actually be worth more closed than open. Serving midlist books of indifferent economics can cost meaningfully more money than agents are paid, particularly after allocating overhead. Annual frontlist effort losses on all but the largest clients eat into what would otherwise be free and clear backlist profits. Agencies should depend upon good computerized operating systems, but many agencies are not up to date.

I had never met Scott Meredith. One thing for sure was that his succession plan for his business was a textbook case on how not to do it. By 1991, Scott Meredith was sixty-eight and progressively dying of cancer. He was the sole shareholder of the agency he founded in 1946. His three most senior agents, Jack Scovil, Ted Chichak, and Russell Galen, had worked for him a total of more than sixty years. They handled almost all of the key clients. Meredith in the later years rarely put in time in the office and personally handled only Norman Mailer and Carl Sagan.

Over the years, Meredith frequently promised his senior team that the agency would be "theirs." He didn't, however, commit any of this to paper. After Meredith's death, the three agents tried to work out a deal to buy the agency from his widow, Helen. The negotiations went from bad to worse. When Scovil, Chichak, and Galen decided to set up an agency under that name, the original Scott Meredith Literary Agency was no more. Dozens of their clients followed for new projects, Carl Sagan decided to ask Mort Janklow to represent him, and Norman Mailer selected Andrew Wylie. The agency continued to be the agent of record for nearly 1,500 titles still in print and represented a wide range of clients and rights.

I realized from my first meeting with Helen Meredith that making the deal would be as much about emotion as money. Helen

Meredith spent parts of this and other meetings in tears. When not in tears, she expressed anger, typically directed at the departed agents. Whenever a subject with the least bit of complexity was discussed, she would retreat, a move which I began to feel was more of a negotiating tactic than a question of understanding. It was soon apparent that neither Helen nor her two grown children were interested in operating the business. Control of the business was vital from my point of view. If I was going to take the risk, I would have to run my own show.

We struck a deal with a $400,000 front payment and a royalty of 10 percent of gross revenues for seven years. Since the agency was grossing a (declining) base of $1.5 million in revenues, this would work if overhead could be kept in line. To make certain that third-party payments to authors and others were current, the front money was to be escrowed. Scott Meredith had made hundreds of thousands of dollars of loans to dozens of his clients. Collecting on this would be Helen Meredith's risk and responsibility. The acquisition would be of assets, so that any problems in the old corporation would not be mine. I had just enough money to swing the deal without a financial backer.

The negotiations and due diligence for the Scott Meredith deal were withheld from IMG. I had drafted an announcement memo for my IMG colleagues, since I literally had to buy the agency late one August afternoon and assume a management role the following morning. While I offered a full transition to IMG, I doubted that they would ask me back on premises (they didn't). By leaving IMG, I had broken an employment contract. Within days, Mayo Clinic advised IMG that they planned to follow me to Scott Meredith. I negotiated a friendly termination agreement by sharing some of the commissions from Mayo projects in exchange for an IMG commitment to share commissions on business I would refer to them in the future. Most of the people I worked with at IMG, including Mark McCormack, acted collegially and professionally as our paths crossed in the future. Barry Frank, I think, felt betrayed.

I was fortunate enough to have a friend, Leslee Dart, one of the leading movie publicists, who offered to handle publicity for a few days. *Variety* ran a nice piece. More important, the *New York Times* in its business deals column ran a piece that suggested that I had paid more than $2.5 million for the agency. I had refused to comment on numbers, but Scovil, Chichak, or Galen must have offered guidance based on what the deal would have cost them. The high price, of course, made the acquisition seem important. There was a grammatical error in the *Times* story that could have been read to suggest that IMG was an investor. IMG insisted that a correction be run that it was not an investor, so the story ran twice.

In 1997, *Publishers Weekly* published its 125th anniversary issue. Inside, it dedicated an article to the "movers and shakers" of the publishing business over those years. The greats were there, Nelson Doubleday, Alfred Knopf, and others. Only two agents made the list, Mort Janklow and Scott Meredith. Meredith was a very entrepreneurial businessman who made more than his share of enemies. When I opened his safe after the acquisition, I found papers on a dozen litigations, of which he had lost eleven. Nonetheless, he was among the earliest to auction books, pioneered the foreign rights marketplace and subagents networks, and was at the forefront of the packaged novel inspired by public events and people.

Meredith also decided early on that he would not read unsolicited material for free. Any agent of reputation or visibility gets dozens of inquiries a week from would be writers. Publishers refer to these submissions as the "slush pile." While there is the exception—the story of success as a young editor makes a discovery in the slush pile, for decades publishers and agents have done little or nothing with these submissions. Agents typically get their clients by referral or by soliciting authors or celebrities. It is a rare agent who finds his opportunities from the slush pile. Meredith perceived that he could charge a fee for reading these manuscripts if he provided something in return. What he provided was a critique letter, analyzing the strengths and weaknesses of the manuscript. The offer was that if the manuscript was saleable as submitted, the agency would offer to represent it.

This "fee reading service" became controversial in the community. Agents' associations and authors' groups recommended against the use of fee reading services.

Meanwhile, the would-be authors flocked to the service. Meredith's objective for the reading service was to cover the overhead of the agency as a whole while spotting new authors, and this was accomplished for decades. At its peak, the service read more than 3,000 manuscripts annually. The fees varied according to the length of the manuscript and the category (less for poetry and plays, more for fiction more than 100,000 words). I set a flat fee of $450, the average price in the prior confusing fee schedule.

Meredith marketed by direct mail and had a never-ending need for new authors to solicit. One example involved magazines that published fiction. Submissions outnumbered acceptances by hundreds to one. Meredith recruited staffers in the mail room of these publications to clip the return address of the submission envelopes (internally at the agency, these were called "corners") and send them to the agency for a payment of ten cents each. Meredith also encouraged other agents to send along copies of the unsolicited submissions that they received. Since these were names of people with a manuscript, the agency would pay one dollar per name or even more to help another agent empty his in-box.

Were there problems with the reader service? Of course. Meredith's marketing materials, by citing the success stories of his most commercial authors, puffed a bit too much with the suggestion that "this could be you." But few authors write without that fantasy anyway. With thousands of manuscripts passing through the office, there were inevitably some administrative problems and complaints. There were also successes for early work by mystery writers John Lutz and Bill Pronzini, romantic fantasy writer Jennifer Robinson, and Edgar Award winner (for Best First Novel) Will Harriss.

Meanwhile, Meredith himself focused on star authors. In 1959, Meredith signed the novelist Norman Mailer and proceeded to rewrite some of the rules of publishing. Mailer was also a columnist for *Esquire*. Meredith sold *Esquire* a serialization of a novel in progress (published in 1963 as *An American Dream*). No one had tried this since Dickens. A movie sale for $200,000 confirmed the success of the strategy. Mailer also helped Meredith crack the international marketplace for American fiction. In the early 1960s, American writers had relatively modest international and translation rights opportunities. The overwhelming percentage of the copyright's value was in the United States. Publishers tended to control world rights and to gain relatively modest licenses around the world.

Meredith's first step was to deal independently of the American publishers. He withheld world rights and proceeded to sell them market by market himself, establishing along the way a network of subagents in the various countries. Meredith would virtually never again sell world rights to the U.S. publisher. Soon enough, he would have his own full-time in-house foreign rights staff to handle the international traffic. Other agents copied the model and publishers found that they would have to pay a premium advance to control the broader international rights package. Meredith's innovative practice also led to bigger international market deals for American authors. With the passage of time, the value of world rights as a percentage of total copyright value grew. When Janklow, Traum, and I helped Sidney Sheldon and Barbara Taylor Bradford set independent rights dealing records abroad, we were building on the work of Scott Meredith.

Meredith couldn't enter the foreign rights marketplace without controversy. He perceived the need for a prominent agency in Germany to represent a range of American agents. Meredith became a secret investor. Other agents would hardly have signed on to a German agency part equity owned by Scott Meredith. Indeed, when his ownership stake was revealed, there was an outcry and mass threats of a client exodus. Meredith sold his interest.

Meredith also was among the first to see a market for ghostwritten fiction, particularly the roman à clef. In 1966, Senator Thomas Dodd had well publicized problems in Washington. Meredith decided that Dodd's censure circumstances offered a wonderful opportunity for a novel. He had a client, Gerald Green, a decent enough novelist of no great commercial following at the time (Green went on to write the novel which was the basis of the television miniseries *The Holocaust*). All he needed was the "author" with a famous name. One of the best known political columnists of the day was

Drew Pearson. Pearson had been hospitalized. Meredith convinced one of his clients, Bill Adler, to approach Pearson for the endorsement. In effect, Pearson "signed here" for a check for $100,000 for a book he neither wrote nor probably read. The resulting title *The Senator* by Drew Pearson published by Doubleday in 1967 for an advance of $300,000 pretty much invented the political roman à clef. John Ehrlichman (*The Company*), Joe Klein (*Primary Colors*), and hundreds of "authors" should say thank you.

Over the decades, Meredith and his brother Sidney (his one-third partner until 1983) built a publishing factory. At its peak, there were was a staff of twenty-five, one of the largest in the agency business. The deals flowed, more than 25,000 separate domestic transactions and another 15,000 foreign transactions before Meredith's death in 1993 at age seventy. At the end, the "star" clients were Norman Mailer, Carl Sagan, Margaret Truman, and Arthur C. Clarke, although you could do as well on commission with the list of Marion Zimmer Bradley or Philip K. Dick and the earning stream of Aldous Huxley's *Brave New World*. In 1993, more than two hundred new titles would be published with Scott Meredith Literary Agency as the "agent of record."

What interested me as I learned Meredith's story was less the agency at the time of his death and more the story of authors and agents lost over the years. Evan Hunter began as a reader in the fee program. He wrote and Scott Meredith sold *The Blackboard Jungle*. Later, under the pseudonym Ed McBain, he wrote and Scott Meredith sold a series of 87th precinct cop mysteries. Their falling out was so bitter that Evan Hunter was successful in prying loose his backlist. Agents nearly always enjoy the life of copyright returns on books they have sold, whatever the future dispute with a client. There is an unconfirmed story that, in order to secure his release, Hunter had threatened to write a roman à clef that opens with a corrupt literary agent who stole money from his clients.

Meredith sold the first American title for Jackie Collins. *The Stud* sold several million units for New American Library, but Collins never thought that Meredith went to bat for her on future titles. That loss was ultimately Mort Janklow's gain. In the late 1970s, I worked with Jackie Collins and her deceased husband, Oscar Lerman, to get the balance of her British published titles into the American marketplace. John Jakes was another writer whose early books were sold by Meredith but whose commercial success was established elsewhere.

Meredith could also be vindictive. A young Dean Koontz left the agency in 1972 after writing *How to be a Bestselling Writer* for Writer's Digest Press (long before he took his own advice). When Koontz asked Writer's Digest to pay him and Meredith his commission directly, a common practice, Meredith wrote a letter to the publisher, Richard Rosenthal, denouncing Koontz out of anger for acting independently. Rosenthal passed the letter along to Koontz. Koontz never forgave Meredith. When I asked former Meredith clients for quotes for a pamphlet for the agency's fiftieth birthday, Koontz refused and wrote me, "I would consider that equivalent to having a negative piece in a book that mostly celebrated the spirituality and humanitarianism of Al Capone."

Authors weren't all that he lost. A larger general agency is only as good as the agents. Over the years, Meredith hired and groomed very good people. Sooner or later, they left, taking some of the clients with them. The science fiction desk alone spawned several generations of the leading agents in the business—Richard Curtis from the 1960s, whose list includes Harlan Ellison; Ralph Vicinanza from the 1970s, whose list includes Stephen King and the Isaac Asimov estate; and, thanks to the implosion upon Meredith's death, Russell Galen, whose list includes Arthur C. Clarke and the estate of Philip K. Dick. The publishers Don Fine and John Holt also worked for the agency before setting out on their own.

Meredith ran the agency with a variety of idiosyncrasies. For several years in the mid-1960s during Lyndon Johnson's war on pornography, Meredith was rumored to be a target of investigation as a part owner of a pornographic publisher. In theory, some of the clients were supporting themselves writing this type of material under pseudonyms. While you could argue that Meredith was trying to help get otherwise impecunious authors income through writing pornography,

Meredith himself looked after every dime in the operation. When authors submitted return postage with unsolicited manuscripts, it was clipped and held for Agency use. Expense reimbursement clauses in the retainer agreement were interpreted to include the flowers Meredith would send to a client spouse's funeral. Framed in the front of the office was a certificate of thanks for a nominal contribution to the local PBS Station.

Meredith was also obviously a more complicated man than his critics would acknowledge. He loaned substantial sums of money to his clients, often on only a handshake. These loans ranged from up to five thousand dollars for smaller clients to tide them over as they worked to complete manuscripts, up to several hundred thousand dollars for Carl Sagan or Norman Mailer as circumstances indicated. Meredith didn't charge interest for the loans and often waited a considerable amount of time to be repaid. At the time of his death, there were nearly six hundred thousand dollars of loans outstanding to several dozen clients. For these purposes, perhaps out of memories of his own harder times as a young agent and writer, Meredith was a soft touch.

Meredith's sight deteriorated in his final years, to the point that he was nearly blind. Meredith collected Japanese netsuke, the tiny, artfully crafted ivory figures. Collecting netsuke is a rarefied taste and Meredith apparently had a very fine collection. He was a well enough known collector that he would send office employees to bid at Sotheby's or Christie's to avoid running up the price. Meredith was also a talented author far beyond the pulp works he churned out as a young man. He wrote a biography of *George S. Kaufman and his Friends*, which was published to fine reviews but modest sales. While *Writing to Sell* is a how-to, it is a very good how-to, and today's agents would be hard-pressed to write a better account for new or established commercial fiction writers.

Hercules had a harder job on his hands, but during the months after August 1993, I felt like I had walked into an immense stable that I needed to clean. Liability issues were flying around me. I had to keep departure issues with Scovil, Chichak, and Galen from turning into litigation. Several major former clients (most notably Carl Sagan) were very unhappy and needed to work out certain separation issues. Sets of former agents wanted unsold rights back or commission agreements renegotiated or broken.

I decided to keep the Scott Meredith name despite advice from friends to substitute my own. I thought that the name represented "brand," even if the man might not have made me comfortable. I hired Christopher Johnson to design a new logo and pamphlet that would tell the updated Scott Meredith story. We mailed several thousand of those pamphlets in two editions across the community. Over time, I was able to capture the part of the brand I wanted and separate myself from the man I never met. Also, by keeping my name off the door, I had more flexibility to explore a range of other activities.

Systems set up in the 1970s and earlier just weren't appropriate for the computer era. With the help of my deputy, Lisa Edwards, we designed and implemented first-class software systems (a process most publishers are still struggling with). Our accounting bills went down by half, and the questions that hit my desk became few and far between. For the manuscript reading business, we established a careful complaint review procedure which offered follow-up readings and a full chance for the client to air his or her views. My team completely redesigned the marketing materials for the reading program and renamed it, "The Discovery Program for New Authors." The marketing materials focused on examples from the past of the program and assessments of clients. We tested outside mailings and learned that we should communicate with those who first contacted us. I stopped the practice of buying corners and agents' submission letters. We tried hard to market the best of the manuscripts submitted and successfully sold some science fiction and horror titles.

Step by step, I made certain that each member of the staff had responsibilities that were directly aligned with income opportunities. Since our frontlist opportunities were reduced by client defections before I bought the agency, the staff had to be reduced over time. As Mark McCormack had succinctly explained to me, an agent on staff had to produce from his clients about double what they were paid to make the economics of the agency work. The numbers at Scott Meredith unfortunately fell far short of the mark. I let any departing staffer take with them any clients who chose to follow. It was the first time I have ever had to fire anyone. I still managed to keep good relationships with most of the agents I had to let go. When reporters talked to former employees during the Random House/RosettaBooks litigation, they had good things to say.

When you buy an agency like Scott Meredith, you hope that hidden among the thousands of titles and rights are happy financial surprises. I found a few. One of the best ways to breathe new life into a book is to make a successful movie. *Contact,* the novel by Carl Sagan and his wife, Ann Druyan, had been in development for many years. When I bought the agency, annual royalties were less than five thousand dollars and my commission less than five hundred dollars. Then came *Contact* the movie starring Jodie Foster. Pocket Books promptly reissued the paperback with movie artwork on the cover, the book shot briefly to number one on the mass market fiction bestseller list, and, instead of five hundred dollars, my commission amounted to about fifty thousand dollars.

The second surprise was an Arthur C. Clarke contract. My final deal with Scovil, Chichak, and Galen split commissions on unfinished books of clients who had left the agency for their representation. They had to do the work. I still ended up with most of the economics. The split commissions were itemized by client and contract. One contract omitted, probably because Scott Meredith had kept it a secret, had been entered years before by Arthur C. Clarke with Ballantine Books for *3001,* the third and final sequel in the *2001* series. The *3001* contract called for an advance of $1.5 million, but no money had changed hands, since at the time Clarke had no intention of writing the book. Now approaching eighty, Clarke wanted to write the book and Galen had to work with me as the "agent of record." In a brief telephone call, we agreed to a fifty-fifty commission split. Galen promptly got Ballantine to up their old advance offer to $3 million and I picked up an unanticipated $150,000 commission. The book was briefly a best-seller.

One backlist commission I worked for involved *The Stud* by Jackie Collins. As a general rule in mass market paperback publishing, the publisher with a backlist for an author will outsell a publisher with a stray title by that author by a sizable per title margin. Years before, Warner sold many times more units of Sidney Sheldon's weakest title than Dell could sell of *The Other Side of Midnight,* arguably his best title. The same was true of Judith Krantz's *Scruples* with Warner while the core of her list was with Bantam. With Jackie Collins, Pocket Books was the main publisher. NAL published only *The Stud. The Stud* sold fewer than 2,500 copies per year, less than a tenth of a typical Collins title. After much back and forth, we bought the rights back for *The Stud* and licensed them to Pocket Books for a $50,000 advance and a strong ongoing sale. A Hollywood movie or television miniseries from a backlist title will revive an author's entire backlist—for example, the TNT miniseries of Marion Zimmer Bradley's *The Mists of Avalon.*

The 1,500-title active backlist now smoothly processed 10,000 annual payment entries with one employee's part-time attention. The backlist of the agency, the ongoing discovery program and a reshaped frontlist together with a sensibly structured overhead freed me to invest my time where I wished. As important, I had a place where I wanted to go to work.

In 1946, at age twenty-three, Scott Meredith formed his literary agency. He looked out at a wide range of independent publishers prepared to buy hardcover books and an extensive array of anthology magazines publishing short fiction to nurture and launch writers' careers. Meanwhile, Pocket Books published Dr. Spock's *Baby and Child Care* as an original paperback, and the rack-size mass market paperback business grew out of its success. I was born the following year.

By the time I left for Yale in 1965, Scott Meredith had sold thousands of books and short pieces of fiction. Norman Mailer was a worldwide success. The biggest chain bookseller was Doubleday, with fewer than a dozen stores. There were about a dozen independent, successful mass market publishers, whose genre lines began to cut into the audience for anthology magazines. Publishers were generally a privately held, fierce and independent group, and the conglomerates had yet to discover the publishing business. No one had paid as much as $250,000 in advances for rights to a paperback book (Pocket Books would do the honors with Jacqueline Susann several years later).

When I joined Janklow and Traum in 1973, Dayton Hudson had just begun to build the B. Dalton chain of bookstores with about 20,000 titles each, and Carter Hawley had begun building the Walden chain with about 12,000 titles each. Conglomerates were on the scene—RCA had bought Random House, Gulf & Western Simon & Schuster, MCA Putnam, CBS Fawcett, and so on. Robert Ludlum could sell 250,000 hardcovers and be the number one book in a year James Michener wasn't publishing. The paperback marketplace was king. Books such as *Jaws, The Godfather,* and *The Exorcist* sold more than 10 million copies, and seven-figure paperback rights auctions were frequent events. The anthology magazines for fiction were failing one by one.

In the ten years starting in 1973 that Janklow, Traum, and I were building our agency, Scott Meredith became more and more successful at his. By 1983, when I sold my interest in the agency back to Janklow and went out on my own, Dalton and Walden had more than 1,000 stores each. The paperback houses were growing tired of losing money on most of their seven-figure advances. The paperback sales business was flat. Each year, no more than twenty-five new titles industry-wide shipped 1 million units or more. Sales over 3 million copies were a rare event. Meanwhile, the hardcover book enjoyed ever broader distribution. Discounting and the extended number of points of sale started to open up the hardcover market.

In 1980, Sidney Sheldon was very successful because he could sell 250,000 hardcovers and nearly 3 million paperbacks. The emergence of superstores Barnes & Noble and Borders, with 150,000 titles in the store and warehouse selling clubs with 125 high-selling titles, would change the hardcover landscape. Sidney Sheldon would grow to sell 750,000 hardcovers and the same 3 million paperbacks. Soon enough, each year a handful of new hardcover titles would sell more than 1 million copies and one or two would sell more than 2 million copies.

Before his death in 1993, Scott Meredith may not have recognized the publishing community he had entered as a young man. With the exception of smaller publishers like Workman and Kensington Publishing, there were no leading independent houses. Corporate consolidation would be the rule. The computer ordering systems of the booksellers were beginning to run the business. The publisher could only reach the marketplace by convincing the booksellers to preorder an appropriate number of books, even though the books were returnable. The booksellers increasingly relied on an author's prior sales, indeed even the pace of prior sales, as the determining factor of how many books they would order upfront for a new title. Thus, computer-aggregated sales numbers punished the professionally accomplished author after any book that had a dip in sales. While the numbers reflected the past, they couldn't project the future. The publishers had begun to emphasize large commitment projects at the expense of trying valid smaller projects. Somehow, the chance to lose a large advance was an acceptable risk, but the chance to continue investing in an author's career was not.

Had Meredith lived a few more years, he would have seen Bertelsmann take control of Ballantine, Fawcett, Dell, and Bantam, all once proud independent houses, and with them nearly two-thirds of every mass market science fiction title sold in the publishing business (and more or less similar consolidation in the UK). Bertelsmann would also own or control the marketing of both major book club groups—Book-of-the-Month Club and the Literary Guild. He would have seen three groups—Simon & Schuster (Viacom/Redstone), HarperCollins (NewsCorp/Murdoch), and Penguin (Pearson) scramble to reach $1 billion in annual revenues as the minimum necessary to challenge the much larger Bertelsmann. Other publishers would be a fraction of their size. He would have seen the markets dry up for most beginners and many professional writers with less than stellar sales. And he would have seen the new selling space of the Web and books-on-demand open the playing field on a set of rules yet to be written.

ELEVEN

Backlists and Frontlists

My primary focus for new business was the progressive growth of my ongoing clients. Publishers and agents find that the backbone of their business is the author with numerous successful books and an ever-growing backlist. When Mayo Clinic followed me as a client to Scott Meredith, I worked out a fee-sharing arrangement with IMG on a second edition of the *Family Health Book*. I did the Mayo Clinic publishing work while IMG collected the commissions on the two-book open contract for the *Mayo Clinic Heart Book* and *Complete Book of Pregnancy & Baby's First Year*. My first new assignment was to help Mayo's electronic publishing partner, IVI, renegotiate the terms of an electronic license with Morrow for the *Family Health Book*. When I completed the assignment, I had helped achieve another industry breakthrough—the first seven-figure CD-ROM rights advance for a single title. This was part of Mayo Clinic's step by step move into the electronic world.

My next assignment was to renegotiate the original contract for the *Family Health Book* as the Mayo Clinic team prepared for a substantial editorial revision. Since sales of the first edition had exceeded 700,000 copies at $40 each, there was much to discuss. The final agreement rewrote large sections of the first contract and better reflected Mayo Clinic's role as a book marketer in its own right. The second edition of the *Family Health Book* arrived with great success in 1996. Mayo bought 80,000 books from the first printing, a sign of the growing strength of their direct marketing programs.

Mayo Medical Ventures expanded in many directions, including medical information for the corporate and insurance markets. Their editorial capabilities grew. My challenge was to focus the Mayo team on publishing opportunities that were significant enough to justify their allocation of resources. I knew that any Mayo Clinic book addressing diet would be successful. As an institution, Mayo Clinic shied away from what they called the "d" word, since so many diets were unhealthy. Of course, Mayo Clinic had a major commitment to nutrition, with an entire department and many internally published materials, including recipes, and patients throughout the institution had nutritional plans built into their care.

Because of my representation of Sheila Lukins, from time to time, other cookbook authors were in touch about representation. Michael Levine, the Toronto lawyer who had inadvertently started me on the path to the Pope's column when he suggested Robert Ballard, called to introduce me to Anne Lindsay, who was, and is, the "cooking queen" of Canada. Anne Lindsay has enjoyed tremendous success in Canada with a series of cookbooks and frequently has the formal support of major Canadian medical societies. Her goal was to get more than the modest publication efforts she had achieved thus far in the American market. I explored this goal by bringing Anne Lindsay and representatives of the Canadian Medical Association (the equivalent of our American Medical Association) to Rochester, Minnesota, for day-long meetings with the Mayo Medical Ventures team. The concept was a collaborative project that Mayo Clinic would endorse and market in the United States.

The meeting and some follow-up got the Mayo team to focus on a cookbook, but not the one Anne Lindsay and the Canadians had in mind. While Mayo Clinic credits its physician contributors as editors and trains the editor physicians to act as public spokespeople for its books, the cover credits for a Mayo Clinic book are institutional. There is no "by"-line. So the collaborative project didn't go forward. However, as part of the review of the project, the Mayo team conferred with a colleague at Williams Sonoma. Williams Sonoma has a fabulously successful line of books sold in their stores, by direct response, and to the trade through Time Life. The Williams Sonoma call quickly produced another Rochester meeting.

This collaborative discussion led to a thirty dollar illustrated coffee table book, *The Mayo Clinic Williams Sonoma Healthy Cookbook*. The book has more than 200,000 copies in print. Mayo itself has sold more than 25,000 cookbooks. The negotiations for this project were principally with Weldon Owen, the book packager that handled the Williams Sonoma series. Since I got to spend a considerable amount of time with John Owen, this deal gave me a chance to deepen my own learning about the book packaging world. I made good use of this learning later for projects of my own.

I had long hoped to interest Mayo Medical Ventures in a line of disease-specific books published in trade paperback format. Several attempts to negotiate new major hardcover titles had ultimately gone nowhere in part because the publisher advances, while large, did not adequately cover the costs of preparing the books. The *Family Health Book* sold in record seven-figure numbers. The other titles sold more than 100,000 copies, respectable by any standard, but not enough to earn well beyond their advances. I had already failed to close seven-figure advance deals for multibook hardcover deals, so I focused on the trade paperback opportunity.

Editorially, the Mayo team could assemble a 55,000-word disease-specific trade paperback with several black-and-white line drawings with a small fraction of the resources necessary to deliver a fully illustrated major hardcover title. Trade paperback books are very inexpensive to print. A publishing arrangement that gave Mayo control of these books for direct selling could be very profitable. Controlling electronic rights to its content was very important to Mayo and very difficult to achieve, since any traditional publishing arrangement mandated that the trade publisher control the electronic rights. I knew that if I presented the right partner with the right deal format that a series of books could be created. I also knew that Mayo would finance the deal if that got them the deal structure they wanted.

The right partner was someone with strength in paperback distribution and promotion who would value the association with Mayo Clinic and be flexible enough to negotiate what amounted to a distribution deal. Walter Zacharius, owner of Kensington Books, was that person. Walter Zacharius and Peter Workman were among very few living publishers picked out by *Publishers Weekly* as "movers and shakers" in its 125th anniversary issue. Kensington, a privately held company, is the principal competitor to Harlequin Books in the mass market. When I presented this opportunity to Walter, he personally and eagerly pursued an eighteen-month process to woo and sign Mayo Clinic to a distribution arrangement. The series is now expanding to ten books, with several new titles debuting annually. A typical book has a press run of more than 50,000 copies. Mayo is very successful selling the books in their own world, and Mayo and Kensington work closely to try and build the trade life for the series.

Mayo's publishing program, of course, is about more than profit and loss. The titles represent Mayo Clinic to the public. In part, that extends the educational mission of Mayo Clinic and its wish to encourage good medical habits. In part, the publishing program associates Mayo Clinic in the mind of the public with top quality health information, going to the heart of Mayo's life as a medical institution. Today, you can watch for Mayo Clinic's regular four-page advertising inserts in *Publishers Weekly* or visit their booths at the Frankfurt, London, or Chicago Book Fairs. The third edition of the *Family Health Book* is in preparation. My next goal (an ever harder challenge) is to convince the Mayo team of another worthy extension of their publishing program.

My most productive individual client continued to be Sheila

Lukins, whom I had represented since 1983. After more than ten years as partners, Sheila Lukins and Julee Rosso had decided to go their separate ways in 1991. I had little trouble deciding to continue as Sheila Lukins's agent after the split. Walter Anderson of *Parade* magazine decided to continue the monthly column with Sheila as its sole author. Workman decided to publish Lukins's solo books, the first of which was to interpret food throughout the world in her kitchen. Lukins toured the world working on what would become the *All Around the World Cookbook*. Lukins nearly died of a stroke in 1992, but recovered and wrote movingly of her experience in *Parade*. The publication of *All Around the World* got more media attention than any of Sheila's prior books. The book confirmed her arrival as a solo star in the world of cooking.

After *All Around the World* came the very successful *USA Cookbook*. Lukins traveled the fifty states to interpret the best of America's cooking in her kitchen. The *USA Cookbook* set another industry first. I arranged through Stuart Oran, a friend who had become general counsel for United Airlines, for Lukins to create recipes and menus for United's coach cabin. Run by United's Larry DeShon, the program was introduced on millions of airline trays as Workman launched the book. The corporate tie-in generated lots of publicity both for United and Workman. Sheila prepared recipes for the Lamb Council, for the Catfish Institute, and designed menu programs for newly opened Florida hotels. The United program launched efforts with a series of chefs, and a promotion that would normally last less than a year lasted three. Sheila is well underway with her next cookbook, which promises to be as successful as her others. Representing Sheila Lukins is that professional rarity: combining a gratifying friendship with a business association, a dedicated creative professional, and a serious money-making opportunity. Not your everyday business deal.

Sheila's publisher, Peter Workman, deserved his *Publishers Weekly* 125th anniversary designation as a mover and shaker. He was typically celebrated for clever marketing and packaging presentations of his new books. This often disguised his careful attention to his backlist. Open a publisher's catalog and you will almost always see only the newest offerings. Open a Workman catalog and you will see two-thirds of the pages dedicated to backlist. Check the promotional expenditures of typical publishers and they will be overwhelmingly dedicated to the frontlist. Check a Workman list and you will nearly always see a backlist promotion. Check a typical publisher and they are always thinking about adding titles to next season's list. Not Workman. He will tell you that he is looking for a stronger title for the same size list.

Fifteen years into Sheila's monthly food column for *Parade,* Walter Anderson and I negotiated a five-year contract for her that must be one of the largest magazine contributor contracts in the industry. Soon thereafter, Walter became publisher, a well-deserved promotion. I introduced him to Mayo Clinic, which became a frequent source for medical information. After Carl Sagan died, I also proposed and Walter agreed that Lisa Edwards's client David Levy ultimately become the science editor. Walter also regularly dealt directly with Bill Bradley, whose articles typically ran on the cover. Walter and *Parade* continue to be one of my favorite relationships. I wish only that I had more suitable material. With some clients I had better luck with my material—and more of it to work with.

For example, my better ideas for Roger Tory Peterson somehow cropped up in odd circumstances. What became Easton's 1 million-plus copy selling Roger Tory Peterson leatherbound Field Guide series came out of the ride with Roger on the New Jersey Turnpike. The idea to present what became the beautiful twelve-inch by seventeen-inch facsimile book of Peterson's Field Guide Art came to me driving in traffic from my Connecticut house to Roger's home and studio in Old Lyme, Connecticut. I asked Roger when I arrived if he would cooperate with such a book. He said no one would commit the money to do it. I asked whether he would cooperate if they did. David Ward of Easton Press committed to the project based on a telephone call. Easton ultimately did very well with the books.

Board meetings of the Roger Tory Peterson Institute for Natural History were often scheduled in good birding spots. To reach one of these meetings in Naples, Florida, our small plane encountered terrible crosswinds and turned back to land one hundred miles away. With several other Board members, I ultimately arrived by car. During some part of this awful trip, I thought about a beautiful coffee table book that would be a Roger Tory Peterson résumé of more than fifty years of achievements. Roger was in his mid-eighties. I saw this book as something we could use for decades for Peterson licensing and publishing presentations. Roger agreed to cooperate. I sold the book to Charles Miers of Rizzoli. Rudy Hoaglund, a very talented designer and skilled birder, culled Roger's archives and designed the book. William Zinsser, a wonderful writer who, like me, is not a birder, contributed a first-class text. Published as *The Art and Photography of Roger Tory Peterson, the World's Foremost Birder,* the trade edition generated broad publicity, including a "Man of the Week" interview with Peter Jennings. Easton's signed leather-bound edition promptly sold out.

After Roger's death at age eighty-seven (he was painting the day he died), I got my first opportunity to represent the Field Guides. Roger had represented himself since 1934. With his widow, Virginia, and Roger's protégés Noble Proctor and Pete Dunne, we organized the fifth edition of the *Eastern Guide to the Birds* (to be published in spring 2002). The *Eastern Guide* has been the lead title for the series since its publication in 1934. The book has been named one of the one hundred most important books of the twentieth century by the New York Public Library. Houghton Mifflin published a facsimile edition of the 1934 edition to emphasize its importance. The fifth edition will arrive twenty years after the fourth edition and invigorate the series for decades to come.

The Roger Tory Peterson collectibles licensing programs had quieted down by the mid-1990s, even though MBI referred in its corporate materials to a company built on three licenses—Norman Rockwell, M. S. Hummel, and Roger Tory Peterson. My goal for some time was to relaunch the Peterson licensing program in a major way. I also thought it was important to maintain centralized licensing control over the Peterson name and archive. Rockwell, for example, was licensed through the family for the major Bradford

Exchange program, through the *Saturday Evening Post* covers for the MBI program, and through the Museum in Stockbridge, Massachusetts, for other programs. Hummel's paintings were the basis of the collectible Hummel figurines. But the rights-holders included the owners of the painting images in two dimensions on the one hand, and the figurine company for three dimensional images on the other.

The circumstance that led to the major Peterson license was again a difficult trip. I traveled with Ardith Grandbouche, very talented businesswoman, on a two-city West Coast day of meetings to explore an interesting vitamin regime book. The project never happened, but since we had hours to talk in airplanes and cars, I learned that Ardith was coincidentally an investor in Proprietary Media, a company formed to explore cause marketing opportunities for the American Zoo & Aquarium Association (AZA). The AZA represented nearly 190 zoos and aquariums in the United States and Canada. The member institutions had 130 million annual visitors and nearly 10 million active contributors. Nonetheless, their corporate support programs were modest and not unified, their gift shops, measured on a dollar per visitor basis, unproductive, and their need for funding ever escalating. Proprietary Media had a long-term contract with the AZA to maximize their private sector opportunities without compromising their mission. They had already commissioned Kermit Love, the creator of Big Bird, to create "Aza," the character who would represent AZA.

Ardith arranged for me to meet Natasha Rabin and Jeffrey Moritz, the talented principals of Proprietary Media. I proceeded to spend months convincing them and their team that an alliance with the Roger Tory Peterson name and archive would be great for both parties. The first breakthrough came when they realized that two-thirds of the AZA board were avid birders and Peterson fans. The second key reading was the number of senior people within the AZA world whose lives, professional and personal, had been touched by Roger. The third, and more morbid observation, was that Roger in death could be a "legend" and avoid any competitive feelings among accomplished naturalists at the various institutions.

I wanted the broadest possible role for Roger Tory Peterson and his archive in the AZA world. The visibility and remuneration could be enormous and continuing. The on-site selling opportunities had implications for the Houghton Mifflin book series and any other merchandise we could create. The sponsorship tie-in opportunities at the core of Proprietary Media's skill-set and revenue objectives were exciting. I needed an idea to persuade Proprietary Media and the AZA to adopt this broad role. My pitch became that Roger as a "character"—animated on their Web site, created as Kermit Love had created Aza—could teach photography to children and families and that Roger as a character could join the "AZA family."

This concept excited Proprietary Media and the AZA. Ultimately, we negotiated a long-term master license that committed Proprietary Media to significant investment in digitizing and marketing the Peterson photographic and motion picture archive. The license contemplated a range of sponsorship opportunities for the Peterson character and tie-ins for existing Peterson publishing efforts. We planned to find a range of ways to develop and market new Peterson products. The license was announced with fanfare at the 2000 annual meeting of the approximately 2,000 senior executives of zoos and aquariums in the United States. As we head toward the 2002 release of the fifth edition of the *Eastern Guide,* all of this will be widely marketed. Unfortunately, Virginia Peterson, who guided these efforts, died in April 2001. If life is fair, she will see this all in the spirit of the butterflies she loved so deeply.

One of the advantages of owning your own agency is that you can select the projects you wish to represent. In 1994, a Yale classmate Norman Resnicow called to ask if I could help his father, Herbert Resnicow, with a new project. Herb Resnicow had come late in life to writing after a successful career in construction. He became active as a mystery writer, often collaborating with the likes of Tom Seaver or Pele. Resnicow had a dozen ideas, but one got my attention: a murder mystery series with New York City Mayor Ed Koch as a detective in City Hall. I thought that this was would be perfect for Walter Zacharius and I knew that Sheila Lukins, a good friend of Ed

Koch, could get me an introduction.

Zacharius was ready to buy two books for $100,000 each if I could get Ed Koch to agree. Resnicow and I went to visit Koch in his New York City law offices. Koch graciously heard us out, said he was interested but that there was a problem: He was represented by William Morris. I said that I could work with his William Morris agent and split the commission, or that William Morris could waive their commission on this deal and I could handle it all. Koch thought that central responsibility made more sense, and with us there in the room, he placed a call to Robert Gottlieb, then William Morris's top literary agent, and insisted on a commission waiver. I hoped that I wouldn't have occasion soon to ask Gottlieb for a favor for Easton Press. I commented to Koch that I could see how he had been effective in union negotiations.

The Koch murder mystery series was a lot of fun, clouded only by Resnicow's death before Zacharius committed to books three and four. One of my most amusing author/publisher meetings involved taking Koch to meet a team of Kensington people led by Zacharius to discuss the launch of the first book. Zacharius explained that they had researched renting a hot air balloon in Central Park. Regulations forbade the balloon rising above a certain number of feet. The balloon would be decorated with the title and jacket of the book. Koch jumped in and said this reminded him of an evening as mayor and an anniversary for the circus. A trainer was walking around with a live tiger and someone shouted out, "The Mayor should pet the tiger." Koch said, "The Mayor will not pet the tiger." The man in the crowd tried again, "Is the Mayor a coward?" Koch answered, "The Mayor is not a coward but the Mayor is not a schmuck." Zacharius went with a more traditional promotional plan.

Resnicow wrote the manuscript for the first Koch book, *Murder at City Hall*. Wendy Wasserstein, the playwright, gave the book an excellent review in the *New York Times*. Resnicow took Koch to a meeting of the Mystery Writers Association, where Koch enjoyed presenting himself as a mystery writer. We were all following in Scott Meredith's footsteps from *The Senator* by Drew Pearson.

Meanwhile, a good book could transform the identity of the author. My Yale urban mentor Alexander Garvin had spent nearly twenty-five years of his life documenting planning issues in seventy-five American cities. He had his own six hundred photographs and a long text detailing what was right and wrong about twentieth-century urban planning. This was an important work. Trade publishers admired the manuscript but backed away from the scale of the project. Increasingly, trade houses were leaving to the university presses the more serious works of nonfiction which over the years had become the spine of their backlists. The university presses were themselves introducing commercial criteria (often misguided) where merit used to be the governing rule.

I asked my uncle Nathan Glazer, who knew Garvin's work in general, to read the manuscript. He was impressed and gave a strong testimonial quote. He also forwarded the manuscript to the Harvard University Press with his support. The editor at Harvard also endorsed the book. His editorial board turned the book down on the logic that there was not a broad enough market interested in the subject of cities. We recruited McGraw-Hill Companies to publish the book. They produced a handsome book, which used all of Garvin's photography. The book, titled *The American City: What Works, What Doesn't*, won a wide range of awards, including an award from McGraw-Hill for best publishing project in its division. The book has gone through several printings, has been profitable for McGraw-Hill, and will stay in print for many years.

The publication and publicity transformed Garvin from a man with a worthy and complex resume into Alexander Garvin, author of the award-winning book *The American City*. Now a member of the New York City Planning Commission, Garvin is frequently invited to speak and consult across the country. He also heads a group trying to figure out the planning implications of New York City as host to a future summer Olympics Games. His students at Yale are lucky enough to develop proposed plans for parts of New York City and present them over a weekend to a panel of high-level officials and professionals. Books do not have to be best-sellers to make a difference for their authors, nor do they have to be best-sellers to make a difference for society.

My friend Ellen Chesler had a similar experience after publishing *A Woman of Valor*, a highly praised biography of Margaret Sanger, the birth control activist. While Ellen and I were disappointed by the lack of marketing support from Simon & Schuster despite strong front-page reviews, the book vaulted Ellen into a visible group of biographers of women and helped it make it possible for her to serve George Soros's foundations in their domestic and international initiatives for women.

Jerry Traum's friend Joe Jaworski (son of Leon Jaworski, the Watergate prosecutor) spent years writing an amazing personal business journey book published as *Synchronicity*. Rejected by the larger houses, who couldn't relate to its personal message, the book has sold more than 75,000 copies and achieved everything its author hoped it might.

The transforming book was every bit as satisfying from my perspective as the book that hits the best-seller list. Curiously enough, if you check the best-seller lists of decades ago, you will find very few books that matter today either as a matter of impact or as a matter of sales. Fortunately, I could afford to make an effort when I wished. That was the true freedom I valued.

TWELVE

....

Civil Society

Bill Bradley called me each year or so after he was elected to the Senate in 1978 to discuss writing a book. The conversation would go something like this: Bradley would describe his then current thinking about a book. I would ask if he was open to collaborative help. He would say no, that any book of his would be only his written words. Then I would ask whether he saw himself having the time to invest in writing a book. He would say, "Not really." We would take the opportunity of the call to catch up on other subjects.

In the spring of 1995, Bradley called me to say that he had, in fact, completed a manuscript after three years of work at night and had a contract on his desk from Knopf, but felt he needed my advice. He invited me to Washington to have dinner with him and his wife, Ernestine. I learned at dinner that Ernestine was the only person other than Bill who had seen the manuscript. The contract was a result of Bradley's relationship with Jonathan Segal, who had been his editor for *Life on the Run* and now worked at Knopf. Bradley had described the book in a meeting at Knopf, but had shown them nothing. Paul Gitlin, Bradley's longtime agent (whose most prominent client was Harold Robbins), had negotiated a $400,000 advance for the book.

Bradley confided in me that night that he had decided not to run for reelection to the Senate in 1996, but that the timing and manner of his retirement and announcement were still to be determined. He wanted the announcement of publication of the book to be part of the retirement announcement. It was clear to me then, as he said later publicly, that he was retiring from the Senate, but not from public life. To accept the book advance or not was not a simple question. Under Senate ethics rules, it was clear that a Senator could publish a book with a legitimate publisher and keep any advances and royalties without limit. Bradley had a letter from the Ethics Committee to that effect about the Knopf offer.

However, Newt Gingrich, the Republican Speaker of the House of Representatives, had just pushed the public appearances limit by accepting a $4 million advance from HarperCollins, when its parent, Rupert Murdoch's NewsCorp, had substantial regulatory concerns. Curiously, no such issues had been raised years before when Random House, owned by S. I. Newhouse, had signed a seven-figure advance with then Speaker of the House Tip O'Neill. At the time, Newhouse and his brother Donald had pending the largest estate tax dispute ever with the Internal Revenue Service. It settled favorably, but no one questioned the appearance of conflict.

The Gingrich deal colored the issues. Bradley was not personally wealthy. Senators have virtually no legitimate ways to supplement their government income, one reason why so many Senators are independently wealthy to start with. The money offered Bradley was attractive. Again, the problem was that there was no way to solve the appearances issue if you took an advance. Bradley and I independently agreed that the press would question him about how much he was paid upfront for the book. If the answer pointed to any significant fixed amount of money, he would be lumped with Gingrich and attacked on all sides. The only solution was to take an advance of one dollar.

I thought I could negotiate some commitments from Knopf which would make a poor royalty performance for the book unlikely. First, I urged Bradley to let Knopf read the manuscript. Should Knopf not be enthusiastic or want too substantial a set of editorial changes, now was the time to find out. We could always get another publisher. If Knopf was enthusiastic, I thought I could get two commitments without telling them of Bradley's future plans. First, we could get a specific publication date of January 1996, which would tie in nicely with the Senate retirement press conference. Second, we could get a commitment of "lead" title treatment, which simply meant the book would be Knopf's number one nonfiction title effort that month. The combination would hopefully assure a best-seller.

Books that hit the *New York Times* hardcover nonfiction bestseller list tended to need a minimum printing of 100,000 copies. After returns, a book might net fewer copies than that if the appearance on the list was for a few weeks and only near the bottom. Hardcover books had a suggested retail price of about twenty-five dollars. The royalty rate to the author was typically 15 percent of the retail selling price. So a hardcover author stood to make more than $3.50 per copy on sales net of returns. A best-seller likely meant a value close to $350,000, more if the book did better yet as a best-seller with additional values from the book club, paperback sales, and foreign rights. Bradley and I met with Paul Gitlin, who had negotiated the initial offer, to work out my role. We shook hands that with the circumstances Gitlin and I would split the commission. Knopf quickly agreed to what we wanted. Jonathan Segal worked well with Bradley in editing the manuscript over the summer. All of the arrangements were set for the book's launch.

Bradley called me again to Washington for an informal Chinese takeout dinner at his home to discuss whether he should challenge Bill Clinton for renomination in 1996 and/or whether he should consider running as an independent candidate for president in the 1996 general election. Doug Berman, one of Bradley's closest political confidants, chaired the informal session. I thought Bradley was really testing himself and the idea rather than seriously considering making a race. It was already too late to think about the early primaries. The state by state delegate filing issues were complex and required tremendous organization, and, of course, challenging a sitting president was no simple task. The independent option had to deal with the reality of Ross Perot, who did ultimately run. There was no room for two independent candidates.

Bradley formed a small circle including Peter Goldmark, whom I knew from my Lindsay days, to monitor political developments for the next few months. I found the prospect of a challenge to Clinton exhilarating and told Bradley that I would make any necessary adjustments with my business to work at his side. Our planning group (including Bradley) spoke by conference call a few times and exchanged briefings, but it was clear to me that this was not the real thing. What most interested me was Bradley's total comfort with the idea of challenging Clinton. This was, of course, before Monica Lewinsky and his impeachment were even on the public horizon. Bradley, I think, simply didn't think much of Bill Clinton, the man or the president, and felt that he could do a better job. I agreed.

Meanwhile, Anita Dunn, Bradley's expert communications adviser, arranged a brilliantly staged two-day press event for his resignation from the Senate. The statement emphasized that while he was resigning from the Senate, he was not resigning from public life. At the press conference the day after the announcement (I learned that you get a two-day story by announcing and taking no questions on day one and then calling a press conference to discuss the announcement on day two), Bradley spoke about the book. A reporter immediately asked about the advance. When Bradley said, "One dollar," it was not even referenced in any of the stories. Bradley spoke about the book in some detail, so the planned publication received enormous national visibility.

To keep the Senate announcement confidential, we couldn't brief Knopf in advance, and contrary to what publishers normally like to do, the author rather than the publisher, was, in effect, announcing the book. I had to do some fencing with the Knopf publicity people, but the results excited everyone.

Bradley as an author wanted to get involved with every detail of the publication process. He attended a publicity planning meeting, the direct opposite of my experience with Nixon. At the meeting, Bradley asked, "What is the best thing that would support the launch of the book?" The answer, "A twenty-minute piece on one of the prime time television news shows." Bradley's follow-up question, "Which one?" Then silence. I stepped in to point out that typically the publisher can't get their authors on any of these shows, and the idea of choice is more than a little uncommon. Bradley chose Diane Sawyer and *20/20*. The resulting interview helped launch the book.

The book, *Time Present, Time Past*, was published in January 1996 to good reviews and excellent coverage. The book was on the *New York Times* best-seller list for fourteen weeks, rising as high as number four. It was a success in every sense. Bradley did everything he could to bring the book to the attention of the public. This included a series of calls to Len Riggio, the owner of Barnes & Noble, who has a serious interest in politics. As for the book itself, I loved reading it, partly because of my political interests from Yale days onward and partly years of admiration for Bradley. In his acknowledgments, Bradley wrote, "I thank my agents: Paul Gitlin, who kept getting deals too generous for me to accept, and Art Klebanoff, who knew why I wouldn't accept them." This was not an endorsement likely to bring me commercial clients, but gratifying nonetheless.

Gitlin, meanwhile, refused to pay my half of the commission, calling me "Bill's friend," whom he thought was working for free. Bradley intervened, since the handshake had been in front of him. Gitlin tried to buy me off with a promise of $5,000. Rather than fight, I accepted. Gitlin then failed to pay again. The net effect of Gitlin's behavior was that I didn't have a commission on *Time Present, Time Past* (although I did have the public credit), but I did have Bill Bradley as a future client. I would have made the trade any day.

Late in 1996, Bradley came for a rare visit to my office. My guess was that he would run for president in 2000. Since it had been more than twenty years between *Life on the Run* and *Time Present, Time*

Past, and since I knew he would insist on writing his own material and had very little free time, I asked Bradley how he felt about a visual book on a basketball theme which could be based on a short-ish essay (under 15,000 words). I told him that I thought I could get him a $100,000 advance for the essay. Knowing how careful he was in decision making, I got him to commit in principle to the project if I could deliver the deal, which I doubt he thought was likely. With one telephone call to Peter Workman, I had the buyer for what became *Values of the Game.*

Bradley joined me for a meeting with Workman and Ann Bransom, the publisher of Artisan Publishers imprint that published the book. We set up a schedule that would permit the book to become Artisan's lead title for fall 1998. Bradley wrote a wonderful series of short essays relating the aspects of the game of basketball to life itself. For business people, there were the issues of leadership, management, and entrepreneurship. For families, the essays represented the heart of family values. For basketball fans, of course, there was Bradley on the game itself. For voters, there was Bradley's background in a thematic book without once explicitly dealing with a political subject.

Artisan published the book with Workman flair. Walter Anderson published a piece from the book as a cover story in *Parade.* Television and print coverage was fabulous. The pictorial book at thirty dollars hit the *New York Times* best-seller list, rose as high as number four, and stayed more than ten weeks on the list. In an extremely unusual development, Broadway Books bought the right to publish the text only in paperback form for a $200,000 advance. Bradley's handwritten inscription in my copy read, "To Art Klebanoff, who made the book possible." The book became not only part of Bradley's résumé for a presidential race, but a fundamental part of his life when the contest was over.

As Bradley organized for his presidential race, my wife, Susan, and I did what we could to help. We raised money and urged others to do so. I attended some early planning meetings and heard two good humored pledges—one to maintain his very informal jacket attire and the other to avoid plastic surgery for extra skin under his chin. I pledged to try and organize a campaign "first"—an illustrated manifesto that would convey the message of the campaign. In publishing terms, this would be a miniature of *Values of the Game*. Workman signed on again as the publisher.

The book became a small symbol of the campaign itself. All went pretty smoothly in the early going. When it came time to accelerate the process and push for publication, Bradley's campaign team balked, out of fear that the book might be "off-message" when published. We put the book on hold. By the time there was any reconsideration of the book, Bradley had already withdrawn from the race.

No doubt Bradley made mistakes in the race (and he will be first to admit it), but my own feeling is that the core Democratic voter was simply too loyal to Clinton to change horses in the context of prosperity at home and peace abroad. Bradley was right that he was the stronger general election candidate, but I am not sure that he could have persuaded the Democratic primary voter to agree with him, or even to vote on that basis if they did. I did get the curious opportunity to witness Moynihan endorse Bradley with a forceful explanation: "because Gore is a good fellow, but can't be elected president." Moynihan proved right, although not by much.

Bradley called me the day after his withdrawal to thank me for my help. I told him important people here and abroad would still look to him for leadership and inspiration and that the race, no matter how disappointing, had opened doors of opportunity for this next phase of his life. In terms of my personal relationship, we were able to reassemble the campaign book and have Workman publish it in the fall of 2000 as *The Journey from Here*. The themes within the book (and the campaign), best summarized as "a Civil Society" (government, the not-for-profit sector, and people working together for a purpose), had been Bradley themes for years.

As the license with Proprietary Media and the American Zoo & Aquarium Association took shape, I realized that there was a strong role for Bradley with the AZA since what they were pursuing with the cause marketed effort represented the very Civil Society Bradley wrote and spoke about. Here was a major representative of the not-for-profit sector looking to influence the environmental policies of government, yet motivate the individual conduct of millions of citizens. The themes of *Values of the Game* also resonated with a range of programs the AZA ran for children, particularly when the themes were extended to protecting the planet. I conceptualized and negotiated a license for Bradley to become a spokesperson for the AZA, an appointment that was announced at the Shedd Aquarium in Chicago in May 2001. Part of the arrangement invited Bradley to solicit appropriate sponsorships for the AZA by introducing Proprietary Media to chief executive officers of the target companies.

When Natasha Rabin and Jeffrey Moritz met Bradley for the first working meeting, there was a good chance to see Bradley's self-deprecating humor in action. A friend of Natasha Rabin's had wanted to introduce her to Bradley as a date during his Princeton years. She had declined because he was too tall. After Natasha told the story, Bradley told a story of his own. He had apparently told his parents that he would come East to look at Princeton for school if he could go to Philadelphia and appear on *Dick Clark's American Bandstand*. Bradley had watched the show in St. Louis and wanted a chance to dance with the attractive girls. When he appeared, the girls found him too tall, so Bradley explained to Natasha that her reaction was hardly unique.

When Hillary Clinton was elected to the Senate and considered her book deal, Bradley's approach to the $1 advance for *Time Present, Time Past* could have been her standard. Instead, we had the spectacle of broadcast meetings in the White House with publishers and an advance of $8 million. When Gingrich took a large book advance from HarperCollins, whose owner Rupert Murdoch had regulatory dealings with the federal government, the negative reaction forced withdrawal of the advance proposal. When Hillary Clinton took double that advance from Simon & Schuster, whose parent Viacom and owner Sumner Redstone have at least as broad a range of regulatory dealings with the federal government, the reaction, in general, was to leave her alone. I might have enjoyed the fee on Hillary Clinton's book, but I wouldn't have traded clients.

Bradley's political loss and Moynihan's decision to retire in 2000 did not leave me without a friend in the Senate. My wife and I promised to run Chuck Schumer's first fundraiser the moment he chose between the Senate and Gubernatorial races in 1998. The $50,000 we raised was a small part of Chuck's $17 million-plus war chest, but it made us feel good. In the primary, Schumer defeated the initially far better known Geraldine Ferraro and Mark Green by more than two to one, and went on to defeat three-term Senator Al d'Amato, upsetting the predictions of a wide range of political pundits.

I knew enough about electoral campaigns to keep my advice for Chuck at a distance. I did toss in the occasional memo. I did get to talk to Chuck shortly before the primary when the result seemed assured. All of the networks cover the "victory" statement briefly. Politicians often waste this air time with thank-yous to everyone in sight. I urged Chuck to use the air time to sound his themes against d'Amato and save the thank-yous until the cameras were off. He made a very effective statement that was widely covered and sounded the themes of the very combative general election. While Susan and I had been in Chuck's suite on primary night, we had a commitment to be in London for the night of the general election. With the victory, we collected the international papers and framed the clippings.

Mainly due to impeachment hearings delays, it took us a few months to schedule a small celebratory dinner. Our scheduling was influenced at least twice by the failure to get clearances from Henry Hyde as the Judiciary Committee hearings dragged on before Chuck's swearing in as Senator (Chuck would be one of the few to vote on Clinton's impeachment in both the House and the Senate). Our relationship didn't change, although the context did. Because of my wife's role with the Breast Cancer Research Foundation (chaired by Evelyn Lauder of the Estee Lauder Companies), the Estee Lauder CEO Leonard Lauder invited us to their home (decorated with their collection of Picassos and Braques) to "meet" Chuck and donate one thousand dollars toward his 2004 war chest. I would like to think there is more than enough time for Chuck to cross my business path again, as he did in 1983 when he sent Sheila Lukins to me as a client.

THIRTEEN

··

Brand Extensions

There can be a great deal more to measuring the success of a book project than the number of copies sold. And there can be much more opportunity for the agent than the commission as "agent of record" for the book. No client better illustrated these truths than Mike Bloomberg. I met him in 1995 through my friend Bernice Kanner, who covered the advertising and marketing worlds for *The Bloomberg, Bloomberg News,* Bloomberg Radio, and Bloomberg Television. I had given Bernice informal advice through the years on her career and introduced her to Walter Anderson (*Parade* became one the magazines for which she wrote). By introducing me to Bloomberg, she definitely returned the favor.

Bloomberg is the closest business model to what the founders of Dow Jones or Reuters were one hundred years before him. He had left Salomon Brothers ten years before with a $10 million check and set out to form a business that would provide real-time data to stock and bond traders on Wall Street. He convinced Merrill Lynch to back him, built the better mousetrap, and then marched step by step to a large worldwide business. I had heard about the business from Wall Street friends who spoke about his machine, *The Bloomberg,* as though it was their best friend. At a $15,000 per year minimum subscription, it had to be a good friend, and it is. One need only to visit the reception area of Bloomberg's Park Avenue headquarters or wander through his large, Princeton campus–like setting to understand that this is a business of the next century. Each work station lets a reporter go directly to radio or on-line. The television signal is produced by the on-air reporter with a sophisticated array of technological options at his fingertips. You feel the energy before you talk to anyone. The offices are alive.

When I first met Mike Bloomberg, he was uncertain about whether he wanted to write a book. We talked off and on. Myles Thompson, then the executive editor of John Wiley & Sons, who had shepherded George Soros and a book about Warren Buffett into bestsellers, was doing his best job of persuasion. Finally, Bloomberg called to discuss how we might work together since he was ready to write a book. Private meetings were frequently held outside his offices since Bloomberg's desk was in an open space like everyone else's. His small meeting space had glass walls, so many people knew who he was meeting and for how long. The communal conference spaces were also glass, to encourage short meetings.

Bloomberg's favorite meeting spot was Kaplan's deli. It was across the street from his office, and he could see his guest come in the front door. So we met at Kaplan's. Bloomberg had a request no other client has ever made. Since he was giving the royalty proceeds of the book to charity, he didn't care about an advance (that I had heard occasionally), but he insisted that he have the absolute right to cancel the project until the last possible moment. That right of cancellation was his primary contractual concern. As for paying me, his comment was, "I don't like paying commissions. I want your best advice without concern about whether the project goes forward." I said, "I don't argue with billionaires and, if I can tell others we are working together, you name the numbers and I will say yes." He laughed. After a meeting with his Princeton team, I was handed a consulting agreement, which I signed as submitted.

Matt Winkler, the head of *Bloomberg News,* helped Bloomberg put together a draft of the manuscript. This was one of the occasions to which I was invited to be a reader as well as an agent, and I was happy to offer my advice. The book was originally scheduled for publication by Wiley in fall 1996. Wiley set aside two pages in its catalog. Everyone was excited. There was one small problem. Bloomberg became convinced that the manuscript could be better if he put more time into it and his schedule didn't give him the time before the deadline for fall books. Precisely what Bloomberg had wanted to protect against had happened. I advised him that his publisher would be disappointed (it was) but everyone would support him (they did), and his increased efforts would make for a better manuscript (they did). More important, his name was on it, it would be a long time before he was likely to do another book, and he should feel good about it.

We canceled the fall publication. The book was published in the spring of 1997 after Bloomberg felt much better about the manuscript. The reviews were excellent, from *Fortune* to the *New York Times.* International publishers signed up and Bloomberg had successful launches in London, Berlin, Paris, Tokyo, and elsewhere. The book serves as a platform for Mike Bloomberg the man and Bloomberg the company here and abroad. The book also pushed Bloomberg's strong view that those who succeed financially should give something back, preferably while they are young and alive to enjoy it. In Bloomberg's case, in addition to broad-based philanthropy, he has given $100 million to his alma mater, Johns Hopkins, where he is now Chairman of the Board of Trustees. While the book's revenues have been modest, in some hard-to-define way the book has helped make both Bloomberg's personal reputation and the company grow.

Bloomberg has been nice enough to include my wife and me at several literary oriented charitable benefit tables his company has purchased. At a dinner to benefit PEN, the international writers organization, Bloomberg was singled out from the podium for his generosity. As he sat down, he commented to the table, "We must have overpaid for that table." On another occasion, he and Marjorie Scardino, the chief executive officer of Pearson, were honored by Literacy Partners. Bloomberg, Scardino, and I happened to be walking up the steps to the New York State Theater in Lincoln Center together. Bloomberg introduced me and said, "He's my literary agent. I have no idea what literary agents do." Bloomberg must have felt some level of comfort with what I did, since our consulting agreement is now entering its fifth year. I haven't been able to persuade him to consider another book ("The first was so successful, why take the risk?").

I don't think that Mike Bloomberg or any of his colleagues were thinking too seriously about the 2001 New York City Mayoral race as we worked on what has become a basic "résumé" book about the man. As the political possibility became more of a reality, I found myself at a Bloomberg reception announcing an Al d'Amato/Ed Koch show on Bloomberg Radio and talking for half an hour with Bloomberg and his pollster Doug Schoen. I have known Doug Schoen since his Harvard days. Doug wrote quite a good early biography of Moynihan. I had helped him source it and gain Moynihan's trust to cooperate. Doug had built a very successful political polling company that included Bill Clinton and Bill Gates among a broad range of clients.

Schoen was nice enough to brief Bloomberg about my political background and even to say that I could have built the business that he had if that had been my choice. We talked a bit as a trio about the upcoming race. I had a chance to offer again my simple advice to run on his résumé. Mike Bloomberg would be attacked for being a billionaire. He had earned it himself. It was, after all, the ultimate American dream. He would be attacked for failure to make full financial disclosures. Obviously, as a billionaire, he made a lot of money. Relevant to his public interests were his charitable commitments. Those would come under attack as calculated attempts to buy political support. I strongly advised him to stand up proudly just as he argued in his book. In his race for Mayor, the jacket photo became the basic

Bloomberg photo and the book itself was frequently referenced.

Bloomberg did become involved directly and indirectly in my first efforts as a book packager. My IMG experiences with the America's Cup book and with Hertz and the Williams Sonoma titles with Mayo Clinic had convinced me that there were opportunities in book packaging. As a book packager, you take the book through the whole process of editorial and production. Sometimes you risk your own capital (as IMG did on the America's Cup book), sometimes you rely upon the commitments of others (the Hertz book), and sometimes you have a blend (Mayo Clinic committing to buy books as part of the Williams Sonoma package). Some packagers hire agents to place their books with trade publishers, but more often than not perform the agenting function themselves. It is unusual for an agent to act as a packager.

The move into packaging was a natural progression for me. I had my own experience and a great deal of confidence in Christopher Johnson, the designer I had worked with on Hertz and the Scott Meredith repositioning. I had worked with trademarks, companies, designers, sources of distribution, public relations advisers, and publishers—pretty much everyone you would need to make these projects happen. Now I had a chance to test these relationships in action.

From my collectibles work, I was aware that the American Express desk diary program was one of the largest, most successful direct response book programs anywhere. I also knew that *The Economist* diary program at a much higher price point was very profitable for Pearson. I felt that a Bloomberg desk diary program could be very successful, particularly if accompanied by a CD-ROM (to reinforce the electronic Bloomberg audience) and designed as attractively as *The Economist* but priced competitively with American Express. I knew that Bloomberg magazines and the Web site had large reach and that the ongoing efforts to solicit advertising for the magazines and the Web site could offer bulk sale opportunities for the diary.

Bloomberg agreed to partner on the *Bloomberg Desk Diary and Reference Center 2000*. David Wachtel, who heads wide range of

Bloomberg's business divisions, supervised the project. I took the publishing risk, Christopher Johnson handled the design, and Bernice Kanner oversaw the editorial. The accompanying CD-ROM was built by the company Scott Klososky had formed after the Haldeman diaries project. The diary was first-rate, but we couldn't assemble the right combination of special sales, response from Bloomberg's on-line and magazine audience, and a trade edition from the Universe division of Rizzoli to make the economics work. The diary would, however, lead me in an entirely unpredictable way into serious Web companies.

The indirect connection between Bloomberg and my initiatives in book packaging was sourced in a referral. Bloomberg sent Richard Hurd, a New Jersey businessman, to see me about a publishing project. While the first project we discussed didn't work out, I learned that Hurd had access to Doug Hyde, the latest in a series of family CEOs of Oshkosh B'Gosh, the manufacturer of children's clothing. I saw a chance for us to approach Oshkosh B'Gosh to package books for them. We invited Christopher Johnson to join us in a pitch meeting in Oshkosh, Wisconsin. The key to the meeting was our offer to take the developmental risk if Hyde would commit to presenting the work to one of his leading clothing retailers. The principal Oshkosh retailers were Kids "R" Us, Sears, Penney and Federated Stores (Macy's, Bloomingdale's, and so on).

We convinced Doug Hyde to let us form Genuine Article Publishing Group, which would be dedicated to packaging books for Oshkosh. We and Oshkosh would both do very well if the publishing program was successful. Part of the deal contemplated that Oshkosh would sell the books prominently in their own 110 retail stores. Christopher Johnson handled design and production, and Bernice Kanner was our editorial director. The fourteen books we developed had the benefit of extensive focus group testing. With the help of Walter Anderson, we also secured the endorsement of the National Center for Family Literacy and its founder, Sharon Darling. For Christmas 1999, we introduced the first fourteen Oshkosh titles in the 110 owned and operated Oshkosh stores and at Toys "R" Us,

Kids "R" Us, and Babies "R" Us.

The better titles promptly sold through their initial 25,000-copy press runs. These numbers were high for a children's series, particularly for one in such narrow initial release. Simon & Schuster agreed to expand this concept into a thirty-title mass market series with a launch in the fall of 2001. Our primary objective of helping Oshkosh extend its brand into children's publishing had been achieved. Our parallel objective of creating a book packaging company to support the project did not work out, as Oshkosh grew more comfortable assuming responsibility itself.

Christopher Johnson and I went on to form a partnership to explore packaged book projects. In addition to the Oshkosh series and the *Bloomberg Desk Diary,* we pitched projects without success. We wanted the American Film Institute to create a tie-in book for its 100 Greatest Movies project. We asked Christie Hefner and her senior team at *Playboy* for permission to create a series of coffee table books combining commissioned essays from leading fiction writers on a sexual theme with archival photographic, line illustration, and cartoon imagery. We made a strong presentation to create a 100-year anniversary book for Pepsi, so strong, in fact, that Christopher Johnson left the room with other marketing assignments from Pepsi. Our book proposals were more than strong enough. We simply didn't persuade the partner. In May 2001, Christopher sold his business to Magnet Communications, a unit of Havas North America. This would open yet more future opportunities.

I increasingly realized that the wave of technology changes here and coming represented opportunities in publishing. I had never been an early adopter of technology. In 1979, Linda Goodman presented us with an IBM Memory typewriter. If I remember correctly, the machine cost more than $5,000, barely handled twenty pages of memory, couldn't cut and paste, and took two people to lift it up. In 1988, my assistant Mary Jo Valko talked me into doing all of my own word processing with the argument that she couldn't take dictation and work at the same time. My choice was a machine, or training and paying a second assistant. That computer cost more than $7,500 and had very limited flexibility. Bernice Kanner had embarrassed me into adopting e-mail or risk my client relationship with the Bloomberg team, one of the first companies to be hard to find by letter or fax.

In 1998, the Toronto lawyer Michael Levine introduced me to Mitchell Bring, a successful Web architect whose core work involved creating on-line economic development packages for state governments and utilities, typically with IBM as his partner. Mitchell, trained as a (physical) architect and a teacher, wanted to find a way to use his electronic skills to transform the consumer experience on the Web. Mitchell and I agreed to swap our respective expertise until we figured out how to do something useful together. Mitchell walked me through a series of development deals with IBM, including prospects with McGraw-Hill and the *Book Review* section of the *New York Times*. Months of effort persuaded me that the big companies didn't know much that small companies couldn't execute faster and cheaper.

While I was educating myself with Mitchell, developing the CD-ROM for the *Bloomberg Desk Diary* gave me a chance to work closely again with Scott Klososky, who had created the CD-ROM with Sony for *The Haldeman Diaries*. In 1999, Scott's company was transforming itself into a company which would specialize in a proprietary form of Webcasting (television on the computer). Klososky's team was confident that they could make this computer experience interactive, a major advance. The initial round of $3.5 million of financing was closing and Klososky was looking for Board members who could broaden the "convergence" opportunities for the company. We agreed that I would join the Board, bringing my publishing and direct response expertise. The resulting company, Webcasts.com, aimed to become a leader in interactive broadcasting for the computer user. This was the first time I had served on a for-profit Board. The experience stretched every aspect of my knowledge and relationships. It was also a great fun.

One application of Webcasting technology involved "enriched e-commerce." For example, now when you visit the site of Amazon or barnesandnoble.com, the screen shows you title lists and book jackets. With enriched e-commerce, you might view interviews with the authors, or excerpts from television appearances about the book, or critics speaking to the book's strengths. For authors who have published many books, a promotion might link to their entire body of work. Any of the titles would be only a click away while you are still watching the author speak. You will be able, if so programmed, to read excerpts from the books, or hear them read as in books on tape. The multimedia interactive experience, available now twenty-four hours per day, seven days per week, changes the promotional landscape. Also, authors or entrepreneurs will be able to promote particular books or categories of books using enriched e-commerce, and perhaps gain even more marketplace attention than the established electronic booksellers. The audience potential is limited only by the imagination and the alliances of the broadcaster. If the viewer has to find the originating Web site, audience is likely to be very small. If the viewer is attracted on high traffic Web sites, audience can be very large.

To save time and money, today's better known author sometimes tries a satellite tour to promote a book. A satellite tour involves the author sitting for a day in a studio as local newscasters throughout the United States conduct brief interviews one at a time. If you are Colin Powell or Nancy Reagan, in hot demand to the local media, this medium works very effectively. If you are a hopeful, you might end up soliciting hundreds of local news broadcasts to find out that your $15,000 day in the studio gets you covered in only a few small markets. Webcasting may become the future media tour of choice. First, its content and capability is enriched and produced to suit by some combination of the author and publisher. Second, unlike daily television, the Webcast is archived and available as long as it is maintained on a Web site. Third, costs of producing a quality Webcast fit within the budgets of publishers and, like certain co-op advertising models for print, can be shared with the e-booksellers. Most important, a Webcast includes e-commerce, so you can measure precisely the number of copies sold against the investment. You can't do that with a book party.

I went on the Webcasts.com Board in spring 1999. At my introduction, Christopher Johnson helped with the company's identity and trade presentation. In less than a year, the company faced a choice between a private round of financing and a merger that would offer a faster path to the public markets. The company voted for the merger and Webcasts.com became a division of iBeam Broadcasting. iBeam promptly went public with Morgan Stanley as its lead underwriter for ten dollars per share in May 2000. The stock zoomed to twenty-nine dollars (and analysts filed reports recommending purchases up to thirty-five dollars per share) and promptly fell to fifty cents per share. As a Board member of the acquired division, I was "locked up" until May 2001. I had the experience of watching my block of stock fall from a solid seven-figure number to a not-so-solid five-figure number. The company's business progress and prospects were, in fact, very good, but that didn't seem to help in a terrible stock market. I learned a lot, but would have felt yet better, of course, had the money materialized.

Oshkosh, the exploration of projects with Christopher Johnson, the search with Mitchell Bring for a practical electronic consumer oriented project, and trying to help Webcasts.com become a large company pushed my personal learning curve and challenged me in precisely the way I wished to be challenged. New assignments—such as representing the family of H. W. Janson, author with his son, Anthony Janson, of the forty-year-old *History of Art,* the art history text that is the single most successful title in the Harry Abrams backlist, the growth of Proprietary Media and the American Zoo & Aquarium Association, and the events with David Clark's Education Powers Our Planet EPOP—present new challenges.

All of these projects extended my role as agent for the situation. With Bloomberg, I was his agent for the book and his partner for the diary. With Scott Klososky, he began as a client with *The Haldeman Diaries,* became a vendor for the CD-ROM of the *Bloomberg Desk Diary,* then CEO of the company whose Board I joined and, most recently, a vendor possibly again for RosettaBooks. Christopher Johnson has been a vendor, a partner, key to my introduction to

Webcasts.com, and critical to RosettaBooks. Mitchell Bring began as a partner helping me to learn about virtual space and became a key vendor to RosettaBooks. With both Proprietary Media and EPOP, I was wearing several hats to try and increase everyone's values, including my own.

Juggling responsibilities has long since been second nature. When I moved to International Management Group, my clients adjusted to calling my assistant at her home for one set of questions (typically, where's my check?) and me at the new office for our ongoing projects. When I bought Scott Meredith, my clients adjusted again to my need to focus on reorganizing the agency. And when I started RosettaBooks, and even after I was sued by Random House, my clients focused on our ongoing projects and understood that I had a major time investment in Rosetta.

FOURTEEN

···

Brave E-World

To give RosettaBooks its best chance at success, I tapped as many professional and personal relationships I could. I also used practically everything I had ever learned—the world of American Studies and good research habits from Yale; my political experience with John Lindsay, Pat Moynihan, and Bill Bradley; my early days as a lawyer, certainly including years working with an advertising client; my deal-making as a literary agent and later years as a literary rights buyer and book packager; my experience with the media and with the direct response approach to the collectibles and leather-bound books business; my entrepreneurial experience setting up an agency and later buying and restructuring one; my experience negotiating and developing electronic rights; and my several years of "convergence" work as the digital divide began to change the publishing world.

In 2001, it was not yet clear if the world was ready to adopt electronic reading. Large companies, like bn.com and Gemstar's Reb 1100 and 1200, burned hundreds of millions of dollars. Companies with investments more than $100 million each with data-based electronic models—Questia, Versaware, and Net Library to name a few—hit sizable problems. Many smaller companies shuttered. While Microsoft, Adobe, Palm, and many others continued to invest significantly on the premise that electronic reading would become ubiquitous, the evidence that the consumer shared this view was hard to document. We admired the progress of the University of Virginia, which offered free downloads of 1,600 public domain titles. By spring 2001, there were more than 350,000 downloads per month. The "best-sellers" were science fiction (Jules Verne and H.G. Wells), not surprising when one thinks about the group early adopters.

I remain convinced that the world will adopt electronic reading, sooner rather than later and in a broader way than even most of the optimists suspect. The curve of adoption of new technologies attractive to the consumer has gotten shorter and shorter—television caught on much faster than radio, desktop computers, laptops, the Web, e-mail, each faster still than the technology that preceded it. If electronic reading reaches critical mass, the adoption curve will be rapid and the range of reading that hits the screen will be broad. The arrival of the tablet computer in 2002 may be the mass event which makes this possible—a larger screen than handheld computers, full operating system functionality, wireless Web hook-ups, twenty-four-hour battery life, high resolution color displays, more memory and quicker speeds than today's well configured laptop, access to many wired environments that offer twenty-four-hour instant communication, and a price tag under $1,000.

As the appliances improve and include electronic reading software programs as part of the standard machine configuration, the consumer will experiment more and more with electronic reading. This is essentially how Adobe built the adoption of Acrobat. Today, Acrobat is nearly universal, mainly since it is preloaded on most desktop and laptop computers sold. Not so long ago, the consumer had to take the step of downloading the program for free, causing Acrobat to take some time to reach critical mass.

Who in the book publishing community shares a commitment to the development of electronic reading? Curiously enough, the textbook publishers are far ahead of trade publishers in this regard. If you are looking for the interesting experiments, look to the schools and Pearson, McGraw-Hill, and Houghton Mifflin. Despite their image as conservative companies, they are at the cutting edge of electronic efforts. Some efforts involve the sale of content in the classroom. Some enable the teacher to teach in a far more interesting way. Some discourage the use of used texts by continually updating material. Some customize materials for particular applications. Some provide interactive bulletin boards and the like for student and teacher. The text houses are not only experimenting themselves, but licensing a wide range of third parties to explore the electronic use of their content.

Contrast the trade publishers. Their efforts to date with electronic publishing mimic the printed world in which their experience is grounded. Electronic editions are priced near the price of printed editions. There is virtually no third-party title licensing, and tens of thousands of rights are warehoused. Rather than experiment with cross-promotions, industry leaders like Random House spend their resources suing start-ups like RosettaBooks and creating ill will with their most important constituencies—authors and their representatives. Some observers even think that the trade publishers would like to slow or reverse the trend toward electronic reading.

What is behind this attitude? Part of it reflects a history of doing things the way they have always been done. The recording industry managed to change its consignment selling practices several decades ago. Not the trade publishing industry, which stands perhaps alone as the only major business in which retailers have a free right to return what they purchase (one prominent editor referred to the shipment of books as "gone today, here tomorrow"). Rights-holders in most intellectual property businesses are paid on net receipts, since that is the cash flow the distributor can measure (and the rights-holder can audit). Not the trade publishing industry, in which royalties are paid on "retail selling price," even though the publisher's cash flow is about half of suggested retail price from the bookseller and the typical consumer pays a steep discount from the suggested retail price at the cash register. Most entertainment businesses invest heavily in their backlists, whether it is the film industry's constant promotion for rereleases, "director's cuts" with DVDs, videocassette collections or the like, or the recording industry's push for "greatest hits" collections from their best-selling artists. Not the trade publishing industry, in which profile efforts to promote the backlist stand out be exception, which proves the publishers' informal rule—a good book sells itself.

Some specific factors may help explain the trade publishing community's slowness to embrace electronic publishing. There is the corporate accident that cross-ownership does not seem to be a significant factor in the adoption of electronic reading. AOL Time Warner obviously has a massive stake in the Internet. But AOL does not have a significant presence in electronic reading. And Time Warner, whose trade division is relatively small (one-tenth the sales of Random House), had entered a joint marketing agreement for its book clubs managed by Bertelsmann shortly before the AOL deal took place. Bertelsmann has massive investments in perhaps five hundred electronic companies (including 40 percent of bn.com and a modest interest in Gemstar) but no parallel interests with the major electronic hardware and software companies. Simon & Schuster's parent Viacom has huge television interests (CBS, MTV, and others) and 2,400 radio stations, but no significant electronic hardware or software company. HarperCollins parent NewsCorp (Rupert Murdoch) has electronic interests, but has been cutting back in these areas rather than investing. Pearson has the anomaly that its textbook divisions are leaders in electronic experimentation, while its trade division Penguin, as of summer 2001 had yet to even launch an electronic publishing line (though that didn't stop Penguin from joining the amicus publishers who filed a brief against Rosetta).

At the same time, the major electronic hardware and software companies are remarkably free of cross-ownership ties to publishers. Microsoft has its own press, but principally to publish books in print and electronic formats technically related to the computer world. Adobe and Palm have no ties to trade publishers. Sony, Panasonic, Hewlett Packard, Apple, Sharp, Ikea, Intel—none have a trade publishing tie. This absence of cross-ownership has contributed to the divide between technology friendly people and the typical executive in trade publishing, who is not particularly computer literate and is perhaps even hostile to the digital world.

A second, often overlooked fact is that the trade publishing community did rush to embrace CD-ROMs in the 1980s and lost a substantial amount of money doing so. The trade publishers in the 1980s believed that the CD-ROM, delivered to the desktop computer at home, would become one of the largest of their business extensions. Rather than act by license and let someone else (who was also much more technology savvy) build the product and take the risk, trade publishers started to release a trickle and then a torrent of product. Most was so badly produced that it became known as "shovelware," i.e., the pages of a book had just been shoveled into a CD-ROM. The consumer market collapsed. While publishers had been busy focusing on the fizzling electronic market, they missed the chance of a generation to build lines of traditional books products for the emerging home computer marketplace with distribution strength in emerging hardware and software channels. Instead, companies like IDG claimed the new topics and channels of distribution with the Dummies series right from under the nose of trade publishers. As Mark Twain said, a cat once burned on a hot stove will never sit on a cold stove.

However, the main reason publishers avoided electronic publishing in my view was fear of the new. Trade publishers have always been slow to adopt technology. Until relatively recently, royalty statements for authors were not computerized. In production offices, publishers often rejected manuscripts on disks, since their process preferred to typeset, a far more expensive process. Digital processes to separate images for color photography, a standard practice in the magazine business, were often rejected in the book business in favor of the far more expensive hand separation process in the (mistaken) belief that the quality of the traditional process was better than the digital technology.

I lived through one striking example of this mind-set with Mayo Clinic and its hardcover publisher, William Morrow, then owned by Hearst. Morrow prepared the layouts of the Mayo books by hand. Thus, if a change was needed that affected pagination, an entire batch of pages needed to be "repasted" by hand. In one meeting during which such changes were discussed, I thought the Morrow production manager would faint. For its own purposes Mayo had adopted standard software packages such as QuarkXPress. You could easily control your own design and layout, make changes, and have those changes "roll through" the title with the software package doing the work. Mayo took on these tasks for itself, mainly for quality control, and we arranged appropriate reimbursements for costs that would have been the publisher's. In a major review meeting with senior executives of Hearst about Mayo's future publishing, which included executives from the magazine group, these executives were amazed that their book group was using production techniques they had long since abandoned. So much for corporate synergy, at least for trade publishing production.

Publishers were clearly afraid that electronic publishing would change their business. They had a right to be concerned. Authors could definitely reach markets directly through electronic publishing, involving much larger risks and difficulties if attempted through paper publishing. Retailers, like bn.com (and possibly Amazon), could become formidable competitors to acquire new work directly from authors. Electronic publishing threatened the bricks-and-mortar retail booksellers, the backbone of publishing. The more the trade publisher pushed electronic delivery, the more the brick-and-mortar people had to push back, although the more creative of the booksellers, such as Powells, were moving aggressively to establish their own electronic selling presence. Electronic publishing invited competition from a new community of deep pocket players, like Microsoft, Adobe, Palm, Sony, Intel, Yahoo, and many others who could elect at a moment's notice to get serious about electronic trade publishing. And as the Random House/Rosetta litigation illustrated, electronic publishing might leave the publishers needing to reacquire rights to the most valuable selling printed books in their backlists.

Publishing, like all businesses, was and is subject to market changes that simultaneously create challenge and opportunity. After World War II, Bertelsmann survived as a tiny Bible publisher that had printed propaganda for the Nazi war machine. With the insight that door to door selling of books could be an international business, Bertelsmann built a phenomenal network of book clubs, the business core of what is now one of the largest media empires in the world. While today Bertelsmann is the world's largest English-language publisher as a result of a wave of acquisitions, it is their book club base that funded that strategy.

Penguin built itself to the formidable presence it is today by acquisition, but its focus is strictly trade publishing. Simon & Schuster, even with its invention of the mass market paperback, was a small company when acquired by Gulf & Western. Dick Snyder built the company through acquisitions and trade growth. Sumner Redstone of Viacom sold off the textbook and professional pieces of Simon & Schuster, but the remaining trade piece that Snyder built is a formidable business. Rupert Murdoch acquired several serious publishers to form HarperCollins and sharpened the trade focus by selling off educational units. Holtzbrinck, an active competitor of Bertelsmann in the German magazine marketplace, bought St. Martin's Press, Farrar, Straus & Giroux, and Henry Holt to stake itself to a serious American trade presence. Even so, the opening of its major new warehouse was noted by proud statements of the number of returns it could handle efficiently in one day!

Time Warner, like Bertelsmann, pushed both book club (Book of the Month) and trade publishing interests. The book clubs grew when there were few bookstores, relatively narrow book choices available, and no discounting. As bookstore chains grew, choice grew to the superstore's 150,000 titles, discounting became commonplace, and ultimately Amazon and bn.com offered millions of titles at your fingertips for rapid delivery. What, then, was the mission of the book club? To survive, even Time Warner needed a partner and Bertelsmann became the manager of a joint venture incorporating all of the major book clubs.

These conglomerates represented one fundamental change—consolidation in the trade publishing business. This consolidation carried over into the retailing and distribution businesses as well. Barnes & Noble, built from a series of acquisitions including the Dalton chain from Dayton Hudson, and Borders, initially part of K-Mart and built from the Walden chain, both had revenues more than $3 billion annually. Amazon was reaching an astounding $1 billion in on-line (printed) book sales after only a few years in business. Wholesalers Ingram, Baker & Taylor and AMS (specializing in the warehouse selling clubs) each grew within sight of $1 billion in annual revenues. Independent distributors, who controlled most of the racks for placing mass market paperbacks, changed from 300-plus independent owners across the country to a handful with major market share, led by family-held Anderson Merchandisers, which also became the principal distributor of books for Wal-Mart.

Behind the consolidation were far more basic changes. In the 1970s, the publishing industry was convinced that the mass market publisher was the future, indeed that the hardcover might even become extinct (as it did in France). Books like *Jaws, The Godfather,* and *The Exorcist* sold more than 10 million copies and attracted the attention of the movie studios, some of whom bought publishers (MCA/Universal buying Putnam; RCA, which then owned NBC, buying Random House; Gulf & Western which owned Paramount buying Simon & Schuster; and NewsCorp, which later owned Fox, buying HarperCollins). The hoped-for synergies did not materialize. In fact, the mass paperback has been a flat business without unit growth for more than twenty years. A title that sells 5 million copies today (John Grisham, perhaps, after the first release and the later movie release) is few and far between.

Meanwhile, the threatened hardcover has exploded over the past twenty years into a mass-marketed commodity. In the mid-1970s, a Robert Ludlum title that sold 250,000 hardcover copies had a good chance of becoming the number one title for the year (unless James

Michener had a strong 500,000-copy seller). Now a 2 million-copy seller may finish only in the top three and a 250,000-copy hardcover may make only the top thirty titles for the year. Why? The growth in sales outlets and discounting practices help immeasurably. Also, the availability of more and more media outlets presents that many more opportunities to promote books. Larry King, Charlie Rose, a dozen television magazine shows, the television tabloid shows, a range of talk radio shows—these are all relatively recent phenomena and all help spread the word that a lively book has arrived.

While the mass market edition was flat and the hardcover was exploding, the trade paperback edition emerged as a business unto itself. Trade paperbacks are basically hardcover editions in size and format, with paper covers instead of hardcover bindings. Jason Epstein of Random House developed the trade paperback, originally focusing on the educational market (Vintage). Since the books are bigger than rack-size mass market editions, they cannot fit in the slots where most mass market books are sold. Over the last twenty years, however, the trade paperback, with the advantage of significantly lower pricing than a hardcover book, has become a significant force in publishing. Individual titles can sell seven-figure quantities competitive with mass market editions. Publishers such as Workman focus on the format very successfully, with seven and even eight figures unit programs such as *What to Expect When You're Expecting* and *The Silver Palate* and *New Basics* cookbooks. Even small publishers can thrive in this format—witness the Zagat restaurant rating books and the Chicken Soup series.

These fundamental changes in distribution, media, and format occurred in spite of, rather than because of, leadership from the trade publishing community. Trade publishers financed the growth of the chain booksellers with their consignment selling practices and then found themselves beholden to the power of the chains for title placement and risk of returns. The chains gained enough power to sell title placement in the store. Sometimes publishers would ask the chain what they thought of a jacket being considered. The computer tracking of the chains often determined how many copies of an author's next book could be placed. Publishers with relatively poor returns overall could have a hard problem achieving large advance orders for titles, even though the publisher was taking the economic risk.

Mature publishers opened the doors each year with relatively predictable revenue from the backlist. Backlist titles, particularly older backlist, have amortized their cost of acquisition and advances. In general, returns experience is relatively small. Paperback, book club, and foreign licenses generate subsidiary rights revenue without much cost. So the pretax operating margin can be 30 percent or more of revenues. Random House admits in its complaint against Rosetta that 40 percent of its revenues are from backlist titles. For some publishers the percentage is closer to 60 percent. So what happens that turns a 30 percent-plus margin backlist business into companies that typically earn no more than 10 percent of revenues and in off years show a loss? The frontlist.

If the backlist is practically all of the publisher's profits, the front list is a money losing proposition in the hope that future sales of titles that join the backlist will cost justify the effort. One or two high-selling books, particularly in hardcover, can mask the overall economics of frontlist publishing, but at its core, the frontlist effort can be evaluated by how much money it loses, not how much money it makes. There are many reasons for this. One is that publishers advance significant money for unwritten manuscripts that are never delivered. Another is that advances are often much higher than the ultimate performance of the book. And publishers are often copying one another in the type of book they acquire.

Trade publishers conceptually become a bank for the better books—they buy at high prices and risk consignment distribution of the title. The larger trade publishers adopted accounting practices which spread their advances to future years on the theory that income would be received over the years. Of course, the likely future income is clear in the first few months after publication. When advances were too high, this accounting practice pushed losses to future years. Finally in the mid-1990s, this practice caught up with the publishers and write-offs, per publisher, of more than $100 million were commonplace. The publishers had simply deferred coming to terms with frontlist losses. Today's publishing lists are smaller and advances a bit tighter—after some focus on the frontlist. Meanwhile, the backlist continues to get limited attention from personnel, marketing budgets, and the like.

Does the publisher need control of electronic rights to justify its rights commitment to a title? Electronic publishing and events like the Random House–RosettaBooks litigation are bringing into focus many major industry questions. Authors and agents clearly want to make short-term license commitments for electronic rights. This process may lead to a review of the rights relationship between author and publisher in general. With the extension of copyrights to author's life plus seventy years, an author is required to sign what amounts to a one hundred–year contract for modest front commitments and no continuing conditions of performance. Does this make any sense? Will the habits of electronic publishers challenge this structure, particularly with the support of the major retailers?

I have long felt that authors and agents would respond to an offer of serious promotion with the launch of their book by agreeing to lower royalty rates and advances. Coupling this offer with a reasonable term of years would make the author even more cooperative. If pharmaceutical companies can thrive in a competitive environment with protection of fewer than twenty years and still invest hundreds of millions of dollars in research and development, why can't a simple business like trade publishing invest in its authors and renew its rights by proving success?

These are issues of rights, relationships, and dollars. In the final analysis, electronic publishing is about much more. You can argue that the monks used the handwritten Bible as a way to protect the role of priests and their acolytes. The fewer the literate, the fewer to challenge authority. Gutenberg's bible of movable type said that literature was for all. Even in the United States, we have fallen far short of that goal, but without Gutenberg or his equivalent, hardly any Americans would be literate. Computer literacy is also not universal. When I worked at International Management Group, there was a clear divide between those in their fifties (who typically didn't touch a computer), those in their thirties and forties (who had a mixed experience), and those joining the company out of business or law school, who were always computer literate. Palm Pilots began selling to computer savvy business people already computer literate from the office. Now, with 100,000 units sold weekly, their audience is mass consumer and has attracted competition from companies using their operating system (Hand Spring, Sony) and others, starting with Microsoft.

Bill Gates has correctly argued that electronic reading is the great leveler. Any child anywhere in the world can be exposed to the education that now is reserved for the world's elite. Today's software programs will even read books aloud in a reasonably pleasant robotic voice—on the one hand a great advance for those with poor eyesight, but in an environment in which most can't read, an approach that brings books alive. RosettaBooks has, to date, disabled these audio features on its books since the audiobook business will presumably take a dim view of a free feature that removes the need to purchase an audiobook recording.

I got a chance to see this electronic future in action at a Brooklyn high school, the High School for Telecommunications and Technology. Jerry Seinfeld designated the ArtsConnection, on whose Board I had served for more than twenty years, and Pencil, an organization that sponsored the Principal for a Day program in the New York City public schools, to receive the live gate proceeds from his first live concerts after the conclusion of his television show. As a result, Pencil invited Board members of ArtsConnection to participate in their program. My visit to Bay Ridge, Brooklyn, and two follow-up visits were eye-opening. The New York City Board of Education was the largest customer of Bell & Howell and made its Proquest electronic database product available throughout the school system. Few schools took advantage of the service like this high school.

The school had also worked out a variety of impressive alliances with hardware makers and foundations. Much of the building was wired and quite a number of classrooms had thirty computers on desks. Students had their own electronic accounts, and teachers their own addresses and Web pages. More interesting than the electronic capabilities was the curricular plan. One course in social studies used the Proquest database to encourage students to read and produce electronic illustrated reports. The day I was there, they were studying the situation in Kosovo. The class was divided into teams—some representing the UN, others the US, China, Russia, NATO, and the warring factions on the ground. A math class offered sufficiently challenging assignments that one student had programmed a 3-D Rubik's Cube. You could move the pieces around and, once frustrated, the machine would solve the puzzle visually step by step.

The use of technology in these classrooms was far ahead of what my sons were exposed to in their elite private high schools. The most important observation about the Brooklyn school was that all of its accomplishments were achieved working with a highly racially diverse student body with nearly all qualified for the federal lunch program. In other words, Black, Hispanic, poor, many from broken homes, so many mothers themselves that the school ran a nursery so that the mothers could stay in school. These kids, with more disadvantages than most could imagine, were having their lives transformed by dedicated teachers working with the advantage of technology. Most were graduating school with full scholarships to college, even though in many instances they had never taken the forty-five minute subway ride to Manhattan before.

Where does electronic reading fit into this puzzle? At this high school, kids are comfortable reading on screens and the screens are going to get better. Teachers are comfortable with electronic information in the classroom and, over time, they will get more comfortable. Today, this high school, like others, works with books on paper, one copy per title. Library and financial resources are limited. Few titles are added each year in a quantity at which everyone in a class could work with the same title at the same time. Suggesting that kids explore parts of many books to investigate a theme or the work of a particular author presents many difficulties. Availability of e-books at a reasonable price becomes very attractive in such an environment. Indeed, the principal of the school has volunteered a number of his classrooms as test sites for Rosetta. The point is that quality titles will have the support of the educational community to find their way into the classroom, ultimately far more broadly than those same titles are studied and read today. Soon, Rosetta will run "beta" tests in these and other classrooms.

I have been fortunate enough to spend most of my fifty-four years at the edge of change, rarely dependent upon a large organization to define my agenda. I think that the digital divide offers more and more people the chance to be entrepreneurial and agents of change. The steps involve risk, but so does sitting still, as the organization decides one day it needs to be smaller. I have missed out on some financial chances. Mort Janklow is quick to remind me that had I stayed with him my interest in the agency would have become a small fortune. A turn in the road and either author's insurance or wraparound mortgages could have become substantial life annuities. A photograph here or there or a bit of better organization might have taken the Vatican licensing project into a major business in the mid-1980s. A bounce or two and a close colleague might have been President of the United States.

Regrets? Not really. I think Teddy Roosevelt and Richard Nixon are right—life is in the arena. Each time I have passed a five-year birthday marker, my sense of the coming five years is far more exciting than the five years just past. A job suggests perhaps security, and at least at some point, retirement. An agent, particularly one for the situation, seeks independence, challenge, and a chance to give something back. No one should want retirement from that gratification.

Selfless? Not really. But motivation involves much more than a chance to make money. In politics, I want to see good people getting elected, not worry about what it might mean for me. Many of my book projects are about how they might give something useful to others, including the author, rather than simply how my commissions will aggregate. Authors' insurance was fundamentally about helping authors solve a problem (and did, even if my only personal benefit is now that I have become an author). Wraparound mortgage solutions in bulk could have meant tens of millions of dollars for Columbia University, rather than the hundreds of thousands of dollars that were, in fact, generated. Some of my major book projects are for history (Moynihan, Nixon, Haldeman, Bradley), others to help people (Mayo Clinic), some for importance (leather-bound Easton Press editions), others for beauty and the environment (Roger Tory Peterson), and some for fun (Sheila Lukins's cooking, again and again changing the way we eat). Some help businesses (Bloomberg) with the knowledge that his philanthropy helps others. Some just make perennial money (Linda Goodman's astrology) while doing no harm and apparently pleasing millions.

Whether or not RosettaBooks ultimately becomes the business it can, it will play an important role in defining relationships between author and publisher and in framing the development of electronic reading with trade books. When Stephen King released *Riding the Bullet* to major news attention before we had made our preliminary presentations, we worried that we were too late to launch our business concept. With businesses failing around us and the adoption curve of electronic reading around a corner of unpredictable distance away, I could worry that we are too early. But I don't think so, if we can manage to survive the birthing process for us and electronic reading. Obviously, our investments of time and money are about the business, not about a crusade. Having said that, I have been a crusader for change before and am prepared to be many times more. Hopefully, each time out I am better prepared than the time before. What matters most is to rise to the challenge and compete. And rise again.

So, think for a moment whether you can be an agent. Not a literary agent; there are already too many of us. But an agent for change—there are never too many of them, and there is never too much challenge to go around. As an agent for change, you can be an agent for your own situation and, with yet more gratification, perhaps for others.

ACKNOWLEDGMENTS

Barry Malzberg, my colleague at Scott Meredith, and a celebrated writer in his own right, edited the early versions of this book and encouraged me to believe that someone might want to read it.

In his early days assembling TEXERE, Myles Thompson saw that the manuscript had the makings of a business book if I was ready to do the editorial work. Mina Samuels, my TEXERE editor, proves that there are still substantive editors in publishing. She guided me through several rewrites and reorganizations, large and small. The entire TEXERE team helped me enjoy the process. I think they treat all of their authors this way, not just those who happen to be members of their Board of Directors.

My wife, Susan Hirschhorn, put up with the nights, weekends, and trips with the laptop. There is no convenient way to write a book while building a business.

Any errors are mine alone. Life has its errors, as does memory.

INDEX

Index

ABOUT TEXERE

· ·

TEXERE seeks to become the most progressive and authoritative voice in business publishing by cultivating and enhancing ideas that will illuminate the global business landscape. Our name defines the spirit of our vision: TEXERE is the ancient Latin verb "to weave". In an increasingly global business community, we seek to create an intersection where authors and readers can share the best thinking and the latest ideas. We want to leverage the expertise and insights of leading thinkers by weaving them with TEXERE's capability to deliver them to the marketplace.

To learn more and become a part of our community, visit us at:
www.etexere.com
and
www.etexere.co.uk

About the Typefaces
This book was set in *Fairfield* and *Sabon*